STOLEN IDENTITY

MARCELLA WARD

Copyright © 2022 Marcella Ward.

All rights reserved. No part of this book may be reproduced, stored, or transmitted by any means—whether auditory, graphic, mechanical, or electronic—without written permission of both publisher and author, except in the case of brief excerpts used in critical articles and reviews. Unauthorized reproduction of any part of this work is illegal and is punishable by law.

ISBN: 978-1-957203-71-3 (sc)
ISBN: 978-1-957203-72-0 (hc)
ISBN: 978-1-957203-73-7 (e)

Because of the dynamic nature of the Internet, any web addresses or links contained in this book may have changed since publication and may no longer be valid. The views expressed in this work are solely those of the author and do not necessarily reflect the views of the publisher, and the publisher hereby disclaims any responsibility for them.

One Galleria Blvd., Suite 1900, Metairie, LA 70001
1-888-421-2397

DEDICATION

To the Triune God—God the Father,
Jesus the Son, and the Holy Spirit Who was
and Who is and Who is to come!

I also dedicate this book to my husband,
Marty, for his love and support.

CONTENTS

Foreword		vii
Chapter 1	AI—Am Who I Am?	1
Chapter 2	God as Father	8
Chapter 3	Men of Faith in the Bible	19
Chapter 4	Women of Faith in the Bible	36
Chapter 5	The Church	45
Chapter 6	I Have a Dream	60
Chapter 7	Cultural Impact on Identity	72
Chapter 8	Gender Identity	88
Chapter 9	Progressive Agenda	101
Chapter 10	Who Is Jesus?	116
Chapter 11	Identity in Christ	132
Chapter 12	Inheritance in Christ	145
Chapter 13	God's Healing Touch	159
Chapter 14	The Ultimate Showdown	177
Chapter 15	Reflections	186
Chapter 16	Heaven's Perspective: The Best Is Yet To Come	199
Notes		203
About the Author		217

FOREWORD

Could it be that Satan, after his fall, had a plan to thwart the plan of God by stealing something very valuable to God and us? Satan came to steal, kill and destroy. "God said, Let Us [Father, Son, and Holy Spirit] make mankind in Our image, after Our likeness, and let them have complete authority over the fish of the sea, the birds of the air, the [tame] beasts, and over all the earth and over everything that creeps upon the earth. So God created man in His own image, in the image and likeness of God He created him; male and female He created them" (Gen. 1:26-27).

The evil one has been trying to steal mankind's identity since the Garden of Eden. He put doubt into the heads of Adam and Eve by asking them if God *really* had told them that they would die if they partook of the forbidden tree's fruit. He told them that they would become like God if they ate of the fruit and because of their disobedience they were banished from Eden. Their identity was on its way to being lost forever, but God had a plan.

As mankind began to multiply upon the earth, the Nephilim began to emerge. These were offspring from fallen angels who produced offspring form the daughters of men and became known as Nephilim (the giants, the mighty men). Satan wanted to pollute the seed from which Jesus would come to thwart God's plan.

During the time of Noah, God sent a flood to destroy mankind, except for Noah and his family, because of the wickedness of man and because the enemy had been manipulating the DNA of man-kind. The spirit of the Antichrist is still alive and well and is working through this present age to continue to sabotage God's image in us so that the Antichrist can ultimately reign on earth at the end of the age before the Second Coming of Jesus Christ. "As were the days of Noah, so will be the coming of the Son of Man" (Matt. 24:37).

There are many men and women of faith in the Old Testament that knew who their identity was in God—Abraham, Noah, Jeremiah, Elijah,

Daniel, and many more as well as women of faith who knew their identity in God such as Rahab, Ruth, Esther, Mary the mother of Jesus, and many more. There are many, women and men who have taken a stand to preserve who they are, such as Martin Luther King Jr., Rosa Parks, Mother Teresa of Calcutta, and many more.

This book will challenge you to be among those who will stand for who you are in Christ, and don't let the media, the politicians, the political correctness gurus of the world change who you are. There is an agenda out there by the left and the progressives to change your identity from God's image and likeness to making man in *his* own image. Our true identity is in Jesus Christ alone and who He created us to be.

As you read through this book I hope you can fall deeper in love with Jesus the Son of God, God the Father, and the Holy Spirit. If we understand that our true identity is in Jesus Christ, then we will become more like Him so we can be Christ to others. "Let your light so shine before men that they may see your moral excellence and your praiseworthy noble and good deeds and recognize and honor and praise and glorify your Father Who is in heaven" (Matt. 5:16).

We have been given many gifts from the Holy Spirit to help us in our journey using these gifts to glorify God and minister to others. We need to live from heaven to earth claiming and using our authority that God gave us through His Son, Jesus. "And He raised us up together with Him and made us *sit down together* [giving us joint seating with Him] in the heavenly sphere [by virtue of our being] in Christ Jesus [the Messiah, the Anointed One]" (Eph. 2:6).

If we truly understand who we are in Christ, then there will be *no identity crisis* for us because we will live a Christ-centered life in which He will live in us and work through us to accomplish God's great plan of salvation, redemption, and restoration as we will live in His inheritance as sole heirs of His Kingdom upon the earth!

Chapter One

AI—Am Who I Am?

"One goal of AI (Artificial intelligence) is to create an 'other' in our own image. That image will necessarily be partial; thus we must determine what it is in ourselves that computers must possess or demonstrate what it is in ourselves that computers must possess or demonstrate to be considered our "mind children." The question of what we humans might share with such an other has been examined by Christian theologians through the concept of the image of God, in which, according to Genesis 1, human beings were created. Is this image that humans share with God related to the image we wish to share with our own creation in AI?"[1]

Are we attempting to create other beings in our *own* image? Dan Brown, the author of the best-selling *Da Vinci Code*, has collaborated with philologist Friedrich Nietzsche in announcing the death of God, stating that "God cannot survive science . . . Our need for the exterior God that sits up there and judges us . . . will diminish and eventually disappear."[2]

We will embark on a journey throughout this book to look at the schemes and agenda of the enemy, the evil one, to destroy our identity that was given at the beginning of time when God established that we are "created in His image." From Adam and Eve, Noah, Abraham, to Jesus Himself, the devil has attempted to steal who we are by his lies and manipulation. Let's look at what the Bible, the Holy Word of God, has to say about our image.

The Image of God

"God said, Let Us [Father, Son, and Holy Spirit]) make man-kind in Our image, after Our likeness, and let them have complete authority over the fish of the sea, the birds of the air, the [tame] beasts, and over all the earth, and over everything that creeps upon the earth. So God created man in His own image, in the image and likeness of God He created him; male and female He created them" (Gen. 1:26–27).

What does image mean? According to *Webster's Dictionary*, it means "a close or exact resemblance to another."[3] Have you ever heard someone say, "You resemble your father so much"? Yes, I think a lot of us may resemble our mother or our father. When they look at us, they see that person in us. I think that maybe God wanted to have a family, and He wanted to have sons and daughters that He could say resemble Him, and we as sons and daughters would be proud to say that we resemble our Father, our Heavenly Father.

There are many people around the world who have had their identity stolen. Can you imagine someone stealing your identity, which would include your name and all your personal identification that is only yours and yours alone, such as your social security number or your bank account? Let's look back to the Garden of Eden and see how their identity was stolen. Adam and Eve walked and talked with God. Their identity was formed by God and Him alone. They had all that they needed, and they had intimacy with God that one could be jealous of.

Adam and Eve

"Now the serpent was more subtle and crafty than any living creature of the field which the Lord God had made. And he [Satan] said to the woman, Can it really be that God has said, you shall not eat from every tree of the garden? And the woman said to the serpent, we may eat the fruit from the trees of the garden, except the fruit from the tree which is in the middle of the garden. God has said, you shall not eat of it, neither shall you touch it, lest you die. But the serpent said to the woman, you shall not surely die, For God knows that in the day you eat of it your eyes will be opened, and you will be like God, knowing the difference between good and evil and blessing and calamity" (Gen. 3:1–5).

"Can it really be that God has said, you shall not eat from every tree of the garden?" At this time, it appears that Satan was trying to put doubt in Eve's heart, tricking her into eating of the forbidden tree to trap her and steal her identity.

Let's look back at creation. God created the earth and all that is in it including the plants, trees, birds of the air, fish in the sea, and all creeping things. He said that it was good, but something or someone was missing. I think that God, in wanting to reproduce Himself, created man and woman to complement Him and be a part of Him, part of His glory. He wanted us to identify with Him.

The Flood (Nephalim)

Mankind began to multiply upon the earth. "The sons of God saw that the daughters of men were fair, and they took wives of all they desired and chose" (Gen. 6:2). "There were giants on the earth in those days—and also afterward—when the sons of God lived with the daughters of men, and they bore children to them. These were the mighty men who were of old, men of renown" (Gen. 6:4).

"The Lord saw that the wickedness of man was great on the earth, and that every imagination and intention of all human thinking was only evil continually. And the Lord regretted that He had made man on the earth, and He was grieved at heart. So the Lord said, I will destroy, blot out, and wipe away mankind, whom I have created from the face of the ground—not only man, [but] the beasts and the creeping things, and the birds of the air—for it grieves Me and makes Me regretful that I have made them. But Noah found grace [favor] in the eyes of the Lord" (Gen. 6:5).

In the Hebrew language, these "sons of God" were *bene Elohim*.

This term is usually applied to angels (see Job 1:6). Genesis seems to be stating that, somehow, there was a physical union between angels and human women. The unnatural offspring of this union, according to Genesis 6:4, were the "Nephilim." The word *Nephilim* is directly transliterated from the Hebrew. The ancient root of the word implies a "fall." Whatever the word actually means (in some versions of the Bible it is translated as "giants." Scripture describes the Nephilim as "the heroes of old, men of renown." Some theologians believe that "God could simply not allow this corrupt offspring to exist on the earth, and that was part of the reason for the flood."[4]

It appears the "fallen ones," who some people believe to be fallen angels, took on human form and produced offspring polluting the seed from which Jesus, the Son of the Living God, would come from to deliver the world from sin and death. Another form of "identity theft" to deprive mankind from his true identity in God.

The Tower of Babel

Noah's descendants spoke the same language. They settled in a fertile area called Shinar where they decided to build a city with a tower to "reach to the heavens." "And they said, Come, let us build us a city and a tower whose top reaches into the sky, and let us make a name for ourselves, lest we be scattered over the whole earth. And the Lord came down to see the city and the tower which the sons of men had built. And the Lord said, Behold, they are one people and they have all one language, and this is only the beginning of what they will do, and now nothing they have imagined they can do will be impossible for them. Come, let Us go down and there confound [mix up, confuse] their language, that they may not understand one another's speech. So the Lord scattered them abroad from that place upon the face of the whole earth, and they gave up building the city. Therefore the name of it was called Babel—because there the Lord confounded the language of all the earth; and from that place the Lord scattered them abroad upon the face of the whole earth" (Gen. 11:3–9).

As you can see, God was not pleased. They, in essence, were building a monument to themselves. Instead of giving God the glory for their very existence, they chose the arrogance of believing that they essentially could build a tower that would be a gateway to heaven and therefore insinuating that they are gods and not in need of the everlasting God, the one true God. It would be man not in need of a redeemer, Jesus Christ, as the mediator between God and man for their salvation. It would be, essentially, man's way of "buying" his way to heaven through his own deeds.

I Am Who I Am

"And God said to Moses, I am who i am and what i am will be what i will be; and He said, You shall say this to the Israelites: I AM has sent you! God said also to Moses, This shall you say to the Israelites: The Lord, the God of your fathers, of Abraham, of Isaac, and of Jacob, has sent me to you! This is My name forever, and by this name I am to be remembered to all generations" (Exod. 3:14–15).

God was declaring to Moses who He is. He was identifying Himself to Moses. God is saying that

1. He is self-existent: He has His being Himself;

2. He is eternal and unchangeable and always the same, yesterday, today, and forever;
3. He is incomprehensible, and we cannot by searching find Him out: this name checks all bold and curious inquiries about God;
4. He is faithful and true to all His promises, unchangeable in His "Word as well as in His nature; let Israel know this, I AM hath sent me unto you. I Am, and there is none else besides Me. All else have their being from God, and are wholly dependent upon Him. Also, here is a name that denotes what God is to His people. The Lord God of your fathers sent Me unto you. Moses must revive among them the religion of their fathers, which was almost lost; and then they might expect the speedy performance of the promises made unto their fathers."[5]

God gave Moses a commission to deliver His people from the bondage of the Egyptians. He told Moses that he would bring His people out of Egypt to the land of the Canaanite, the Hittite, the Amorite, the Perizzite, the Hivite, and the Jebusite, to a land flowing with milk and honey.

God told him that He knew that the King of Egypt would not let His people go but that He would raise His mighty hand and smite Egypt with great wonders and then the King of Egypt would let the Israelites go.

Moses, being overwhelmed with such a great mandate realized his own weakness and told the Lord that he could not speak well. "And Moses said to the Lord I am not eloquent or a man of words, neither before or since You have spoken to Your servant; for I am slow of speech and have a heavy and awkward tongue. And the Lord said to him, who has made man's mouth? Or who makes the dumb, or the deaf, or the seeing, or the blind? Is it not I, the Lord?" (Exod. 4:10–11). So the Lord met Moses half way and said that he would speak through Moses to Aaron his brother and that Aaron would deliver the message. And with that said, Moses took his wife and his sons and returned to the land of Egypt.

Moses did not really know who God was. God spoke to him in a fiery bush and told him who He is. By telling Moses who He is, He was giving Moses an identity of who he was and that he and his people belonged to God and that God loved them, heard their call and was going to free them from their bondage through an unlikely vessel in Moses who believed that he was not fit for the task because of his speech, but God reminded him that He was the Creator, and He could do all things. Moses had to truly put his trust in the God of Abraham, Isaac, and Jacob. He was not going on this journey alone, but God promised that He would put the words in his mouth and that through his obedience God's people would be delivered. Moses had just received a new identity.

Israel's Identity

"If you will listen diligently to the voice of the Lord your God, being watchful to do all His commandments which I command you this day, the Lord your God will set you high above all the nations of the earth. And all the blessings shall come upon you and overtake you if you heed the voice of the Lord your God. Blessed shall you be in the city and blessed shall you be in the field. Blessed shall be the fruit of your body and the fruit of your ground and the fruit of your beasts, the increase of your cattle and the young of your flock. Blessed shall be your basket and your kneading trough. Blessed shall you be when you go out. The Lord shall cause your enemies who rise up against you to be defeated before your face; they shall come out against you one way and flee before you seven ways. The Lord shall command the blessing upon you in your storehouse and in all that you undertake. And He will bless you in the land which the Lord Your God gives you. The Lord will establish you as a people holy to Himself, as He has sworn to you, if you keep the commandments of the Lord your God and walk in His ways. And all the people of the earth shall see that you are called by the name [and in the presence of] the Lord, and they shall be afraid of you" (Deut. 28:1–10).

The Sabbath identifies God! It points as a memorial to Whom we are to worship—our Creator God. It was also given as a sign which identifies who the people of God are. Exodus 31:13 says: "Say to the Israelites, Truly you shall keep My Sabbaths, for it is a sign between Me and you throughout your generations, that you may know that I, the Lord, sanctify you [set you apart for Myself]." The Sabbath not only identifies God as the Creator, but He also identifies His believers in Christ.[6]

Most people want to be identified as belonging to the world. They want to fit in. You can see it in the media, Facebook, etc. where people want to show the world how they are "cool," and that they are setting the tone for what we should do or be in this world. The left wants to completely get rid of any knowledge of the Bible or God represented in taking down the Ten Commandments in public places.

A covenant as defined by *Webster's Dictionary* is "An agreement between persons or parties. A solemn compact."[7] It is a contract or an agreement by two parties. "Wherefore the Israelites shall keep the Sabbath to observe it throughout their generations, a perpetual covenant" (Exod. 31:16).

Summary

We are created in the image of God. We are a close resemblance of God created to manifest His glory throughout the earth. When God created Adam and Eve, it appeared that He wanted to share His love, to love and to be loved, and He loved mankind so much that He gave him a will of his own. God did not create robots but people with a free will who would choose right from wrong and also choose to love or be loved by their Creator God. When Adam and Eve chose to not obey God because they were convinced by the serpent that they would be like God, this was the first step in Satan's deception of identity theft, which continued on through the Nephilim who polluted the seed of man and produced giants.

The Tower of Babel was an act of arrogance and defiance of God as they believed they could reach the heavens on their own strength and power. God stopped them because it was only the beginning of what they could do or imagine to do, so God confused their language. Does this possibly sound familiar as far as man going too far in our time through the use of artificial intelligence?

Moses heard from God who he was and what God wanted to do through him even though Moses did not consider himself equipped to do the mandate. God does not always call the equipped, but He always equips the called!

Israel's identity was given to the Israelite's through His covenants and His commandments and in Deuteronomy 28, He outlined for them the blessings and attributes of God's chosen people, but it was conditional for them to obey His commandments.

The enemy, Satan, has from Adam and Eve until now, tried to steal our identity which is in God through Jesus Christ, who is God in the flesh and who is the mediator between God and man. It was because of stolen identity, which occurred in the Garden of Eden through Adam and Eve's disobedience, that Jesus was sent from the Father to purchase our salvation and restore our identity that had been established at creation by God.

Chapter Two

God as Father

"He who does not love has not become acquainted with God [does not and never did know Him], for **God is love**. In this the love Of God was made manifest [displayed] where we are concerned: in that God sent His son, the only begotten or unique [Son], into the world so that we might live through Him. In this is love: not that we loved God, but that He loved us and sent His Son to the propitiation [the atoning sacrifice] for our sins. Beloved, if God loved us so [very much], we also ought to love one another. No man has at any time [yet] seen God. But if we love one another, God abides [lives and remains] in us and His love [that love which is essentially His] is brought to completion [to its full maturity, runs its full course, is perfected] in us!" (1 John 4:8-12).

"As a father loves and pities his children, so the Lord loves and pities those who fear Him [with reverence, worship, and awe]" (Ps. 103:13).

A compassionate God is a loving father. A loving father is willing to sacrifice everything to love and care for his children. God as Father is the epitome of Who God is. God loved us so much that He sent His Son, Jesus to atone for our sins so we would no longer be separated from God because of Adam and Eve's sin. God is still wanting to be in relationship with us just as much as our earthly fathers. He is the template for how a father is supposed to be, act, and do by example.

God's love is unconditional. There isn't anything that we can do that would separate us from His love. Even though our earthly father may abandon us, He will never leave us or forsake us. He is also compassionate, comforting, and loyal. "Sing for joy, O heavens, and be joyful, O earth, and break forth into singing, O mountains! For the Lord has comforted His people and will have compassion upon His afflicted. But Zion [Jerusalem, her people as seen in captivity] said, The Lord has forsaken me, and my Lord has forgotten me. [And the Lord answered] Can a woman forget her nursing child, that she should not have compassion on the son of her womb? Yes, they may forget, yet I will not forget you. Behold, I have indelibly imprinted [tattooed a picture of] you on the palm of each of My hands; [O Zion] your walls are continually before Me" (Is. 49:13-16). His love is continual and will never, never, end.

How do we show our love for our family or our friends? We give them gifts. God is a gift giver. He is the perfect gift giver because He knows us better than anyone else. He also knows what is best for us. "Every good gift and every perfect [free, large, full] gift is from above; it comes down from the Father of all [that gives] light, in [the shining of] Whom there can be no variation [rising or setting] or shadow cast by His turning [as an eclipse]" (James 1:17).

"If you then, evil as you are, know how to give good and advantageous gifts to your children, how much more will your Father Who is in heaven [perfect as He is] give good and advantageous things to those who keep on asking Him!" (Matt. 7:11).

He is a protector and always available. How many of us always felt safe as a child when we were in our father's care? I remember as a child greeting my father as he came home from work. It was a joyful occasion. I knew that with him around I would be safe and secure. God is our protector and our shield, and He is always available.

If God treats us as sons and daughters, He also disciplines us as sons and daughters. What good father does not discipline his children? "And I will be a Father to you, and you shall be My sons and daughters, says the Lord Almighty" (2 Cor. 6:18). "Moreover, we have had earthly fathers who disciplined us and we yielded [to them] and respected [them for training us]. Shall we not much more cheerfully submit to the Father of spirits and so [truly] live?" (Heb. 12:9). The Greek word for *forgive* is "aphete," which means "to let go, leave behind, dismiss, or cancel the debt." God is a forgiving God.[8] How many times did Israel disobey God and He forgave them?[9] When Jesus was asked by one of the disciples how many times he should forgive his brother, Jesus answered seventy times seventy. "If we [freely] admit that we have sinned and confess our sins, He is faithful and just [true to His own nature and promises] and will forgive our sins [dismiss our lawlessness] and [continuously] cleanse us from all unrighteousness [everything not in conformity to His will in purpose, thought, and action]" (1 John 1:9).

What better example of a loving, compassionate, forgiving Father than the Prodigal Son parable in the Bible? "And He said, there was a certain man who had two sons; and the younger of them said to his father, Father, give me the part of the property that falls [to me]. And he divided the estate between them. And not many days after that, the younger son gathered up all that he had and journeyed into a distant country, and there he wasted his fortune in reckless and loose [from restraint] living. And when he had spent all he had, a mighty famine came upon that country, and he began to fall behind and be in want. So he went and forced [glued] himself upon one of the citizens of that country, who sent him into his fields to feed hogs. And he would gladly have fed on and filled his belly with the carob pods that the hogs were eating, but [they could not satisfy his hunger and] nobody gave him anything [better]. Then when he came to himself, he said, How many hired servants of my father have enough food, and [even food] to spare, but I am perishing [dying] here of hunger! I will get up and go to my father and I will say to him. Father, I have sinned against heaven and in your sight. I am no longer worthy to be called your son; [just] make me like one of your hired servants. So he got up and came to his [own] father. But while he was still long way off, his father saw him and was moved with pity and tenderness [for him]' and he ran and embraced him and kissed him [fervently]" (Luke 15:11–20). His father forgave him and celebrated that a son who was lost was now found! He was anxious to see his son return. So anxious that it appears that he was always looking, anticipating his son's return. He probably had already forgiven him before his son had asked for forgiveness.

"Our Father"

"Then He was praying in a certain place; and when He stopped, one of His disciples said to Him, Lord, teach us to pray, [just] as John taught his disciples" (Luke 1:11).

Jesus then taught them the "Our Father" prayer. Do you notice that Jesus said "our Father"? To me this indicates the power of two or more gathering together and gathering together in unity with a common bond— Father. Yes, God the Father. The first person of the Holy Trinity and Jesus His Son united in prayer with us His children. We call Him "Abba," which is even more intimate. Just like a little child would say "Daddy." "See what [an incredible] quality of love the Father has given [shown, bestowed on] us, that we should [be permitted to] be named and called and counted the children of God! And so we are! The reason that the world does not know [recognize, acknowledge] us is that it does not know [recognize, acknowledge] Him" (1 John 3:1). We are His covenant family. We are the family of God.

"Who Art in Heaven"

Heaven is truly our destiny and our home. We are on a journey to the heavenly kingdom God has prepared for His children. We are sojourners on our way to our true home. We know that God dwells there. All things are under His feet, and the earth is His footstool. We acknowledge His abode as we pray to him for all our needs to be met here on earth.

"Hallowed Be Thy Name"

Hallowed means, according to *Webster's Dictionary*, "sanctified, consecrated, greatly venerated, sacrosanct (sacred and inviolable)." He is truly holy. The angels around the throne of God never stop saying, "And one cried to another and said, Holy, holy, holy is the Lord of Hosts; the whole earth is full of His glory!" (Isa. 6:3).

As we pray the "Our Father," we acknowledge His holiness. We honor Him for who He is. Just as a child honors his Father, so we honor Him in this prayer of petition and thanksgiving.

"Thy Kingdom Come"

"God is our Father, but also our King. In His kingship we discover the full meaning of human fatherhood: self-sacrifice, authority, life, compassion, justice, mercy, and love. This is the Biblical meaning of fatherhood"(James Seghers).

In the Kingdom of God, there is joy, peace, love, and there is no illness, grief, or strife. We pray that the Kingdom of God be made manifest upon the earth.

"Thy Will Be Done on Earth as It Is in Heaven"

If we as children of God really took seriously "Thy will be done on earth as it is in heaven," how much better off would we be? We need to seek God's will in everything. Where can we look to find out God's will? We can go to His Holy Bible; Bible—*Basic Instructions Before Leaving Earth*! He has given us His Word and commandments. If we follow His Word and commandments, we will avoid pitfalls and pain. Will we avoid every pitfall and pain? No, because we live in a broken world. If we pray with sincerity "Thy will be done on earth as it is in heaven," God will listen and answer our prayers as only He can.

"Give Us This Day Our Daily Bread"

In referring to our daily sustenance the Lord is teaching us that as the Israelites ate manna in the wilderness they still died, but He is the Living Bread that will feed us eternally. Jesus, the Living Bread, is present in the Eucharist; Holy Communion. This is eternal food for our soul. "Your forefathers ate the manna in the wilderness, and [yet] they died. [But] this is the Bread that comes down from heaven, so that [any] one may eat of it and never die. I Myself am this Living Bread that came down from heaven. If anyone eats of this Bread, he will live forever; and also the Bread that I shall give for the life of the world is My flesh [body]" (John 6:49–50). A loving Father always provides for his children.

"And Forgive Us Our Trespasses As We Forgive Those Who Trespass Against Us"

"For if you forgive people their trespasses [their reckless and willful sins, leaving them, letting them go, and giving up resentment], your heavenly Father will also forgive you" (Matt. 6:15). Forgiveness is not easy. So many of us have held grudges toward other people for many years, and where has it gotten us? The only person who is really being hurt is not the person who offended us but ourselves because sometimes bitterness can lead to illnesses. You've heard the old saying, "Unforgiveness is like drinking poison expecting the other person to get sick."

To forgive is not a natural act but a supernatural act. If God has forgiven us, we need to forgive others who have offended us.

"And Lead Us Not Into Temptation"

We are asking our heavenly Father to help us reject temptation. Our flesh is very weak, and we need supernatural strength to help us through all the temptations of life. God is faithful, and He will not allow us to be tempted beyond our strength if we call on Him for help. Even Jesus was tempted in the desert, but He never gave in. "For no temptation [no trial regarded as enticing to sin], [no matter how it comes or where it leads] has overtaken you and laid hold on you that is not common to man [that is, no temptation or trial has come to you that is beyond human resistance and that is not adjusted and adapted and belonging to human experience, and such as man can bear]. But God is faithful [to His Word and to His compassionate nature], and He [can be trusted] not to let you be tempted and tried and assayed beyond your ability and strength of resistance and power to endure, but with the temptations He will [always] also provide the way out [the means of escape to a landing place], that you may be capable and strong and powerful to bear up under it patiently" (1 Cor. 10:13).

"But Deliver Us From Evil"

God gave each of us a free will. Our earthly father can guide us, direct us but it is ultimately we who choose to listen or not listen. Sometimes evil can come upon us because of the choices we make, which are a natural result of turning away from God. We are not asking God to keep us from evil but deliver us from evil. We live in a world that is dominated by the evil one. He is our enemy, and we see evil everywhere, but God can deliver us from evil when we call upon Him to help us.

As Christians, we are in a spiritual battle by virtue of who we are. The carnal world hates us. "Be well balanced [temperate, sober of mind], be vigilant and cautious at all times; for that enemy of yours, the devil, roams around like a lion roaring [in fierce hunger], seeking someone to seize upon and devour. Withstand him; be firm in faith [against his onset—rooted, established, strong, immovable, and determined], knowing that the same [identical] sufferings are appointed to your brotherhood [the whole body of Christians] throughout the world. And after you have suffered a little while, the God of all grace [Who imparts all blessing and favor], Who has called you to His [own] eternal glory in Christ Jesus, will Himself complete and make you what you ought to be, establish and ground you securely, and strengthen, and settle you" (1 Peter 5:8–10).

"Amen"

"We end our prayers with the word *amen*. It is a transliteration of a solemn Hebrew word describing something frim, true, or reliable. At the conclusion of Christian prayer, it expresses our complete trust and surrender to God's will. It is our *fiat*."[9]

Jesus's Relation to the Father and Disciples' Relation to the Father

From the scriptures, we do not know exactly when Jesus first knew His purpose and His calling by the Father. When Jesus was twelve years old, He and His family went to Jerusalem to celebrate the Passover. Jesus remained behind in Jerusalem. His mother and father could not find Him, and after three days they found Him listening to the teachers and asking them questions in the Temple. He must have been asked questions because it is written that they [teachers in the Temple] were astonished at His understanding and answers. When Mary, His mother, told Jesus that they had been anxious looking for Him: "And He said to them, How is it that you had to look for Me? Did you not see and know that it is necessary [as a duty] for Me to be in My Father's house and [occupied] about My Father's business?" (Luke 2:49).

It appeared that Jesus knew that He needed to be obedient to God, His Father; to what extent at this age we do not know from the Scriptures. It says that Jesus, as He grew to adulthood, "increased in Wisdom [in broad and full understanding] and in stature and years, and in favor with God and man" (Luke 2:52).

The great intimacy that Jesus had with His Father is illustrated in this great prayer in John 17: "When Jesus had spoken these things, He lifted up His eyes to heaven and said, Father, the hour has come. Glorify and exalt and honor and magnify Your Son, so that Your Son may glorify and extol and honor and magnify You. [Just as] You have granted Him power and authority over all flesh [all humankind], [now purify Him] so that He may give eternal life to all whom You have given Him. And this is eternal life: [it means] to know [to perceive, recognize, become acquainted with, and understand] You, the only true and real God and [likewise] to know Him Jesus [as the] Christ [the Anointed One, the Messiah], Whom You have sent. I have glorified You down here on the earth by completing the work that You gave Me to do. And now, Father, glorify Me along with Yourself and restore Me to such majesty and honor in Your presence as I had with You before the world existed. I have manifested Your Name [I have revealed Your very Self, Your real Self] to the people whom You have given Me out of the world. They were Yours, and You gave them to Me, and they have obeyed and kept Your word. Now [at last] they know and understand that all You have given Me belongs to You [it's really and truly Yours]. For the [uttered] words that You gave Me I have given them; and they have received and accepted [them] and have come to know positively and in reality [to believe with absolute assurance] that I came forth from Your presence, and they have believed and are convinced that You did send Me. I am praying for them. I am not praying [requesting] for the world, but for those You have given Me, for they belong to You. All [things that are] Mine are Yours, and all [things that are] Yours belong to Me; and I am glorified in [through] them. [They have done Me honor; in them My glory is achieved.]" (John 17:1-10).

Jesus dwelt in heaven with the Father before He even came into the world. Though He was still God, most people only saw Him as a carpenter's Son. He prayed that the visible manifestation of His glory be restored. Jesus manifested the person of the Father to his disciples in His flesh. Jesus said to the disciples that when they see Him, they see God the Father.

"Phillip said to Him, Lord, show us the Father [cause us to see the Father—that is all we ask]; then we shall be satisfied. Jesus replied, Have I been with all of you for so long a time, and do you not recognize and know Me yet, Philip? Anyone who has seen Me has seen the Father. How can you say then, Show us the Father?" (John 14:8-9).

At the core of Jesus's identity is the relationship that He has with the Father. "Do you not believe that I am in the Father, and that the Father is in Me? What I am telling you I do not say on my own authority and of My own accord; but the Father Who lives continually in Me does the [His] works [His own miracles, deeds of power]" (John 14:10).

"He [Jesus] does not simply represent the Father, He presents Him. Such complete union means that Jesus's words and deeds have their source in the Father. Jesus may be the Father's agent but the Father is also the agent at work through Jesus. Jesus does not say however, that He is the Father."[10]

Essentially what Jesus is saying is that He is God in the flesh. Jesus is not acting on His own authority but on Father God's authority. Jesus and the Father are one, so when the disciples see Jesus they are seeing God in human form. The disciples need to grasp Jesus's identity before they can understand who Jesus really is.

"I assure you, most solemnly I tell you, if anyone steadfastly believes in Me, he will himself be able to do the things that I do; and he will do even greater things than these, because I go to the Father. And I will do [I Myself will grant] whatever you ask in My Name [as presenting all that I AM], so that he Father may be glorified and extolled in [through] the Son" (John 12:12–13). Jesus relayed to the disciples who their identity is in Him. Jesus is passing down their inheritance, their true identity in God through Christ.

What greater things is Jesus talking about? Could we, as Christians do greater works than Jesus? It appears that Jesus is talking about the supernatural manifestation of God's miracles coming through us as mere mortals. It could also mean that there would be an exponential multiplication of greater works through the millions of vessels that God would work through for His glory in the thousands of years to come. We are actually sharing in the life of Christ, His identity, through union with Him. The greater things cannot be accomplished without Jesus who acts as mediator with the Father.

Jesus promises that He will do whatever they ask in His Name. When we pray "in Jesus's name," we pray in keeping with His character, His identity with the Father. God's agenda, through Christ, becomes the disciples' agenda. They were to bring Glory to God the Father.[11]

Jesus loves the Father. He gave His life freely for the Father for our redemption. Jesus was completely dependent upon the Father and obedient to Him. Jesus only did what He saw the Father doing and spoke what He heard the Father speaking.

Jesus is our advocate before God. He said that He is the only way to the Father. A major aspect of Jesus's ministry was to mediate the Divine presence. "Jesus is a human presence ["the Righteous One"] in heaven, and He is the Divine presence on earth. The Paraclete [who is Himself distinct from Jesus and not simply Jesus's presence] is to continue that Divine presence among the disciples."[12s]

The Paraclete or the Holy Spirit, the Third Person of the Most Holy Trinity, is the Divine presence among the believers. He is with us and with Him we are glorifying Jesus, who always glorifies the Father and who only speaks the truth to the world. The Holy Spirit bears witness to Jesus Christ. The Holy Spirit is a gift from the Father.[13] Jesus said that it was necessary for Him to go so that the Holy Spirit, the Paraclete would be sent by the Father which did happen on Pentecost fifty days after the Resurrection of the Lord. "But the Comforter [Counselor, Helper; Intercessor, Advocate, Strengthener, Standby], the Holy Spirit, Whom the Father will send in My name [in My place, to represent me and act on my behalf], He will teach you all things. And He will cause you to recall [will remind you of, bring to your remembrance] everything I have told you" (John 14:26).

"The person who has My commands and keeps them is the one who [really] loves Me; and whoever [really] loves Me will be loved by My Father, and I [too] will love him and will show [reveal, manifest] Myself to him. [I will let Myself be clearly seen by him and make Myself real to him.] Judas, not Iscariot, asked Him, Lord, how is it that You will reveal Yourself [make Yourself real] to us and not to the world? Jesus answered, If a person [really] loves Me, he will keep My word [obey My teaching]; and My Father will love him, and We will come to him and make Our home [abode, special dwelling place] with him" (John 14:21-23).

Summary

We know that God is a loving, compassionate, and forgiving Father. He identifies with us through the incarnation of Jesus His Son who came in the flesh to point us to the Father. Jesus and the Father are one. God the Father, Jesus His Son, and the Holy Spirit are one—the Holy Trinity.

God's love is unconditional. He loved us first before the earth was formed and anyone else existed. He is compassionate and loyal. Even an earthly father may abandon his child, the Lord will never leave us or forsake us. He fashioned us in secret:

"Oh Lord, You have searched me [thoroughly] and have known me. You know my downsitting and my uprising; You understand my thought afar off. You sift and search out my path and my lying down, and You are acquainted with all my ways. For there is not a word in my tongue [still unuttered]. But, behold, O Lord, You know it altogether. You have beset me and shut me in—behind and before, and You have laid Your hand upon me" (Ps. 139:1-5).

"My frame was not hidden from You when I was being formed in secret [and] intricately and curiously wrought [as if embroidered with various colors] in the depths of the earth [a region of darkness and mystery]. Your eyes saw my unformed substance, and in Your book all the days [of my life] were written before everything took shape, when as yet there was none of them. How precious and weighty also are Your thoughts to me, O God! How vast is the sum of them! If I could count them, they would be more in number than the sand. When I awoke [could I count to the end], I would still be with You" (Ps.139:15–18).

God has not left us orphaned because He sent the Holy Spirit, the Paraclete, to help and guide us on our journey. He will be with us always even until the end of the age. Come, Lord Jesus, come!

Chapter Three

Men of Faith in the Bible

Abraham

"Now [in Haran] the Lord said to Abram, Go for yourself [for your own advantage] away from your country from your relatives and your father's house, to the land that I will show you. And I will make of you a great nation, and I will bless you [with abundant increase of favors] and make your name famous and distinguished, and you will be a blessing [dispensing good to others]. And I will bless those who bless you [who confer prosperity or happiness upon you] and curse him who curses or uses insolent language toward you; in you will all the families and kindred of the earth be blessed [and by you they will bless themselves]" (Gen. 12:1–3).

God told Abraham who he was and that through him a great nation would emerge and those that blessed him would be blessed and those that cursed him would be cursed. "After these things, the word of the Lord came to Abram in a vision, saying, 'Fear not, Abram, I am your shield, your abundant compensation, and your reward shall be exceedingly great.' Abram means 'a high father' or 'exalted father.' Abraham means 'father of many' or 'the father of a multitude.'[14] How could a great nation emerge from someone who was childless? "And Abram said, Lord God, what can You give me, since I am going on [from this world] childless and he who shall be the owner and heir of my house is this [steward] Eliezer of Damascus? And Abram continued, Look, You have given me no child; and [a servant] born in my house is my heir. And behold, the word of the Lord came to him, saying, This man shall not be your heir, but he who shall come from your own body shall be your heir"(Gen. 15:2–4).

Then the Lord told Abram to look outside at the stars and see if he could count them and told him that just like the stars that no man can count, so it would be with Abram's descendants. Abram believed God even though he was old and the Lord "counted it to him as righteousness [right standing with God]."[15]

Abraham was a man of faith. He was taught to be patient by God for the promise of a child because it was many, many years before the promise was fulfilled—the promise of a country, Canaan; of posterity, descendants that could not be counted and spiritual seed in which all the families of the earth would be blessed.

Abraham trusted that God's promises, even though he did not see all come to pass, believed that God meant what He had said to him. He also trusted God and had faith in God when he was asked to sacrifice his son Isaac; the son of the promise. "By faith, Abraham, when he was put to the test (while the testing of his faith was still in progress). Had already brought Isaac for an offering he who had gladly received and welcomed [God's] promises was ready to sacrifice his only son, of whom it was said, Through Isaac shall your descendants be reckoned. For he reasoned that God was able to raise [him] up even from among the dead" (Heb. 11:17–19).

Abraham knew who he was in God. His very name identified who he was and who he would become when he was given the name Abraham. Each time someone spoke his new name, Abraham "father of many," they were in essence decreeing his new identity in the Lord and proclaiming the miracle of God's calling and promises through a gentle servant of the Lord.

Jacob

"And He said, Your name shall be called no more Jacob [supplanter], but Israel [contender with God]; for you have contended and have power with God and with men and have prevailed" (Gen. 32:28). The angel that had wrestled with Jacob told him this. The Lord God Himself later appeared to Jacob and also told him about the change of his name.

Abraham, as discussed earlier had a name change. He was no longer Abram ("exalted father") but Abraham ("exalted father of the multitudes"). He was no longer to be called Abram because, in so doing, it would reduce him to his prior self and significance.

Jacob and Israel are two different names with two different meanings. When Jacob was born, he was grasping the heel of his elder twin brother,

Esau. Jacob in Hebrew means "at the heel." Another interpretation is when Esau found out he was deceived by Jacob twice he said, "No wonder he is called Jacob ["cunning"]![16] *Double Identity* Chassidic Masters-Parshah.

The Lord said to Rebekah, Jacob's mother, "The Lord said to her, [the founders of] two nations are in your womb, and the separation of two peoples has begun in your body; the one people shall be stronger than the other, and the elder shall serve the younger. When her days to be delivered were fulfilled, behold, there were twins in her womb. The first came out red all over like a hairy garment, and they named him Esau [hairy]. Afterward his brother came forth, and his hand grasped Esau's heel; so he was named Jacob [supplanter]. Isaac was sixty years old when she gave birth to them" (Gen. 25:23–26).

Esau was Isaac's favorite because he was a hunter, and he enjoyed eating the game that he brought home. Jacob was more quiet and dwelled in tents. Esau ended up selling Jacob his birthright for a bowl of lentil stew. One day when Isaac was getting very old, he called Esau and asked him to go out and hunt game for him. He told him to prepare a meal for him so that he could give him a blessing as his first born before he died. Jacob deceived his father by bringing a meal prepared by his mother Rebekah, and she put the skins of the goats she had prepared on his hands and his neck. Jacob received the blessing, and shortly after, Esau saw what had happened and swore to kill Jacob. Isaac sent Jacob away with a blessing and directed him to go to Padan-aram, to the house of Behuel his mother's father and take a wife there.

Jacob left the promised land, which was part of the blessing. One would think that Jacob would have realized that the way he got the blessing was not what God would have planned. Outside of Haran, Jacob has a dream of angels ascending and descending from the earth on a ladder that reaches to heaven. The Lord God appears to him and tells him promises he will give him the land on which he is lying. He will have countless offspring, and He will be with him and keep watch over him and not leave him.

Jacob marries Rachel and becomes prosperous and decides to leave Laban, his father-in-law, and travel to the country of Edom to make amends with his brother, Esau. He becomes fearful when he is told that Esau has four hundred men with him. He is at the end of his rope, and he calls out to God for mercy and reminds God of His promises to him. He sends gifts for Esau ahead of him and while he was left alone, "A man wrestled with him until daybreak. And when [the man] saw that He did not prevail against

[Jacob], He touched the hollow of his thigh; and Jacob's thigh was put out of joint as he wrestled with Him. Then He said, Let me go, for day is breaking, But [Jacob] said, I will not let You go unless You declare a blessing upon me. [The Man] asked him, What is your name? And [in shock of realization, whispering] he said, Jacob [supplanter, schemer, trickster, swindler]! And He said, your name shall be called no more Jacob [supplanter], but Israel [contender with God]: for you have contended and have power with God and with men and have prevailed. Then Jacob asked Him, Tell me, I pray You, what [in contrast] is Your name? But He said, Why is it that you ask My Name? And [the Angel of God declared] a blessing on [Jacob] there. And Jacob called the name of the place Peniel [the face of God], saying For I have seen God face to face, and my life is spared and not snatched away" (Gen. 32:24-32).

The man that Jacob wrestled with was God. It is evident because the new name "Israel" means "he fights with God." When Jacob finally began to trust in God, he is given a new name. "Israel was God's covenant name for the new nation. The name 'Jacob' represents independence from God, and 'Israel' represents dependence on God."[17]

Jacob and his mother had been manipulating Jacob's inheritance. His mother had been given a message from God that "the elder shall serve the younger" (Gen. 25:23). Instead of just waiting on the Lord and trusting in Him to work out His will in His time and way, they both took matters into their own hands. God's will was accomplished, and the name Israel was given to Jacob because God said that he had contended and had power with God and with men and had prevailed. He had a new identity in God, one that had already been decreed in the courts of heaven. It was a mantle that Jacob struggled to achieve, but once he surrendered to the Lord, he received his true calling and purpose.

Joseph

Joseph was the eleventh son of Jacob. Joseph was Jacob's favorite son whom he loved dearly. Joseph was a tattletale, who would bring a bad report about his brothers from the field. His brothers resented this and hated him for it. One day Jacob presented Joseph with a special coat of many colors, and it just reinforced their hatred for him even more. Joseph spoke about his dreams to his brothers, which were prophetic showing that Joseph would one day rule over his brothers. Because of this and many other reasons, his brothers plotted his death, but Reuben the eldest brother convinced them to deceive their father in thinking that he had been slain by beasts. They cast him into a pit and noticed that a caravan of Ishmaelites coming from Gilead and decided to sell Joseph.

Joseph was sold to a high-ranking Egyptian named Potiphar. Joseph became a faithful servant, but one day Potiphar's wife tried to seduce Joseph, and he rejected her, and because of this she falsely accused him of attempted rape and he was thrown in prison. In prison he interpreted the dreams of two prisoners, and two years later the king had a dream and told Joseph his two dreams and Joseph interpreted the dreams and advised the king to start storing grain in preparation for a great famine. Because of Joseph's great wisdom, he was made a ruler in Egypt second to the king[18]

Jacob sent ten of his sons to go to Egypt to buy grain when the famine struck. Joseph's brothers met him in Egypt but did not recognize him. Joseph tried to conceal his identity, but he could not any longer and decided to reveal his identity to them after he told everyone else to leave the room. "And Joseph said to his brothers, I am Joseph! Is my father still alive? And his brothers could not reply, for they were distressingly disturbed and dismayed at [the startling realization that they were in] his presence. And Joseph said to his brothers, Come near to me, I pray you. And they did so. And he said, I am Joseph your brother, whom you sold into Egypt! But now, do not be distressed and disheartened or vexed and angry with yourselves because you sold me here, for God sent me ahead of you to preserve life. For these two years the famine has been in the land, and there are still five years, more in which there will be neither plowing nor harvest. God sent me before you to preserve for you a posterity and to continue a remnant on the earth, to save your lives by a great escape and save for you many survivors. So now it was not you who sent me here, but God: and He has made me a father to Pharaoh and lord of all his house and ruler over all the land of Egypt" (Gen. 45:3–8).

Joseph's true identity was not a shepherd boy, nor a father's favorite child. His purpose came through a time of rejection, pain, and suffering. If Joseph had never been thrown into the pit, and falsely accused and sent to prison, he would never have been able to fulfill his destiny, which was to save God's chosen people. Sometimes the things that happen in our lives only happen because they are molding us and directing us into our destiny. In Romans 8:28 it says, "We are assured and know that [God being a partner in their labor] all things work together and are [fitting into a plan] for good to and for those who love God and are called according to [His] design and purpose."

Moses

It was providential for Moses to escape being killed by a mandate by the King of Egypt for the midwives to kill a baby if it is a male. His mother put him in a basket in the river, and Pharaoh's daughter found him and kept him and raised him as her own son.

Moses, the son of a Hebrew slave, lived the first forty years of his life as a Prince of Egypt. He was schooled in the Egyptian schools, and when he was forty he developed a relationship with the Israelites who he considered his brethren.

Moses began to identify with the Hebrew slaves and saw himself as a Hebrew. He saw an Egyptian beating an Israelite and Moses killed the Egyptian. In the eyes of the Hebrew slaves, Moses was not their savior, and his attempt to identify with the Hebrew slaves was a failure.

Moses had to flee after the Pharaoh threatened to arrest him and kill him as a traitor. He was rejected by the Hebrews, and he lost his Egyptian heritage. He was a man without a heritage or country. He escaped to the land of Midian. He was a stranger in a foreign land.

Everything about his new life was foreign to him: the food, customs, lifestyle, language expectations, family, and view of the world. Moses became a shepherd, which the Egyptians considered an abomination. He needed to do this to support his wife and family.

At the age of eighty, forty years later, God appeared to him in the burning bush and told him who he was: "I Am Who I Am," and he told Moses his purpose. "And I have declared that I will bring you up out of the affliction of Egypt to the land of the Canaanite, the Hittite, and the Amorite, the Perizzite, the Hivite, and the Jebusite, to a land flowing with milk and honey" (Exod. 3:17). The Lord had heard the cries of His people in Egypt, and it was His plan to free them and use Moses as their leader to do it. God promised that He would be with him through signs and wonders.[19]

Needless to say, Moses was not too enthused for he knew that he was weak and not qualified. "And Moses said to the Lord, O Lord, I am not eloquent or a man of words, neither before nor since You have spoken to Your servant; for I am slow of speech and have a heavy and awkward tongue. And the Lord said to him, who has made his mouth? Or who makes the dumb, or the deaf, or the seeing, or the blind? Is it not I, the Lord? Now therefore go, and I will be with your mouth and will teach you what you shall say" (Exod. 4:10-12). What an identity crisis! Moses, whose identity seemed to have changed so many times, was given a new identity or purpose for his life, and he did not have to worry about what he was to say or do because God Almighty would be the one to direct his steps from now on, and because of his obedience, Moses did accomplish the deliverance of God's chosen people.

Gideon

Because the Israelites had done evil in the sight of the Lord by being disobedient to the Lord, He gave them over into the hand of the Midianites for seven years. The Midianites and the Amalekites would come and destroy the crops of the Israelites. The Israelites began to cry out to the Lord for Him to save them. God was angry because of their disobedience.

"Now the Angel of the Lord came and sat under the oak [terebinth] at Ophrah, which belonged to Joash the Abiezrite, and his son Gideon was beating wheat in the winepress to hide it from the Midianites. And the Angel of the Lord appeared to him and said unto him. The Lord is with you, you mighty man of [fearless] courage. And Gideon said to him, O sir, if the Lord is with us, why is all this befallen us? And where are all His wondrous works of which our fathers told us, saying, Did not the Lord bring us up from Egypt? But now the Lord has forsaken us and given us into the hand of Midian. The Lord turned to him and said, Go in this your might, and you shall save Israel from the h and of Midian. Have I not sent you?" (Judg. 6: 10-14).

Gideon begins to describe to the Lord how unfit he is and "I am the least in my father's house" (Judg. 6). He was telling him that he came from a poor humble family. The Lord promised that He would be with him and Gideon would smite the Midianites "as one man" (Judg. 6).

Gideon asked for a fleece, a sheepskin and asked God to make the fleece full of dew, but the ground around the fleece dry. God answered his prayer and the ground was dry the next day and the fleece was wet, and then he asked for the opposite to happen and it did. In modern day terms "putting out a fleece" is something we ask God as a sign to confirm His word to someone.[20]

The army that Gideon had, thirty-two thousand men, was too much for the Lord and he asked Gideon to pare down his army. Gideon asked the men to return home if they were afraid of the battle and twenty-two-thousand men left. With only ten thousand left, God told Gideon to test the wisdom of the rest and told him to choose only those who when they drank from the water at the river, kept guard of their surroundings. Only three hundred did this, and this was the army that Gideon used to defend and defeat the Midianites.[21]

As instructed by God, Gideon blew his trumpet and broke a pitcher containing a lamp and the soldiers were to do the same. The soldiers yelled out, "The sword of the Lord, and of Gideon." This created the men in the enemy camp to become confused and they began fighting those around them instead of Gideon's army! The soldiers who had been sent away met up with the enemy on their way home and began to defeat them. Israel lived in peace and worshipped God for the next forty years because of their fear of Gideon.[22]

Gideon, even though he considered himself to be unqualified and weak, trusted in the Lord because of what the Lord told him step-by-step. God wanted Israel to know that it was He and not Gideon and his men who defeated the enemy.

David

David was one of eight sons of Jesse. He was a shepherd boy who was perfectly content to do what he had been doing. King Saul had been disobedient to the Lord and because of this he was rejected by God. God told Samuel to anoint another king of Israel. Samuel was afraid that Saul might kill him if he did this, but he went trusting in the Lord. Samuel went and looked at one of the seven sons of Jesse, Eliab who was the eldest son and thought he must be the one God has chosen.

"But the Lord said to Samuel, Look not on his appearance or at the height of his stature, for I have rejected him. For the Lord sees not as man sees; for man looks on the outward appearance, but the Lord looks on the heart" (1 Sam. 16:7). This is what the Lord told Samuel who looked upon one of Jesse's sons because he was looking at the outward appearance. His family had probably thought so little of David that they did not even consider asking him to come when Samuel visited, but the Lord did not choose any of the sons that were present but when David was called the

Lord told Samuel that David was the one and Samuel anointed him with oil, and the Spirit of the Lord came upon David from that day forward.

The men of Israel were terrified of Goliath. "And David said to the men standing by him. What shall be done for the man who kills this Philistine and takes away the reproach from Israel? For who is this uncircumcised Philistine that he should defy the armies of the living God?" (1 Sam. 17:26).

Saul had been informed by David's brother Eliab what he had said. "When David's words were heard they were repeated to Saul, and he sent for him. David said to Saul, Let no man's heart fail because of this Philistine; your servant will go out and fight with him. And Saul said to David, Youi are not able to go to fight against this Philistine. You are only an adolescent, and he has been a warrior from his youth. And David said to Saul, Your servant kept his father's sheep. And when there came a lion or again a bear and took a lamb out of the flock, I went out after it and smote it and delivered the lamb out of its mouth; and when it arose against me, I caught it by its beard and smote it and killed it. Your servant killed both the lion and the bear; and this uncircumcised Philistine shall be like one of them, for he has defiled the armies of the living God! David said, The Lord Who delivered me out of the paw of the lion and out of the paw of the bear; He will deliver me out of the hand of this Philistine. And Saul said to David, Go, and the Lord be with you!" (1 Sam. 17:31–37).

When David was confronted with Goliath, he stood his ground, and because of his faith and trust in the Lord he came only with five smooth stones and put them in his shepherd's pouch and a sling in his hand. Goliath mocked him because he was but an adolescent with nothing more than a sling and some stones. "Then David said to the Philistine, You come to me with a sword, a spear, and a javelin, but I come to you in the name of the Lord of hosts, the God of the ranks of Israel, Whom you have defied. This day the Lord will deliver you into my hand, and I will smite you and cut off your heard. And I will give the corpses of the army of the Philistines this day to the birds of the air and the wild bests of the earth, that all the earth may know that there is a God in Israel. And all the assembly shall know that the Lord saves not with sword and spear; for the battle is the Lord's and He will give you into our hands" (1 Sam. 17:45–47).

David knew who he was in God and who he belonged to, and he put his trust in Him. It was not his battle but the battle was the Lord's. David was just an instrument that used five small stones and a slingshot to defy the mighty Goliath. David was not who others told him who he was, but he was now a champion who took on the giants of the day.

Elijah

Elijah was from Gilead. He was regarded as a wilderness dweller, because of many factors, such as his trans-Jordanian connections and his identifying apparel, "They answered, He was a hairy man with a girdle of leather about his loins. And he said, It is Elijah the Tishbite" (2 Kings 1:8). He had great physical endurance. He was devoted to the Lord and was bold to speak out about what is right. He stood up to the priests of Baal. He had a strong concern for Israel.

Elijah spoke out against King Ahab because he had followed the Baals instead of being faithful to the Lord. He challenged King Ahab to assemble 450 prophets of Baal and four hundred prophets subsidized by Jezebel, the queen. He challenged the king and queen to a test to show who the true God was.[23] Both Elijah and the prophets of Baal were to put together a meat offering, and the god who answered by fire and consumed the fire would be the true God. God answered with fire from heaven and consumed the offering, the wood, the altar, and the dust and the water of the altar of Baal! He ordered the prophets of Baal to be slain.

Elijah took flight when he heard that Jezebel was angry over the deaths of the prophets. He fled into the wilderness. He became depressed and discouraged, and the Lord sent an angel that provided food and drink for him. The angel told him to go to Mt. Horeb in Sinai to find shelter in a cave. While he was there, the Lord spoke to him; not in the fire, not in a powerful wind and not in an earthquake but in a "still small voice" (1 Kings 19:12). The Lord told him to anoint Jehu to be king of Israel.

Elijah stood up to the status quo in his time, the worshipers of Baal who worshiped false gods. Elijah stood his ground and obeyed what God had told him to do. "Behold, I will send you Elijah, the prophet before the great and terrible day of the Lord comes" (Mal. 4:5). Jesus was regarded by some of the Jews as Elijah. "Now when Jesus went into the region of Caesarea Philippi, He asked His disciples, Who do people say that the Son of Man is? And they answered, Some say John the Baptist; others say Elijah; and others Jeremiah or one of the prophets" (Matt. 16:13–14)

Jeremiah

Jeremiah was one of the priests at Anathoth in the territory of Benjamin. The Lord spoke this message to Jeremiah:

"Before I formed you in the womb, I knew [and] approved of you [as My chosen instrument], and before you were born, I separated you and set you apart, consecrating you; [and] I appointed you as a prophet to the nations. Then said I, Ah, Lord God! Behold, I cannot speak, for I am only a youth. But the Lord said to me, Say not I am only a youth; for you shall go to all to whom I shall send you, and whatever I command you, you shall speak. Be not afraid of them [their faces], for I am with you to deliver you, says the Lord. See, I have this day appointed you to the oversight of the nations and of the kingdoms to root out and pull down, to destroy and to overthrow, to build and to plant" (Jer. 1:5–8:10).

Here again, just like many men of God before him, Jeremiah did not feel qualified to carry out the will of the Lord, but the Lord promised that He would be with him and put His words in his mouth. "Then the Lord put forth His hand and touched my mouth. And the Lord said to me, Behold; I have put My words in your mouth" (Jer. 1:9).

Jeremiah went about preaching the words of the covenant to the people. There had been reform under Judah's King Josiah bringing religious observances back to the Jewish people. Jeremiah was called to restore that which had been lost. He had been appointed to reveal the sins of the people and the consequences of ignoring. Tragedy came when righteous King Josiah died suddenly.

Jeremiah told the people that the effects of sin would be that God would remove His blessings. There would be famine and starvation, and they would be taken captive into a foreign land. He was persecuted because he had been speaking out. Even his own family conspired against him. The new king and the king's men did not want to hear these warnings, so he was thrown into a cistern but was saved by an official who persuaded the king to free him.[24]

Despite the persecution, Jeremiah knew he had to speak God's message. "If I say, I will not make mention of [the Lord] or speak any more in His name, in my mind and heart it is as if there were a burning fire shut up in my bones. And I am weary of enduring and holding it in; I cannot [contain it any longer]" (Jer. 19:9).

Jeremiah's message to the people of God was both a warning and also hope for the nation. He gave them hope through the time of the Babylonian captivity and beyond. Jeremiah prophesied that God would bring a remnant back to Judah rebuilding Jerusalem and the temple; raise up a descendant of David to serve God and to guide His people—a reference to the coming of Jesus; He would bring a remnant back to Israel a second time and God would heal the wounds of His people and restore His covenant with them and plant His people back in their land again.[25]

Daniel

As a child Daniel was brought to Babylon along with other Hebrew children to serve in a barbaric system. Daniel also brought his faith in God with him. He revealed the meaning of a dream to King Belshazzar and was elevated to a high position in the kingdom.[26] Daniel did not forget his faith and continued to pray as usual.

The leaders of the new King Darius were jealous of Daniel and plotted against him. "Then said these men, We shall not find any occasion [to bring accusation] against this Daniel except we find it against him concerning the law of his God. Then these presidents and satraps came [tumultuously] together to the king and said to him, King Darius, live forever! All the presidents of the kingdom, the deputies and the satraps, the counselors and the governors, have consulted and agreed that the king should establish a royal statute and make a firm decree that whoever shall ask a petition of any god or man for thirty days, except of you, O king shall be cast into the den of lions" (Dan. 6:5-7).

Daniel, defiantly went into his house and opened the windows and prayed just as he always did. He did not go in secret it appears because he opened the windows for everyone to hear! Daniel knew very well what the consequences would, be but he was faithful to God. He did not compromise.

King Darius was concerned about Daniel being thrown into the lion's den and apparently knew something about Daniel's God. "Then the king commanded, and Daniel was brought and cast into the den of lions. The king said to Daniel, May your God, Whom you are serving continually, deliver you! And when he came to the den and to Daniel, he cried out in a voice of anguish. The king said to Daniel, O Daniel, servant of the living God, is your God, Whom you serve continually, able to deliver you from the lions? Then Daniel said to the king, O king, live forever! My God has sent His angel and has shut the lions' mouths so that they have not hurt me, because I was found innocent and blameless before Him; and also before you, O king, [as you very well know] I have done no harm or wrong" (Dan. 6:16–22).

As a result of Daniel's courage and determination to serve his God, he was again elevated by the king and decreed that the God of Daniel is the living God and a Savior and Deliverer who works signs and wonders and by Whose power He delivered Daniel from the lion's den.

Jonah

Jonah was a prophet of God who was God's instrument to carry out God's will on the earth. God called Jonah to Nineveh to repent and that God's mercy would follow repentance. "Now the word of the Lord came to Jonah son of Amittal, saying, Arise, go to Nineveh, that great city, and proclaim against it, for their wickedness has come up before Me" (Jon.1:1).

Jonah decided to flee after hearing the commandment of the Lord. He tried to run from his calling from God. Anyone who truly knows God, knows that you cannot run from Him. Jonah must have known this but decided to run anyway.[27]

He decided to board a ship to go to Tarshish to "escape" from God's calling. God sent a great storm that rocked the ship. The sailors prayed to their god with no avail, so the ship's master awoke Jonah and rebuked him for not praying to his God for help. They were convinced that someone on the ship was causing God to get angry, so they cast lots and it fell on Jonah. They began asking him questions, and he finally confessed that he was a Hebrew and a prophet of the true God. He also admitted that he was running from God, and when they asked him why and what should they do, Jonah said to throw him over and they did.[28]

God prepared a fish to swallow Jonah. "Then Jonah prayed to the Lord his God from the fish's belly. And said, I cried out of my distress to the Lord, and He heard me; out of the belly of Sheol cried I, and You heard my voice. For You cast me into the deep, into the heart of the seas, and the floods surrounded me; all Your waves and Your billows passed over me. Then I said, I have been cast out of Your presence and Your sight; yet I will look again toward Your holy temple" (Jonah 2:1–4).

So the Lord heard Jonah's prayer and the word of the Lord came to him and God told him to go to Nineveh and preach and cry out to it what He would tell him. "And Jonah began to enter into the city a day's journey, and he cried, Yet forty days and Nineveh shall be overthrown! So the people of Nineveh believed God and proclaimed a fast and put on sackcloth (in penitent mourning), from the greatest of them even to the least of them" (Jon. 3:4-5).

The king made a proclamation that every person and beast not eat or drink for a period of time and turn away from evil so that God revoke His sentence upon them. God saw their hearts and that they turned away from evil and God revoked His sentence.

God gave Jonah a second chance. Even though he disobeyed God initially, He knew Whom he was and gave the warning to the people of Nineveh. We can never run away from God. God is very merciful even to the unbelievers because He wants all mankind to come the knowledge and the saving power of God through Christ.

John the Baptist

John was born to aged parents, Zacharias and Elizabeth. Elizabeth was related to Mary the mother of Jesus. The Angel Gabriel had appeared to his father informing him that his prayers were going to be answered by the birth of a son, and he was to call him John. The birth of a son is not extraordinary, but his parents were beyond child bearing years. It was also foretold that John would be filled with the Spirit of God.[29] "For he will be great and distinguished in the sight of the Lord. And he must drink no wine nor strong drink, and he will be filled with and controlled by the Holy Spirit even in and from his mother's womb. And he will turn back and cause to return many of the sons of Israel to the Lord their God, And he will [himself] go before Him in the spirit and power of Elijah, to turn back the hearts of the fathers to the children, and the disobedient and incredulous and unpersuadable to the wisdom of the upright [which is the knowledge and holy love of the will of God]—in order to make ready for the Lord a people [perfectly] prepared [in spirit, adjusted and disposed and placed in the right moral state]" (Luke 1:15-17).

John did not really fit into to society at that time. He dressed in a "camel's hair" garment, and he ate locusts and wild honey. He stood out among the wealthy of the time. He was a loner and did not seek out the multitudes but they sought him out.[30]

John had a mission, and the mission as had been foretold was the "preparer." He was to prepare people for the coming Messiah. The prophets Isaiah and Malachi had said that someone would come to prepare the way for the coming of the Messiah. John consistently said that he was not the promised Messiah, nor was he Elijah come in the flesh.[31]

John administered a baptism that was "for the forgiveness of sins" (Mark 1:4). When Jesus came to him to be baptized, John hesitated. "But John protested strenuously, having in mind to prevent Him, saying, It is I who have need to be baptized by You, and do You come to me? But Jesus replied to him, Permit it just now; for this is the fitting way for [both of] us to fulfill all righteousness [that is, to perform completely whatever is right]. Then he permitted Him. And when Jesus was baptized, He went up at once out of the water; and behold, the heavens were opened and he [John] saw the Spirit of God descending like a dove and alighting on Him. And behold, a voice from heaven said, This is My Son, My Beloved in Whom I delight" (Matt. 3:14–17). John continued teaching about the coming kingdom and the need to repent. When John proclaimed that the kingdom was at hand, he meant that it was near.

Even though John's life was caught short because he was beheaded by orders of Herod, his life had purpose, and he did fulfill what had been prophesied many centuries before he was born and the Angel Gabriel's words to John did come to pass even in worldly terms he was not great, he was great in the eyes of the Lord. "Truly I tell you, among those born of women there has not risen anyone greater than John the Baptist; yet he who is least in the kingdom of heaven is greater than he" (Matt. 11:11).

Peter

There's a little bit of the apostle Peter in most of us. He was enthusiastic, outgoing, gregarious, and transparent. It was very evident that he did love Jesus. He was also strong-willed and impulsive at time. He even showed some pride.[32] When Jesus asked the disciples "Who do people say that I am?" in Mark 8:27, Peter blurted out the truthful answer, "You are the Christ [the Messiah, the Anointed One]." Jesus told them not to tell anyone and told them that He would suffer many things and be tested and rejected by the elders and be put to death, but Peter rebuked Him. "But turning around [His back to Peter] and seeing His disciples, He rebuked Peter, saying, Get behind Me, Satan! For you do not have a mind intent on promoting what God wills, but what pleases men [you are not on God's side but that of men]."

In the Garden of Gethsemane, Jesus told His disciples that they would fall away and stumble deserting Him. "Peter declared to Him, Though they all are offended and stumble and fall away because of You [and distrust and desert You], I will never do so. Jesus said to him. Solemnly I declare to you, this very night, before a single rooster crows, you will deny and disown Me three times. Peter said to Him, Even if I must die with You, I will not deny or disown You! And all the disciples said the same thing" (Matt. 26:33–35). As we know from the scriptures, Peter's words did not match up with his actions because he denied Christ three times.

Peter's brother Andrew introduced him to Jesus. Andrew told Peter that he had found the Messiah, the Anointed One. "Andrew then led [brought] Simon to Jesus. Jesus looked at him and said, You are Simon son of John. You shall be called Cephas—which translated is Peter [Stone]" (John 1:42). Jesus was already giving Peter a new identity.

After the crucifixion of Jesus, Peter knew that he had betrayed the Lord because he began to weep. After the Resurrection of Jesus, He appeared to them many times and as if seeming to allow Peter to redeem himself from his betrayal, the Lord asks Peter: "When they had eaten, Jesus said to Simon Peter, Simon, son of John do you love Me more than these [others do—with reasoning, intentional, spiritual devotion, as one loves the Father]? He said to Him, Yes, Lord, You know that I love You [that I have deep, instinctive, personal affection for You, as for a close friend]. He said to Him, Feed My lambs" (John 21:15). Again, Jesus asked him two more times.

He then told him to tend His sheep and feed His sheep. Jesus was giving Peter a new calling. He was reaffirming what He had already seen in Peter all along.

After receiving the infilling of the Holy Spirit on the Day of Pentecost, Peter was no longer self-centered and vain. He was no longer afraid as well as all the other disciples who locked themselves in the upper room. Peter became a role model and a humble servant-leader, having a shepherd's heart.

Summary

Abraham and Joseph found themselves in a new land. Abraham was asked by God to leave his country and go to a land that He would show him. A man who had no offspring would be a man whose descendants would be more numerous than the stars in the heavens. Joseph was forced to go to another land because of his brother's jealousy. Sold as a slave and living in Egypt, he was unjustly accused of a crime, sent to prison only to be elevated to a high position because of his interpretation of a King's dream. His identity hidden, even his brothers didn't recognize him, but his purpose from the Lord had already been planned by the Almighty God.

Moses and Gideon did not consider themselves capable of doing what God called them to do yet they endeavored, with the help of the Lord, to accomplish what He had purposed for them. The faith of Abraham was constant even though He did not live long enough to see the promises of God.

Overlooked by even his own family, David, a shepherd boy, slew the giant and was the one who became King. David encouraged himself in the Lord when things got rough. He looked at his victories not his failures. Elijah stood up to the status quo and challenged King Ahab and the prophets of Baal. Just like David, even in his weaknesses God still used him.

Jeremiah and Daniel stood up to the authorities and were faithful to God. God very distinctly told Jeremiah who he was and what he would do. Daniel knew Whom he was and continued to faithfully pray to the Lord God even if it meant death. Even though Jonah knew what he was supposed to do, he tried to run away from it, but in the end he obeyed the Lord and the city of Nineveh was saved from destruction. John the Baptist prepared the way for the Lord. Even in his mother's womb he was appointed to this destiny and Peter, though at times proud and impulsive, was given a mandate from Jesus to "feed My sheep" (John 21:17).

Chapter Four

Women of Faith in the Bible

Rahab

Rahab was an Amorite and had a name of an Egyptian god. The meaning of her name was *insolence, fierceness,* or *spaciousness.* According to the genealogy of Jesus Christ, Rahab was married to Salmon, and she became the mother of Boaz, who married Ruth and whose son Obed became the father of Jesse who was the father of King David. Salmon was a prince of the house of Judah and thus Rahab married into one of the leading families of Israel.[33]

Rahab was known as "the harlot," which is the Hebrew term *zoo-nah* and the Greek word *pome*, which means "harlot." Rahab had her own house in Jericho and somehow learned the facts of the Exodus of Israel.[34] When two spies from Joshua asked her for cover, she knew they were men of God, and she decided to protect them. "And she said to the men, I know that the Lord has given you the land and that your terror is fallen upon us and that all the inhabitants of the land faint because of you. For we have heard how the Lord dried up the water of the Red Sea for you when you came out of Egypt and what you did to the two kings of the Amorites who were on the [east] side of the Jordan, Sihon and Og, whom you utterly destroyed. When we heard it, our hearts melted, neither did spirit or courage remain any more in any man because of you, for the Lord your God, He is God in heaven above and on earth beneath" (Josh. 2:9–11).

Rahab then asked the men to swear that she and her family would be saved because of her kindness to them. Rahab had faith in the God that had performed great signs and wonders. She began to identify with the people of God. She exhibited a tremendous amount of courage, knowing full well that if they had discovered what she had done she would have been killed at the hands of the King of Jericho. She saved the spies because she knew that they were servants of the Lord. It was her faith in the one true God that enabled Rahab to do what she did.

The one-time harlot had entered into the royal bloodline of Jesus Christ, the Savior, the King of Kings, and the Lord of Lords! Rahab had a change of heart and mind when she met Joshua's men who asked for safety. In a few moments of time, because of Rahab's decision to hide these men and bring them to safety, she became a symbol of redemption in which all who come to Him can receive forgiveness of sin and become a new creation in Christ Jesus.

Ruth

Boaz asked Ruth, "Who are you?" (Ruth 3:9). Who was Ruth? She was a Moabite woman who had left her country after her husband had died. She could no longer be called the wife of Elimelech, her husband.

Naomi, Ruth's mother-in-law went with her two daughters-in-law to her birth place, Bethlehem. Naomi told them to return to their mother's house, but Ruth refused to go. "Then they wept aloud again; and Orpah kissed her mother-in-law [goodbye], but Ruth clung to her. And Naomi said, See, your sister-in-law has gone back to her people and to her gods; return after your sister-in-law. And Ruth said, Urge me not to leave you or to turn back from following you; for where you go I will go, and where you lodge I will lodge. Your people shall be my people and your God my God. Where you die, I will die, and there will I be buried. The Lord do so to me, and more also, if anything but death parts me from you" (Ruth 1:14–17).

In their culture, a woman derived her identity through her father, her husband, or her son. In this new culture Ruth was referred to as 'the woman.' Ruth had no husband and no sons, but Naomi had a relative of her husband's, a man from the family of Elimelech, whose name was Boaz. They were hungry, and they went to glean from the field. Boaz, who owned most of the land, asked who she was and a servant answered that she was a Moabite girl who came with Naomi. Boaz was not only looking for her name but her identity. Boaz knew there was a family connection, and that is maybe why he was so kind to her. He had been made aware of her kindness to her mother-in-law since the death of her husband having come to a people unknown to her. Ruth had two identities, a Moabite woman and a daughter-in-law.[35]

Boaz accepted Ruth for who she was. He acted quickly so that the way to marrying her would be cleared. He met with the other near-relative, and after discussion and negotiation, he was given the right to take care of Naomi and Ruth because he was now owner of all the property that belonged to Naomi's dead husband and dead sons. Soon after Ruth and Boaz married she gave birth to Obed.

Esther

Esther was an orphan who had been raised by her cousin Mordecai. Her very name, Esther, means *hidden*. Her Jewish name given to her by her parents was Hadassah, which means "myrtle." A myrtle tree is a tree that is plain looking, but when bruised and crushed its leaves release a fragrance. An unlikely candidate who became the Queen of Persia, God chose Esther to bring deliverance to the Jews when they were destined for destruction.[36]

During the reign of Ahasuerus (Xerxes) who reigned from India to Ethiopia whose throne was in Susa, the capital of the Persian Empire, he made a feast for all his princes and courtiers. After seven days of merriment, when the King was full of wine, he commanded the seven eunuchs to bring Queen Vashti before him to show how beautiful she was. She refused to come, and therefore the King in his anger divorced her and sent out a royal decree that all beautiful young virgins be gathered and brought to the King's house so that he would have a new queen. Esther was one of those virgins and was brought to the King's house. She soon won favor from the King and became Queen keeping her identity as a Jewish woman secret. All along, Mordecai had been concealing his identity and had encouraged her to do the same.[37]

Haman, the Agragite, was promoted by the King and was above all the princes in the kingdom. One day Mordecai did not bow down to him, which infuriated Haman who also found out that Mordecai was a Jew and convinced the King to eliminate all the Jews. Mordecai knew that Esther alone could save the Jewish people. There was a problem—Esther had not been summoned to the King in his royal presence for thirty days. The consequences of that could mean that she would be punished by death. Mordecai sent messengers to convey his words to Esther.[38] "For if you keep silent at this time, relief and deliverance shall arise for the Jews from elsewhere, but you and your father's house will perish. And who knows but that you have come to the kingdom for such a time as this very occasion?

Then Esther told them to give this answer to Mordecai, Go, gather together all the Jews that are present in Shushan, and fast for me; and neither eat nor drink for three days, night or day. I also and my maids will fast as you do. Then I will go to the king, though it is against the law; and if I perish, I perish. So Mordecai went away and did all that Esther had commanded him" (Esther 4:14-17).

It was Esther alone who could save the Jewish people. She needed to approach her husband, the king, and when he saw her, she obtained favor in his sight. He asked her what her request was and she said, "let the king and Haman come this day to the dinner that I have prepared for the king" (Esther 5:4). At the dinner, the king asked Esther what her petition was and what was her request and he said that he would even give her half of the kingdom. She requested another dinner on the next day.

The next day, Haman came to the dinner, and the king asked Esther what her petition was, and she said, "If I have found favor in your sight, O king and if it pleases the king, let my life be given me at my petition and my people at my request. For we are sold, I and my people, to be destroyed, slain, and wiped out of existence! But if we had been sold for bondmen and bondwomen, I would have held my tongue, for our affliction is not to be compared with the damage this will do to the king" (Esther 6:4). The king asked her who this person was, and she said Haman, an adversary and an enemy. Haman was punished and hanged at the very gibbet that he had built for Mordecai.

The Jewish people in Persia were saved, and there was great rejoicing because an Esther—a Jewish maiden, who concealed her identity, had been given the birth name, Hadassah by her parents. Hadassah means *myrtle*, which is a plant that releases a fragrance when it is crushed. She became a deliverer who was not afraid to die if need be to save her people. She went from a Jewish maiden to the Queen of Persia. Today the festival of Purim is celebrated to commemorate the courage of Esther and the deliverance of the Jews.[39]

Mary, the Mother of Jesus

"Now in the sixth month, the angel Gabriel was sent from God to a town of Galilee named Nazareth, to a girl never having been married and a virgin engaged to be married to a man whose name was Joseph, a descendant of the house of David; and the virgin's name was Mary. And he came to her and said, Hail, O favored one [endued with grace]! The Lord is with you! Blessed [favored of God] are you before all other women! But when she saw him, she was greatly troubled and disturbed and confused at what he said and kept revolving in her mind what such a greeting might mean. And the angel said to her, Do not be afraid, Mary, for you have found grace [free, spontaneous, absolute favor, and loving-kindness] with God. And Listen! You will become pregnant and will give birth to a Son, and you shall call His name Jesus" (Luke 1:26-31).

She did not understand because she had never had intimacy with any man and the angel told her that the Holy Spirit will come upon her and the power of the Most High will overshadow her and the holy offspring shall be called the Son of God. He said that with God nothing is impossible and no word from God is without power! "Then Mary said, Behold, I am the handmaiden of the Lord; let it be done to me according to what you have said. And the angel left her. Mary, not really knowing what this would entail, with complete trust in God, said 'yes' and surrendered her life and her body as a temple for the creation of the incarnate Son of God. Mary had received a message from heaven that would change her life and her purpose that only the enfolding of the magnitude of her journey could only be 'keeping within her herself all these things [sayings], weighing and pondering them in her heart'" (Luke 2:19).

After Mary went to visit her cousin Elizabeth who was now six months pregnant in her old age, the baby within Elizabeth's womb leaped and then Elizabeth said, "Blessed [favored of God], above all other women are you! And blessed [favored of God] is the Fruit of your womb!" (Luke 1:42).

"And Mary said, My soul magnifies and extols the Lord, and my spirit rejoices in God my Savior. For He has looked upon the low station and humiliation of His hand-maiden. For behold, from now on all generations [of all ages] will call me blessed and declare me happy and to be envied! For He Who is almighty has done great things for me—and holy is His name [to be venerated in His purity, majesty and glory]!

"And when the time came for their purification [the mother's purification and the Baby's dedication] came according to the Law of Moses, they brought Him up to Jerusalem to present Him to the Lord" (Luke 2:22)

"And Simeon blessed them and said to Mary His mother, Behold, this Child is appointed and destined for the fall and rising of many in Israel and for a sign that is spoken against. And a sword will pierce through your own soul also—that the secret thoughts and purposes of many hearts may be brought out and disclosed" (Luke 2:34–35). How Mary's heart, although rejoicing in the special time and blessing, must have grieved because of the prophecy of a "sword will pierce through your own soul" (Luke 2:35).

At the foot of the cross, as Mary knelt and gazed on her precious Son whom she had loved so much, she may have found herself remembering the words of the prophet that a sword would pierce her very soul. It was her Son who at the cross looked at His grieving mother and gave Mary a new role as mother of John and John now accepting Mary as his mother. "So Jesus, seeing His mother there, and the disciple whom He loved standing near, said to His mother [dear] woman, See, [there is] your son! Then He said to the disciple, See, [there is] your mother! And from that hour, the disciple took her into his own [keeping, own home]" (John 19:26–27).

Mary Magdalene

Mary was very devoted to serving the Lord and she was one of the many Marys mentioned in the Bible. This shows us that Jesus loved to use women to spread the Gospel. The very first person that Jesus appeared to after the Resurrection was Mary. She was also the first person to tell the disciples to proclaim that Jesus was alive.[40]

Mary Magdalene was from Magdala, which identified her place of birth. There is no record of her marital status, age, or her parent-age. It appears that she was of high standing in the community and lived in comfortable circumstances, but she suffered from periodic insanity. The Bible says that seven demons were cast out of her by Jesus. After this deliverance she was then ready to become one of the most devoted disciples of Jesus Christ.[41]

Mary left her home in Magdala to serve Jesus. She had a new identity—she was no longer the woman who was delivered from seven demons, but a follower of the Messiah and helped sustain Him and His ministry. "And also some women who had been cured of evil spirits and disease: Mary, called Magdalene, from whom seven demons had been expelled; And Joanna, the wife of Chuza, Herod's household manager; and Susanna; and many others, who ministered to and provided for Him and them out of their property and personal belongings" (Luke 8:2–3).

Even at the cross, Mary did not abandon Jesus like most of the disciples had. She stayed no matter what the cost along with Mary the mother of

Jesus and Mary the mother of James. She was persistent and faithful in her walk with Jesus.

Mary was the first at the garden tomb to be a witness for the most important event in world history—the Resurrection of Jesus Christ! She, along with other faithful women, had been given this special privilege. "But Mary remained standing outside the tomb sobbing. As she wept, she stooped down [and looked] into the tomb. And she saw two angels in white sitting there, one at the head and one at the feet, where the body of Jesus had lain. And they said to her, Woman why are you sobbing? She told them, Because they have taken away my Lord, and I do not know where they have laid Him. On saying this she turned around and saw Jesus standing [there], but she did not know [recognize] that it was Jesus. Jesus said to her, Woman, why are you crying [so]? For Whom are you looking? Supposing that it was the gardener, she replied, Sir, if you carried Him away from here, tell me where you have put Him and I will take Him away. Jesus said to her, Mary! Turning around she said to Him in Hebrew, Rabboni!—which means Teacher or Master" (John 20:11-16). This shows what a great love she had for her Master because even in His death, she came to care for His precious body and was overcome by sorrow.

Jesus then told her to go to His brethren and proclaim the greatest good news of all time! Jesus does make all things new. In Mary's great love and devotion to Jesus He rewarded her with the privilege of being the person to announce the good news. She was made a new creation in Christ

Woman at the Well

"Presently, when a woman of Samaria came along to draw water, Jesus said to her; Give Me a drink—For His disciples had gone off into the town to buy food—The Samaritan woman said to Him, How is it that You, being a Jew ask me, a Samaritan [and a] woman, for a drink?—For the Jews have nothing to do with the Samaritans—Jesus answered her, If you had only known and had recognized God's gift and Who this is that is saying to you, Give Me a drink, you would have asked Him [instead] and He would have given you living water" (John 4-10).

As you can see by the Gospel reading, Jews were not supposed to speak to Samaritans. Without a husband present, men weren't permitted to speak to woman, and a Rabbi should not be speaking to a "shady" lady such as her. Jesus offered her living water. She asked if He was greater than Jacob who gave them the well. "Jesus answered her, All who drink of this water will be thirsty again. But whoever takes a drink of the water that I will give him shall never, no never, be thirsty any more. But the water that I will give him shall become a spring of water welling up [flowing, bubbling] [continually] within him unto [into, for] eternal life" (John 4:13-14).

She asked Jesus to give her this living water but still thought that it was the natural water, not supernatural water. Jesus told her to go get her husband and she admitted that she had no husband. He also told her that she had been married five times before and that the man she was living with was not her husband.

Jesus began to teach her about true worship and that God is a Spirit and that "those who worship Him must worship Him in spirit and in truth" (John 4:24). She told Him that she knew the Messiah was coming. "Jesus said to her, I Who now speak with you am He" (John 4:26). She became excited and ran to town and told the people that she had met a man who knew everything she did. "So the people left the town and set out to go to Him" (John 4:30).

She had been confronted with the truth and the identity of the person, Jesus, who had been speaking to her. In a few minutes, a casual meeting at the well with the Son of the Living God, an ordinary Samaritan woman who no Jew was supposed to speak to; a woman who was not allowed to speak to a man unless her husband was present and a "shady" woman who had no business speaking to a Rabbi, began to proclaim the Good News to the people in her town and in so doing became an evangelist for the Kingdom of God. Jesus knew who she was, but He offered her who she could be in Him.

Summary

These women of faith knew who they were and who they needed to be to fulfill their purpose for the Kingdom. Rahab and Esther were women who even in the face of death decided to protect the Jewish people. Rahab "the harlot," was no longer attached to that name because in an instant because of her decision she changed her destiny to become part of the royal blood line of Jesus Christ.

Ruth and Mary Magdalene left their homes to follow a path that would lead them in God's will for their lives. Ruth was completely stripped of her own identity with no husband or family or country by her own decision but ended up receiving even more than she had before also becoming part of the royal bloodline of Jesus Christ.

Mary, the mother of Jesus, in her lowliness as a maiden, was now asked to conceive in her womb the Son of God. Her "yes" must have been an earthquake to the demons in Hell because salvation was on its way and her "yes" not only changed who she was but changed the destiny of the whole world through salvation in Jesus Christ.

The woman at the well reminds me of all of us who may not be seeking the Lord in our lives but how Jesus comes to us where we are at, knowing our many sins and failures, and He is still reaching out to us, to change us, renew us, and save us.

Chapter Five

The Church

Social and Historical Impact of Christianity

Christianity is responsible for the way our society is organized and for the way we currently live. So Extensive is the Christian contribution to our laws, our economics, our politics, our arts, our calendar, our holidays, and our moral and cultural priorities that historian J. M. Robers writes in the *Triumph of the West*, "We could none of us today be what we are if a handful of Jews nearly two thousand years ago had not believed that they had known a great teacher, seen him crucified, dead, and buried, and then rise again."[42]

In the area of value for human life, Christianity has been a beacon throughout the ages. The Bible says that we are created in the image and likeness of God. The rights for the unborn, women, slaves, and many other oppressed individuals including Christians themselves has been evident in Church history.

A woman was the property of her husband in ancient cultures. Women had a low status in society, and newly born female babies were sometimes left to the elements to die. In Roman society a woman could not go more than two years without being married. A Christian woman was not forced to remarry and was cared for by the community. The Church allowed widows to keep their husband's estate. Women were given greater security because a Christian man needed to marry her if he wanted to live with her.

In pagan cultures infanticide was applauded. In Rome, if you killed your own child, it could be considered a noble act. Because of a view of the sanctity of life, the Christian church forbade such things. There were instructions from a document, Didache, in the early church that contained instructions against abortion.

Even though some Christians owned slaves, they participated equally in worship and the community. They were also given property rights. Christians were the first people to speak up against slavery and some purchased slaves so that they could set them free. Slavery was ended by some Christian activists. William Wilberforce is credited with ending international slave trade.

Telemachus, who was a fifth-century monk has been credited as a significant force in ending the gladiator spectacles. Missionaries have also been credited with stopping cannibalism in some primitive cultures.

It has been recorded that prior to Jesus there was practically no trace of compassion and mercy through charitable efforts. Jesus emphasized caring for the ill and the weak and the lowliest. A good example is the Good Samaritan (Luke 10:33–34) "But a certain Samaritan, as he traveled along, came down to where he was; and when he saw him, he was moved with pity and sympathy [for him]. And went to him and dressed his wounds, pouring on [them] oil and wine. Then he set him on his own beast and brought him to an inn and took care of him." There are charitable organizations outside of faith based but there are many good examples such as the Salvation Army, religious hospitals, Samaritan's Purse (Franklin Graham), etc.

Christianity has promoted heterosexual monogamous love and a lasting relationship between husband and wife for procreation and the upbringing of children who are taught Christian values. The family takes on a central role in Christianity and has been an example of love and compassion throughout history. Jesus was born into a family. His mother and father loved Him and brought Him up in the Jewish doctrine and laws.

Education has its roots in the Protestant Reformation. The impetus for literacy was to promote the reading of the Bible in which Christians find their moral compass for life in this world through its teachings. The Puritans passed the first law to require education for the masses.

The law was called the Old Deluder Satan Act. This referenced the devil who Christians believe can get a foothold into our lives because they do not know scripture. Children's reading texts in schools included the Bible. In the 1800s the illiteracy rate was fourteenth of 1 percent.

There are forty million people today, estimated, that are illiterate in the United States. All but one of the 123 Christian universities during the colonial era were Christian institutions.

Our constitutional government and judicial system has its roots in biblical doctrines. At least fifty of the fifty-five signers of the US Constitution were Christians. Constitutional checks and balances in our system was a result of biblical principles. The Ten Commandments as the rule of law rather than man, traces back to the Old Testament. The Declaration of Independence states that we have unalienable rights given to us by our Creator. Judicial, legislative, and executive branches of the government can be traced back to Isaiah 33:22. The Bible has also influenced the concept of fair trials and the presence of witnesses.

The influence of Christianity on the arts has been tremendous. It has influenced Christian writers such as Dante, Chaucer, Shakespeare, Dickons, Milton, etc. Handel and Bach wanted to honor God through their music. The beautiful cathedrals in the world were influenced by the beauty and grandeur of the influence of Christianity.[43]

Cultural Christianity

Christianity, as stated before has had a major influence on our country as a whole reflected in our charity, our laws, the concept of family, and the elevation of women and the oppressed. It has also played a major role in its influence on the arts and education.

So it appears that Christianity has shaped our culture, but is Christianity continuing to shape our culture, or is our culture shaping our Christian beliefs? Are you a biblical Christian, or are you a cultural Christian? Are we trying to have the best of both worlds by compromising our beliefs as a Christian? We seem to be adopting many of the values of the world. We have been exchanging the truth and the absolutes of God for the lies of the enemy. We have become saturated in the material world and seek after fleshly desires.

We use God as an ATM. God, I want this; God, I want that. We make God who we want Him to be, not Who He is. How many of us who call ourselves Christians are born again and read and know the scriptures?

In the parable of the sower there are four groups of hearers of the Word of God:

1. The first group is the non-Christian or unbeliever.
    Matthew 13:19: "While anyone is hearing the Word of the kingdom and does not grasp and comprehend it, the evil one comes and snatches away what was sown in his heart. This is what was

sown along the roadside." Jesus is making it clear that not everyone who hears the Word of God accepts it.

2. The second group is the cultural Christian, Type "C." The "C" stands for counterfeit faith. It is a faith that is not genuine. "Not everyone who says to Me, Lord, Lord, will enter the kingdom of heaven, but he who does the will of My Father Who is in heaven" (Matt. 7:21).

    "As for what was sown on thin [rocky] soil, this is he who hears the Word and at once welcomes and accepts it with joy; Yet it has no real root in him, but is temporary [inconsistent], lasts but a little while; and when affliction or trouble or persecution comes on account of the Word, at once he is caused to stumble [he is repelled and begins to distrust and desert Him Whom he ought to trust and obey] and he falls away" (Matthew 13:20-21). These people are what we would call cultural Christians because they have not been rooted in their faith enough to actually defend the faith or endure hardships because of it.

3. The third group is a cultural Christian, Type "D." Type "D" is for defeated faith and is type of Christian who lives in defeat. There is hardly a difference between his/her lifestyle and that of the world. They are Christian in name only.

    "As for what was sown among thorns, this is he who hears the Word, but the cares of the world and the pleasure and delight and glamour and deceitfulness of riches choke and suffocate the Word and it yields no fruit. There is little difference between this Christian and the people in the world. The temptations of the flesh in the world are sought out more than the fruits of the Spirit. They seem more influenced by what the world is saying than what God is saying in His Word. They may have faith but have not made Jesus Lord over their lives" (Matthew 13:22).

4. Biblical Christian. A person who trusts in Christ. They have given their lives to the Lord and trusted in Christ for their salvation. They are obedient to the Word of God and God's principles.[44]

    "As for what was sown on good soil, this is he who hears the Word and grasps and comprehends it; he indeed bears fruit and yields in one case a hundred times as much as was sown, in another sixty times as much and in another thirty" (Matthew 13:23). This person is a Biblical Christian who has truly made Jesus the Lord over their lives. They stick out in a crowd because they are salt and light. They do not compromise to worldly desires and pleasures but stand for the Cross of Christ no matter what.

"I appeal to you therefore, brethren, and beg of you in view of [all] the mercies of God, to make a decisive dedication of your bodies [presenting all your members and faculties] as a living sacrifice, holy [devoted] as a living sacrifice, holy [devoted, consecrated] and well pleasing to God, which is your reasonable [rational, intelligent] service and spiritual worship. Do not be conformed to this world [this age] [fashioned after and adapted to its external, superficial customs], but be transformed [changed] by the [entire] renewal of your mind [by its ideals and its new attitude], so that you may prove [for yourselves] what is the good and acceptable and perfect will of God even the thing which is good and acceptable and perfect [in His sight for you]" (Rom. 12:1-2)

Yes, Paul is begging his brethren not to become, in our words, "cultural Christians." Will the Church change the culture and be a great influence as it has in the past or will we allow the culture to change the Church.

What are some of the "symptoms" of a cultural Christian? (Adapted from *"Our Culture is a Corrupting Influence on the Church!)*

1. Acceptance of homosexuality lifestyle. "Do you not know that the unrighteous and the wrongdoers will not inherit or have any share in the kingdom of God? Do not be deceived [misled]: neither the impure and immoral, nor idolaters, nor adulterers, nor those who participate in homosexuality" (1 Corinthians 6:9-11). Homosexuality is increasingly being tolerated in churches.
2. There are many "sipping" saints. Alcohol in moderation is acceptable, but too many Christians are drinking as much as their non-Christian friends. In Ephesians 5:18, it says, "And do not get drunk with wine, for that is debauchery, but ever be filled and stimulated with the [Holy] Spirit."
3. No biblical standards for movies or TV. "I will behave myself wisely and give heed to the blameless way—O when will You come to me?

I will walk within my house in integrity and with a blameless heart. I will set no base or wicked thing before my eyes. I hate the work of them who turn aside [from the right path]; it shall not grasp hold of me" (Ps.101:1–2).

Market-driven churches that seem more like a business than a place of worship. Magnificent buildings that cost millions of dollars with an emphasis on prosperity teaching instead of a servant attitude, which does not include—"What can I get out of this community?" It's all about me, not the great commission that Jesus professed to the disciples just before His Resurrection.[45]

Nashville Statement

A hundred and fifty conservative Christian leaders signed a statement released recently in August 2017. It is a statement affirming beliefs on human sexuality, which includes that "marriage is between one man and one woman" and that approval of "homosexual immorality" is sinful. It is referred to as the Nashville Statement. "We affirm that it is sinful to approve of homosexual immorality or transgenderism and that such approval constitutes an essential departure from Christian faithfulness and witness," Article 10 reads. "We deny that the approval of homosexual immorality or transgenderism is a matter of moral indifference about which otherwise faithful Christians should agree to disagree." In another statement it reads, "Our true identity, as male and female persons, is given by God. It is not only foolish, but hopeless to try to make ourselves what God did not create us to be."

These statements immediately outraged LGBTQ and LGBTQ-affirming Christians, seeing it as an attack on their understanding of the faith. Several progressive Christian groups issued counter statements against it. Even though conservative Christian groups have agreed with Biblical beliefs about marriage there are moderate and progressive brethren that have gone in a very different direction. The United Church of Christ has affirmed marriage equality. The Episcopal Church, Evangelical Lutheran Church in America, and Presbyterian Church (USA) and some others ordain LGBTQ persons and are allowing these ministers to perform same-sex marriages.

Brennan Breed, who is an assistant professor of Old Testament at Columbia Theological Seminary, states, "For me as a Christian, we are not a religion that is bound to a particular time and place, a particular language, a particular culture." He also stated that part of how Christianity works is that it adapts because of new interpretations of scripture or tradition. This I would argue would be a cultural Christian's view of the world rather than a Biblical view.[46] In Matthew 19:4–5, Jesus responded when asked about divorce, "And said, For this reason a man shall leave his father and mother and shall be united firmly (joined inseparably) to his wife, and the two shall become one flesh? So they are no longer two, but one flesh. What therefore God has joined together, let not man put asunder [separate]." "God created man in His own image, in the image and likeness of God He created him; male and female He created them" (Gen. 1:27).

Free Speech vs. Hate Speech and Freedom of Religion

Free speech, according to the Constitution of the United States of America, is a right. Apparently in this day and age it is not a Christian's right. It's now a criminal matter to quote the King James Bible in Britain! The UK culture's definition of free speech and tolerance now seem to demand silence for those who disagree and believe in the Bible. The prosecutor's statement reflects what religious freedom means to secularists: "'To say to someone that Jesus is the only God is not a matter of truth.' Be warned: this is also what secularists are forcing on America. Secular ideology is not about having equal rights but about having superior rights for those in power to eradicate Christian speech."[47]

Two street preachers (Michael Overd and Michael Stockwell) were convicted in Bristol of a public order of offence. The prosecutor said that publicly quoting the King James Bible should "be considered to be abusive and is a criminal matter." They were accused of the Crime and Disorder Act of 1998 of using "threatening or abusive words or behavior or disorderly behavior within the hearing or sight of a person . . . and the offence was religiously aggravated."[48]

In July 5, 2004, Ake Green, a Christian Pastor, was sentenced in Kalmar, Sweden, to one month in jail under Sweden's law against hate speech because of his sermon condemning homosexuality. He appealed the conviction on February 11, 2005, and the decision was overturned and he was acquitted. He never served any jail time.[49] His comments were drawn from Biblical texts, which dealt with the sin of homosexuality. It appears that those that reject Biblical truths are silencing preachers all because of tolerance and diversity. Advocates for the normalization of homosexuality have many people behind them, but advocates for Biblical sexuality and the traditional family are left without a voice. Sweden passed a hate speech statute in 2002, which said that "church sermons" are also subject to the law's restrictions. This also leads to eradicating any criticism of homosexuality. Criticism is driven by the culture that it could be harmful to emotional health.[50] I guess "safe spaces" in America reflect this attitude.

Freedom of speech appears to be a right only for the left. Their goal is to silence all those who disagree with them. One would ask, "Where is the Church?" There are many preachers who are afraid to speak out because of the Johnson Amendment, Section 501 (C) (3) of our nation's tax code, which gives tax exempt to a church as long as they don't participate or intervene in publishing or distributing for any political campaign on behalf of a candidate or opposition of a candidate for public office.[49] President Johnson proposed the amendment to restrict free speech of pastors and churches. It was during that year that he was up for reelection, and he wanted to put a stop to some nonprofit organizations that were supporting his opponent.[51] Our nation has had a history of clergy preaching about political issues. During the American Revolution, independence was preached from the pulpits. This brought about courage and enthusiasm. The minutemen were a result of the preaching from the pulpits.

Peter von Muhlenberg was known as the "fighting parson of the American Revolution." He was the pastor of the German/English-speaking Episcopal Church in Woodstock, Virginia. It was there that he received a letter from George Washington in which he requested that regiments be raised for a Revolutionary Army. His sermon for the following Sunday was based on the scripture from Ecclesiastes 3:1-8: "A time to love and a time to hate, a time for war and a time for peace."

On May 31, 1775, Samuel Langdon, D.D., president of Harvard College in Cambridge, preached a sermon titled "Government Corrupted by Vice and Recovered by Righteousness." The following is an excerpt from that sermon:

> We have lived to see the time when British liberty is just ready to expire, when that constitution of government which has so long been the glory and strength of the English nation is deeply under-mined and ready to tumble into ruins; when America is threatened with cruel

oppression, and the arm of power is stretched out against New England, and especially against this colony, to compel us to submit to the arbitrary acts of legislators who are not our representatives, and who will not themselves bear the least part of the burdens which, without mercy, they are laying upon us . . .[52]

On Thursday, May 4, 2017, President Trump signed an executive order asking the IRS to use "maximum enforcement discretion" over the regulations of the Johnson Amendment. This amendment applies to churches and nonprofits. Trump had promised to dismantle the Johnson Amendment, which essentially bans these organizations from political speech and activities. "The open season on Christians and other people of faith is coming to a close in America and we look forward to assisting the Trump administration in fully restoring America's First Freedom," Family Research Council President Tony Perkins said in a statement.[53]

Freedom of Religion

Everyone in the United States has the right to practice his or her own religion, or no religion at all, according to the First Amendment of the Constitution of the USA. The First Amendment to the Bill of Rights states, "Congress shall make no law respecting the establishment of religion, or prohibiting the free exercise thereof." Free exercise is meant to protect citizens' religious and moral beliefs not just within the four corners of a church. It was meant to give the church freedom to influence the common good. It was never meant to give the government power to censor the church or restrict whatever it deemed necessary to participate in.[54] The churches led the fight against slavery in the 1840s and segregation in the 1950s and 1960s through the leadership of Martin Luther King.

Chase Windebank, a senior at Pine Creek High School in Colorado Springs, thought that he could use study hall time to hold a prayer meeting. It was permitted at the school for a few years and was attended by up to ninety people. Then in the fall of 2014 the administration took a different view and officials said that prayer meetings could only take place before school begins and after school ends.

Windebank complained, and with the help of the religious Alliance Defending Freedom (ADF), he sued. He claimed that the school had violated his constitutional rights by excluding prayers from an "open time" for students where they can "express themselves."

Pinecrest has now eliminated its seminar period for academic reasons, "having nothing to do with Windebank and his lawsuit."

Windebank claims that he "struck a blow for the First Amendment." He also said, "I'm actually quite excited that I was able to take this stand and be able to make a victory for free speech in public schools. Not just for me because I filed this lawsuit. For those after me as well, being able to express what they believe."

Pine Creek's counsel was confident about the case and they agreed to a dismissal when Windebank "voluntarily abandoned" his claim. Robert J. Zavaglia Jr., an attorney for the district said in a statement, "Pine Creek High School has never had, and does not have, a policy in place which restricts students' rights to associate at lunch, and by extension to meet with others and discuss faith, pray, or talk about the news of the day from a Christian perspective." As such, no nonexistent policy was revised to achieve the suit's abandonment.

Matt Sharp of the ADF wrote in an e-mail, "From day one, this case has been focused on the District's decision to not only prevent Chase and the other students from praying together, but also the District's position that students cannot gather for prayer at any time during the school day."[55]

Another case in which an individual is standing up for his civil rights because of his religious beliefs is Jack Phillips, owner of Master Piece Cake Shop in Colorado. The Supreme Court has agreed to hear the case resulting in what could be a landmark decision of a person's right to refuse same-sex couples services on freedom of speech based on religious grounds.

A discrimination lawsuit was filed by Charlie Craig and David Mullins, which won in the state courts. Phillips argued that the First Amendment freedom of expression and religion protected his right to refuse to make a cake, but the Colorado Supreme Court upheld the decision.

Phillips petitioned the United States Supreme Court in December 2016 and on June 26, it agreed to take the case.

Jack Phillips continues to stand on his faith and the faith of his family. In a statement in 2015, he has said, "If it were strictly just a business thing and we lost a lot of money, then conceivably it would be. But because of the situation, where this is a fight for our faith first and our freedom also, we're both in the same fight, and the whole family encourages each other. So, no, it's actually made us stronger. It's a spiritual battle. We're not fighting, God's fighting. And He's using us at the same time."[56]

The Kingdom of God

The Kingdom of God is also the same as the Kingdom of Heaven. "Thy Kingdom come, Thy will be done, on earth as it is in heaven." We pray almost every day when we pray the "Our Father." In Mark 1:15, Jesus said, "And saying, The [appointed period of] time is fulfilled [completed], and the kingdom of God is at hand; repent [have a change of mind which issues in regret for past sins and in change of conduct for the better] and believe [trust in, rely on, and adhere to] the good news [the Gospel]." Jesus was constantly teaching about the Kingdom of God. The disciples were sent to proclaim the good news of the Kingdom.

The Kingdom of God is much broader than the Church and includes every area under rule and authority of God. The Kingdom of God is spiritual. It encompasses every area of our lives.[57] We have our feet firmly planted on the earth, but our hearts, souls, and spirits are between heaven and earth as we journey under the rule of the Kingdom of God.

How does one become part of the Kingdom of God? He is born into the Kingdom through a spiritual birth. Jesus said in John 3:5, "I assure you, most solemnly I tell you, unless a man is born of water and [even] the Spirit, he cannot [ever] enter the kingdom of God." As citizens of the Kingdom, we are coheirs with Christ and share in His inheritance.

We are given authority in the Kingdom because of our inheritance. As Christians bring different aspects of their lives under the will of God, they extend the rule of God into areas of life where they have authority. When the government becomes the main provider for the family, it is usurping the authority given to Christians by God.

The kingdom of darkness is everything outside the Kingdom of God, and it is controlled and ruled by Satan. This kingdom is characterized by disunity and chaos. As we can see in our time and is evident in the past, these two kingdoms have been at war with each other since Cain and Abel. As Christians withdraw from their rightful spheres of authority, ideas have developed that politics for example is an area where Christians should not get involved. Where was the church when Roe V. Wade was enacted? Where was the Church when prayer was taken out of schools?

Instead of building the Kingdom of God, the church has retreated from the world. The church has hidden in the four walls and become a place to worship but has not become a force in the Kingdom. Satan is happy to have us stay in the four walls of the church. Did Jesus just stay in the synagogue and preach? No, He went out on the highways and byways and preached the gospel. He not only proclaimed it; He demonstrated it by healing and delivering people. Jesus Christ is the embodiment of the Kingdom of God. He demonstrated it and talked about it. He said that the Kingdom of God is within you. It is spiritual, and it is who we are in Christ. It is Christ living in us and living His life in and through us.

The Body of Christ is more than just a Church. It is a Kingdom that has the authority given to it by Jesus Christ to be a positive force in the world, to proclaim the gospel, to heal the sick, and to be an example of the love of God here upon the earth.

The Persecuted Church

So many of us here in the United States seem to only look at the Body of Christ essentially within our own shores, but the Body of Christ is throughout the world, and it is suffering great persecution. In the early Church, many of the disciples died for their faith. One year after the crucifixion of Jesus, in the year AD 34, Stephen, was stoned to death. During this period around two thousand Christians suffered martyrdom. Even though there were many martyrs during this time, it did not slow the growth of Christianity.[58]

More Christians died for their faith in the twentieth century than all other centuries of church history combined. Justin D. Long, quoted in an article by Dan Wooding, "Modern Persecution," said, "During this century, we have documented cases in excess of 26 million martyrs. From AD 33 to 1900, we have documented 14 million martyrs."

More than 1.3 million Christians and other non-Muslim people have been killed in Sudan, a South African nation. "Individual Christians, including clergy, have over the past few years . . . been assassinated, imprisoned, tortured and flogged for their faith."[59]

In recent years, much of the persecution has for the most part taken place in Islamic nations. Under Uganda's president Idi Amin, he and his followers tried to set up an Islamic state. The population consisted of many, many Christians, and as a result his regime began a systematic killing of Christians. By the end of his reign of terror, three hundred thousand believers had been murdered.

China is a nation that is persecuting Christians, particularly in the underground church, but this has not stopped its growth. It is estimated that there are around 50 million Christians in China. Some estimates are as many as ninety million. These numbers are increasing despite hostility and opposition from the Chinese government. There has recently been a campaign of persecution against Christians who are not registered in the official state church.[60]

"Convert and live or die" is the message that radical Islam has echoed to the masses that will not adhere to their principles. ISIS militants have forced Iraqi Christians to leave their homes and have suffered persecution with harassment, unfair taxes, arrests, banishment, violence, and of course death. Countless Christians have been beheaded and crucified because they have refused to give up their faith.[61]

From 9/11 to other terrorist attacks here in the United States such as Fort Hood in 2009; Boston Marathon in 2013; San Bernardino in 2015 and Orlando, Florida, in 2016 even though not directly directed at Christians, the ideology behind these terrorist attacks is still against the Judeo-Christian ideology of the West. Although some in the media are not quick to label these events as Radical Islamic inspired, the reality is self-evident.

Persecution for Christians is a fact and it has been happening since Jesus, the founder of our faith, walked the earth and preached the Good News about who our rightful identity is in Him. The world and the enemy hate this truth and have been trying to stifle and do away with it, but the Christian message will go on as long as Christians have breath and resolve to stand for the truth!

Summary

Christianity has had a profound influence in shaping the world through its moral and cultural impact on our laws, judicial system, economics, politics, and sanctity of life. It has elevated the rights of women; built and established hospitals and charities; promoted education, which emphasized the Bible as a moral compass; promoted heterosexual monogamous love and the lasting relationship between a man and a woman and the upbringing of children who are taught Christian values. It has also had a great influence on the arts and literature. It has been a force that has elevated not only the individual to his or her God-given abilities but also the downtrodden and the helpless.

Is Christianity continuing to shape our culture, or is our culture shaping Christianity? There are many different "types of Christians today." There are those who accept the Lord, read His Word, and live a life manifesting the fruits of the Holy Spirit in their everyday lives. There are those that hear the Word, but the trappings of the world take hold and they are only Christian in name. There are those who hear the Word but reject it, and there are those who "pick and choose" what they will follow that fits in with their agenda.

There are "market driven" churches that seem more like a business than a church. A church where people go to get fed and it's "all about me" and what I can get out of the community. There are those who are easily swayed by the culture and the media to accept lifestyles that are not Biblical because they don't want to be labeled a "hatemonger."

The Nashville Statement by Church Leaders has become an issue for some. All they are doing is reaffirming Biblical principles. They are taking a stand where no one else is willing to, and unfortunately other denominations are taking issue with their declaration. We must all come together in unity as the Church, the Body of Christ, and take a stand for God's Word. We need to be a Church on fire, not like the Church of Laodicea, "So, because you are lukewarm and neither cold nor hot, I will spew you out of My mouth!" (Rev. 3:16).

Free Speech is a right that is quickly being taken over by the left. They appear to be the judge and jury of what is acceptable speech and what is hate speech. It looks like hate speech is anything they do not want to hear, and the term is used as an attack on Christianity. We need to stand up and not let them get the upper hand because this is a precursor, in my opinion, to justifying the shutting down of Christian values and making them the fringe in our culture, which has and will lead ultimately to more persecution if we do not stand up and push back.

Freedom of religion is part and parcel of free speech. You can't have freedom of religion if you are not allowed to exercise your free speech. Many Christians are being persecuted and prosecuted because they have been willing to take a stand for their faith; not compromising it just because the world seeks to crush their beliefs.

The persecution of Christians throughout the world has not stopped and will not stop as long as the Body of Christ is a strong voice and an example to those who would be seeking the truth. "Blessed [happy—with life-joy and satisfaction in God's favor and salvation, apart from your outward condition—and to be envied] are you when people despise [hate] you, and when they exclude and excommunicate you [as disreputable] and revile and denounce you and defame and cast out and spurn your name as evil [wicked] on account of the Son of Man. Rejoice and be glad at such a time and exult and leap for joy, for behold, your reward is rich and great and strong and intense and abundant in heaven; for even so their forefathers treated the prophets" (Luke 6:22—23).

The Body of Christ needs to proclaim the Kingdom of God and come out of the four walls of the church and become an influencer, not a body of people who are influenced by the world. We have been given the authority, by Christ, to be world changers just as Jesus was and because of Him, the world will never be the same!

Chapter Six

I Have a Dream

Martin Luther King Jr.

Martin Luther King Jr., a Baptist minister, was a social activist who led the civil rights movement in the United States from the mid-1950s until his death by assassination in 1968. He was born as Michael King Jr. in Atlanta, Georgia on January 15, 1929. He played a large role in ending the legal segregation of African American citizens as well as the creation of the Civil Rights Act of 1964 and the Voting Rights Acts of 1965.

Martin's grandfather, A. D. Williams, was a rural minister for years and then moved to Atlanta, Georgia in 1893. Michael King Sr., Martin's father, took over as pastor of Ebenezer Baptist Church upon the death of his father-in-law, A. D. Williams in 1931. After becoming a successful minister, he adopted the name Martin Luther King Sr. in honor of the religious leader Martin Luther.

Martin's father fought against racial prejudice not only because he considered it racism but because he thought it to be contrary to God's will. This left a lasting impression on Martin and his siblings. At the age of fifteen, Martin Luther King Jr. entered Morehouse College in Atlanta because he was able to skip both ninth and eleventh grades. Initially he was not interested in becoming a minister like his father, but in his junior year his faith was renewed while taking a Bible class, and in his senior year he had made his decision to become a minister.

Martin's mentor during his years in seminary was the President of Morehouse College, Benjamin E. Mays. He influenced King's spiritual development and was also an outspoken advocate for racial equality and encouraged Martin to view Christianity as a force for social change. During his doctorate he married Coretta Scott. They had four children and in 1954 he became pastor of the Dexter Avenue Baptist Church of Montgomery, Alabama. King was only twenty-five years old when he completed his doctorate.

When Rosa Parks was arrested for not giving up her seat to a white person, Martin Luther King Jr. and some other civil rights leaders planned a city-wide bus boycott. Because of Martin's well-trained family connections and professional standing, he was asked to lead the boycott. He also had a strong credibility with the black community.

He gave the civil rights movement a new face in Alabama. The boycott lasted 382 days as African Americans walked to work even though there was harassment, intimidation, and violence. The African American community took action against the ordinance stating that it was unconstitutional based on "separate is never equal" decision in *Brown v. Board of Education*.

In 1957, Martin Luther King Jr., Ralph Abernathy, and sixty ministers and civil rights activists founded the southern Christian Leadership Conference as a moral authority and power of black churches. They conducted nonviolent protests promoting civil rights reform.

In February 1960, a group of African American students began what became the "sit-in" movement in North Carolina. Sitting at racially segregated lunch counters they would remain seated subjecting themselves to verbal and sometimes physical abuse. Martin continued to support them asking them to use nonviolent methods. In October 1960, he joined other protesters for a sit-in at a department store. They requested lunch-counter service and were denied, and when they refused to leave, Martin and others were arrested. Charges were dropped because Atlanta's mayor realized that it would hurt the city's reputation, but he was imprisoned soon after for violating a traffic conviction. John F. Kennedy made a phone call to his wife, Coretta in which he expressed his concern about the harsh treatment and King was released because of political pressure.[62]

There was a historic march on the nation's capital on August 28, 1963, which drew more than two hundred thousand people at the Lincoln Memorial. He gave his famous "I Have a Dream" speech, which emphasized his belief that all of us created by God would someday be brothers and sisters.

I say to you today, my friends, though, even though we face the difficulties of today and tomorrow, I still have a dream. It is a dream deeply rooted in the American dream. I have a dream that one day this nation will rise up, live out the true meaning of its creed: "We hold these truths to be self-evident, that all men are created equal.

> I have a dream that one day on the red hills of Georgia sons of former slaves and the sons of former slave-owners will be able to sit down together at the table of brother-hood. I have a dream that one day even the state of Mississippi, a state sweltering with the heat of injustice, sweltering with the heat of oppression, will be transformed into an oasis of freedom and justice.
>
> I have a dream that my four little children will one day live in a nation where they will not be judged by the color of their skin but by the content of their character. I have a dream . . . I have a dream that one day in Alabama, with its vicious racists, with its governor having his lips dripping with the words of interposition and nullification, one day right there in Alabama little black boys and black girls will be able to join hands with little white boys and white girls as sisters and brothers.
>
> I have a dream today . . . I have a dream that one day every valley shall be exalted, every hill and mountain shall be made low. The rough places will be made plain, and the crooked places will be made straight. And the glory of the Lord shall be revealed, and all flesh shall see it together. This is our hope. This is the faith that I go back to the South with. With this faith we will be able to hew out of the mountain of despair a stone of hope. With this faith we will be able to transform the jangling discords of our nation into a beautiful symphony of brotherhood. With this faith we will be able to work together, to pray together, to struggle together to go to jail together, to stand up for freedom together, knowing that we will be free one day.[63]

On April 3, 1968, Martin Luther King Jr. was assassinated by a sniper's bullet. This initiated riots and demonstrations in more than one hundred cities around the country. James Earl Ray pleaded guilty and was sentenced to ninety-nine years in prison and died in prison in 1998.[64]

Martin Luther King's life and works has been honored with a national holiday. He was a visionary leader deeply committed to achieving social justice through nonviolent means. His legacy lives on through his words and actions. He knew who he was in Christ and that our Creator loves each and every one of us no matter what color or ethnicity we are. He knew his identity in Christ and that became a vehicle to propel him into the journey that he took as one of the greatest civil rights leader.

Rosa Parks

Rosa Parks was born on February 4, 1913, in Tuskegee, Alabama. Her parents separated when she was two and her mother moved the family to live with her parents, Rose and Sylvester Edwards. Both were strong advocates for racial equality and former slaves.

She attended a segregated one-room school in Pine Level, Alabama, and was taught to read by her mother. African American students were forced to walk to the segregated one-room school-house even though the city provided a new schoolhouse for white students as well as bus transportation. She attended segregated school throughout her school years, and while in the eleventh grade while attending a laboratory school for secondary education, which was led by the Alabama State Teachers College for Negroes, she had to leave to care for her sick mother and grandmother. Never returning to her studies, she got a job in a shirt factory.

At the age of nineteen, Rosa married Raymond Parks, who was a barber and an active member of the National Association for the Advancement of Colored People. With the support of her husband, she earned her high school degree in 1933. She became actively involved in civil rights issues by joining the NAACP and was a post she held until her death in 1957.

In December 1955, Rosa Parks, after a long day of work as a seamstress in a department store, boarded a bus and sat in the designated area for blacks or "colored" only. According to the Montgomery City Code all public transportation must be segregated and bus drivers had the "powers of a police officer of the city while in actual charge of any bus for the purposes of carrying out the provisions" of the code. Under the code, bus drivers had the authority to provide separate seat accommodations for white and black passengers. African American passengers paid at the front of the bus and then got off and reboarded the bus at the back door.

The bus continued to get full of passengers, and the bus driver noticed that two white passengers were standing, so he moved a sign separating the two sections back one row and asked four passengers to give up their seats including Rosa. The bus ordinance did not specifically give drivers the authority to make a passenger give up his or her seat regardless of color, but many bus drivers ignored this, and it was customary to move the sign and if necessary to ask black passengers to give up their seats to white passengers. Rosa protested to give up her seat and was arrested. Rosa had stated at one time that it wasn't so much that she was physically tired that she refused but that she was tired of giving in.

The head of the NAACP, organized a boycott of Montgomery's city buses. Martin Luther King Jr. was also involved as mentioned before. Her trial triggered the Montgomery bus boycott, and it was a huge success. Many of the buses were empty. Many people carpooled or walked or took cabs, but most of them walked to work every day and some as far as twenty miles. Unfortunately, there was retaliation from some segregationists, and black churches were burned, and Martin Luther King Jr.'s house was destroyed from a bombing. In response to the events, legal action was taken with the *Brown v. Board of Education* decision, and in June 1956, the district court declared racial segregation laws (Jim Crow Laws) unconstitutional. It was appealed to the Supreme Court and on November 13, 1956, the court upheld the lower court's ruling. The boycott officially ended on December 20, 1956 after officials had no choice but to lift its enforcement. The Montgomery bus boycott became one of the largest and most successful mass movements against racial segregation in history.

Rosa Parks knew that she did not have to give up her right just because of the color of her skin. She took a stand and because she took a stand she helped give birth to the civil rights movement along with Martin Luther King Jr. It did not come without a price. Rosa lost her department store job, and her husband lost his job because his boss forbade him to talk about his wife or the legal case. The couple moved to Detroit, Michigan. She got a job working as a secretary and receptionist for US Representative John Conyer's congressional office.

Rosa Parks received many honors during her lifetime. She received the Spingarm Medal, the NAACP's highest award, the Martin Luther King Jr. Award, and on September 9, 1996 she was presented the Presidential Medal of Freedom by President Bill Clinton. The next year she received the Congressional Gold Medal, which is the highest award given by the US legislative branch. She has had many places named in her honor and in February of 2013 President Barack Obama unveiled in the United States Capitol building a sculpture honoring her. "In a single moment, with the simplest of gestures, she helped change America and change the world . . . And today, she takes her rightful place among those who shaped this nation's course."[65]

Mother Teresa of Calcutta

Mother Teresa was canonized as Saint Teresa of Calcutta in 2016 and is considered one of the greatest humanitarians of the twentieth century. She was the founder of the Missionaries of Charity, which is a Roman Catholic congregation of women dedicated to helping the poor.

She was born in Skopje, Macedonia, in 1910. She was born into a devout Catholic family. She was baptized as Agnes Gonxha Bojaxhiu. Her mother, Nikola, was very involved with the local church and was a vocal proponent of Albanian Independence. Her father died when she was only eight years old, and she became close to her mother, who instilled in her daughter a great commitment to charity.

When she was twelve years old, she went on a pilgrimage to the Church of the Black Madonna in Letnice, and it was there where she first felt a calling to religious life. When she was eighteen, she decided to become a nun, and she left for Ireland to join the Sisters of Loreto in Dublin. She took the name Sister Mary Teresa after Saint Therese of Lisieux.

She made her first profession of vows in May 1931, and afterward she was sent to Calcutta where she taught at Saint Mary's High School for Girls which was a school for girls from the poorest Bengali families. It is there where she learned to speak Bengali and Hindi fluently. In 1937, she took her final vows.

She taught in India for seventeen years and experienced her "call within a call" by devoting herself to caring for the sick and the poor, and her order established centers for the blind, aged, disabled, and also a leper colony. She experienced this "call within a call" as she was riding in a train from Calcutta to the Himalayan foothills. She said that Christ spoke to her and told her to abandon teaching to work in the slums of Calcutta to aid the poor and the sick.

In January 1948, she received approval from the Loretto Convent to pursue her new calling. That August, she wore the blue-and-white sari that she is so well-known for now and embarked on a journey to care for the sick and "the unwanted, the unloved, the uncared for" (frombiography.com).

She established a home for the dying destitute in an old building that was falling apart, which she convinced the city to donate. She gained canonical recognition to found the Missionaries of Charity with a small number of members which consisted mainly of former teachers or pupils from St. Mary's School. Her congregation grew exponentially and she established a leper colony, orphanage, nursing home, family clinic, and many mobile health clinics.

She opened up her first American-based house of charity in 1971. Mother Teresa spoke at the fortieth anniversary of the United Nations General Assembly in 1985. It was while she was still there that she opened Gift of Love for those afflicted with HIV/AIDS.

She began expanding internationally and by the time of her death in 1997, the Missionaries of Charity numbered more than four thousand in addition to lay volunteers and 610 foundations in 123 countries around the world.

She received many honors and was awarded the Jewel of India, the highest honor for Indian civilians and Soviet Union's Gold Medal of the Soviet Peace Committee. In 1979 she received the Nobel Peace Prize in recognition of her work with the poor and helpless.

Following several years of poor health, Mother Teresa died on September 5, 1997, at the age of eighty-seven. The Vatican recognized a miracle of an Indian woman, Monica Besra, who said she was cured of an abdominal tumor through Mother Teresa's intercession on the one-year anniversary of her death in 1998. On October 19, 2003, in a ceremony led by Pope John Paul II she was beatified "Blessed Teresa of Calcutta."

Pope Francis canonized Mother Teresa on September 4, 2016. The Pope spoke about her life and service. "Mother Teresa, in all aspects of her life, was a generous dispenser of divine mercy, making herself available for everyone through her welcome and defense of human life, those unborn and those abandoned and discarded," he said, "She bowed down before those who were spent, left to die on the side of the road, seeing in them their God-given dignity. She made her voice heard before the powers of this world, so that they might recognize their guilt for the crime of poverty they created" (biography.com).

Her charitable organizations still live on doing great works of mercy touching millions of people. She was always humble about her own achievements. Mother Teresa said, "By blood, I am Albanian. By citizenship, an Indian. By faith, I am a Catholic nun. As to my calling, I belong to the world. As to my heart, I belong entirely to the Heart of Jesus."[66]

Corrie ten Boom

On April 15, 1892, Cornelia Arnolda Johanna ten Boom was born in Haarlem, Netherlands, near Amsterdam. She was the youngest of four children. Her father was a jeweler and watchmaker. She and her family lived in rooms above her father's watch shop. They were a very devout religious family and strict Calvinists in the Dutch Reformed Church. Their faith was the inspiration for their charitable activities such as offering shelter, food, and money to those in need. They held a deep respect for the Jewish community in Amsterdam and considered them "God's ancient people."

Corrie trained to be a watchmaker and became the first woman licensed as a watchmaker in Holland in 1922. She established a youth club for teenage girls providing religious instruction as well as classes in the performing art, sewing, and handicrafts.

The ten Booms' quiet life was interrupted by the "Nazification" of the Dutch people in May 1940. During the war, the Beje house became a place of refuge for Jews and students. The watch shop was a perfect front for these activities. Behind a false wall, a secret room no larger than a wardrobe closet was built into Corrie's bedroom. This space could hold up to six people. This hiding place was used when security sweeps came through the neighborhood. A buzzer would signal danger and allow the refugees about a minute to seek sanctuary in this hiding place.

The entire family became active in the Dutch resistance, risking their own lives by harboring Jews hunted by the Gestapo. Corrie became a leader in the Beje movement overseeing a network of safe houses. It is estimated that through this movement, eight hundred Jews' lives were saved.

On February 28, 1944, the Nazis became aware of the ten Booms' activities, and the Gestapo raided their home. By the end of the day, thirty-five people, including the entire ten Boom family, were arrested. The German soldiers searched the house but never found six Jews still hiding in the secret place. They stayed there for three days before being rescued by the Dutch underground. All of Corrie's family was incarcerated, including her eighty-four-year-old father who soon died in the prison. Corrie's sister Betsie died there on December 16, 1944, and twelve days later Corrie was released for reasons not known.

After the war, Corrie returned to the Netherlands and set up a rehabilitation center for concentration-camp survivors. She also took in those who had cooperated with the Germans during the occupation. She began a worldwide ministry in 1946, traveling to more than sixty countries. She was knighted by the queen of the Netherlands in 1971, and she wrote a best-selling book of her experiences during World War II, titled *The Hiding Place*. The book was made into a movie in 1975 and starred Jeanette Clift as Corrie and Julie Harris as her sister Betsie.

At the age of eighty-five, Corrie moved to Placentia, California. She suffered a series of strokes the next year that left her paralyzed and unable to speak. On April 15, 1983, Corrie passed away. She passed on her birthday, and there is a Jewish traditional belief that states only specially blessed people die on the date when they were born.[67]

Corrie lived out her faith. It wasn't just a faith in words but who she was as a Christian. "Faith without works is dead." She had a compassionate heart that took root because of the seeds planted in her at a young age by watching her mother and father "walking the walk" and also participating in that walk of faith. James 2:14–18: "What is the use [profit], my brethren, for anyone to profess to have faith, if he has no [good] works [to show for it]? Can[such] faith save [his soul]? If a brother or sister is poorly clad and lacks food for each day, And one of you says to him, Goodbye! Keep [yourself] warm and well fed, without giving him the well fed, without giving him the necessities for the body, what good does that do? So also faith, if it does not have works [deeds and actions of obedience to back it up], by itself is destitute of power [inoperative, dead]. But someone will say [to you then], You [say you] have faith, and I have [good] works [if you can], and I by [good] works [of obedience] will show you my faith."

Dietrich Bonhoeffer

Dietrich was one of eight children born into an aristocratic family in Berlin, Germany, in 1906. His father was a prominent neurologist and professor of psychiatry at the University of Berlin and his mother, the daughter of a preacher at the court of Kaiser Wilhelm II. As a child, he was encouraged to read great literature and participate in the fine arts. He was very skillful at the piano, and many thought he would be headed for a career in music, but at age fourteen, he announced that he wanted to become a minister and theologian. The family was not pleased with his decision.

At the age of twenty-one, Dietrich graduated from the University of Berlin and spent some months in Spain as an assistant pastor to a German congregation. He went back to Germany to write a dissertation to grant him the right to a university appointment. He spent a year at New York's Union Theological Seminary, before returning to the post as lecturer at the University of Berlin.

Hitler rose to power during this time and became chancellor of Germany in 1933 and president a year and a half later. Hitler's anti-Semitic rhetoric intensified but so did his opposition, which not only included Bonhoeffer but also theologian Karl Barth and pastor Martin Niemoller. They organized the Confessing Church, which announced publicly the Barmen Declaration (1934) its allegiance first to Jesus Christ: "We repudiate the false teaching that the church can and must recognize yet other happenings and powers, personalities and truths as divine revelation alongside this one Word of God..." (Dietrich Bonhoeffer/ Christian History).

In 1937, Bonhoeffer had written *The Cost of Discipleship,* which was a call for more faithful and radical obedience to Christ and a rebuke of comfortable Christianity. "Cheap grace is preaching forgiveness without requiring repentance, baptism without church discipline, Communion without confession . . . Cheap grace is grace without discipleship, grace without the cross, grace without Jesus Christ, living and incarnate" (Dietrich Bonhoeffer/Christian History).

The government had banned Dietrich from teaching openly, so he taught pastors in an underground seminary. The Confessing Church became increasingly reluctant to speak out against Hitler after the seminary was discovered and closed. Moral opposition became more and more ineffective, so Bonhoeffer began to change his strategy.

He decided to sign up with the German secret service and become a double agent—while he traveled to church conferences over Europe. He was supposed to collect information about the places he visited but instead tried to help Jews escape Nazi oppression. He also became a part of a plot to overthrow, and later assassinate, Hitler. Eventually his resistance efforts (mainly in rescuing Jews) was discovered and on an April afternoon in 1943, two men arrived in a car and drove him to Tegel prison.

He spent two years in prison pastoring fellow prisoners and began outlining a new theology penning lines inspired by his reflections on the nature of Christian action in history. He wrote: "God lets himself be pushed out of the world on to the cross. He is weak and powerless in the world, and that is precisely the way, the only way, in which he is with us and helps us. The Bible . . . makes quite clear that Christ helps us, not by virtue of his omnipotence, but by virtue of his weakness and suffering . . . The Bible directs man to God's powerlessness and suffering: only the suffering God can help."

In another passage, he wrote, "To be a Christian does not mean to be religious in a particular way, to make something of oneself (a sinner, a penitent, or a saint) on the basis of some method or other, but to be a man—not a type of man, but the man that Christ creates in us. It is not the religious act that makes the Christian, but participation in the sufferings of God in the secular life" (Dietrich Bonhoeffer/Christian History).

One month before Germany surrendered, on April 9, 1945, he was hanged with six other resisters. A camp doctor a decade later who witnessed Bonhoeffer's hanging described the scene: "The prisoners . . . were taken from their cells, and the verdicts of court atrial read out to them. Through the half-open door in one room of the huts, I saw Pastor Bonhoeffer, before taking off his prison garb, kneeling on the floor praying fervently to his God. I was most deeply moved by the way this lovable man prayed, so devout and so certain that God heard his prayer. At the place of execution, he again said a prayer and then climbed the steps to the gallows, brave and composed. His death ensued in a few seconds. In the almost 50 years that I have worked as a doctor, I have hardly ever seen a man die so entirely submissive to the will of God" (Dietrich Bonhoeffer/Christian History).

His prison correspondence was eventually published as *Letters and Papers from Prison*. Based on his teachings at the seminary, two other books have been published: *Cost of Discipleship* and *Life Together*, which have remained devotional classics.[68]

Summary

Martin Luther King Jr. played a pivotal role in ending the legal segregation of African American citizens in the United States. Empowered by his faith and convictions, he was willing to step out and take a stand for who he was in Christ and who he was as a human being created by God. He believed in nonviolent resistance and encouraged others to do the same without compromising their identity as a child of God who has "unalienable rights." He had a dream of a different America for himself and his children. An America that would be color blind and respected the dignity of each human being. Rosa Parks's stand against racial inequality was woven into the movement along with Martin Luther King Jr. She exemplified her convictions through action when she refused to give up her seat on the bus. This spurred the Montgomery bus boycott and along with other efforts helped to end segregation. It is the power of one!

Mother Teresa is considered one of the twentieth century's greatest humanitarians. Canonized as Saint Teresa of Calcutta in 2016, her legacy continues on. It was a spark within her soul to help the hopeless and the helpless that became a raging fire as her Missionaries of Charity increased all over the globe. A humble nun, who saw the dignity of each person's life, sought to change the world one lowly person at a time. It was her faith and who she was in Christ that spurred her on to accomplish the love and compassion of Jesus to a hurting world.

Corrie ten Boom risked her own life to help refugee Jews fleeing the Nazis. Her home became a refuge and a hiding place for these people. She grew up in a home where her mother and father were examples of love and caring as they shared what they had with others. Without hesitation, she and her family harbored Jews to keep them safe from the Gestapo. She and her family paid the price when they were imprisoned, and she lost her father and her sister there in the prison, but after she was released, she continued on with her ministry.

There were members in both the German Protestant churches and the Catholic churches who, including the clergy and leading theologians, openly supported the Nazi regime. This sentiment grew in both these church circles as more pressure was put on them. When the protest statement by the Confessing Church was read in the pulpits, the Nazis responded by arresting seven hundred pastors. When the 1837 papal encyclical Mit Brennender Sorge ("with burning concern") was read from Catholic pulpits, the Gestapo confiscated copies throughout the country. Both Protestant and Catholic leadership was compromised with the Nazi state where possible. During this period there was no public opposition to antisemitism or any readiness for church leaders to oppose the regime. There were a few who spoke out but none as bold as Dietrich Bonhoeffer, who gave up his life for the cause.[69] He was not willing to compromise his Christian beliefs and stood up for them. How many of us are willing to stand up for our faith in a faithless world?

Chapter Seven

Cultural Impact on Identity

What is identity? Technically we are not born with identity; it is a socially constructed attribute.

> "The self-concept, which is the knowledge of who we are, combines with self-awareness to develop a cognitive representation of the self, called identity."
>
> —Media's influence on Social Norms and Identity Development of Youth/Sabrina Lea Worsham[70]

Identity Politics / Political Correctness

"Identity politics is a political style and ideology that focuses on the issues relevant to various groups defined by a wide variety of shared personal characteristics, including, but not limited to race, religion, sex, gender, ethnicity, ideology, nationality, sexual orientation, gender, expression, culture, shared history, medical conditions, and other of the many ways in which people differ from each other, and into which they may be classified or classify themselves."[71]

Identity politics has been embraced by the hard political left in the West and some elite moderates within the American power structure. Karl Marx could be thought of as an identity-politics theorist. "When his followers define class consciousness as the development of a class in itself into a class for itself, they effectively describe a process whereby members of a class become aware of themselves as a class and forge a collective identity."[72]

Identity politics is a term that has been used since the sixties and seventies. One goal has been for those feeling oppressed to speak about their oppression in terms of their own experiences to bring this to the forefront. Identity politics is closely connected to the fact that some social groups such as women, ethnic minorities, sexual orientation, etc. by individuals belonging to those groups are more vulnerable to forms of oppression such as cultural imperialism, violence, powerlessness, marginalization, etc. In the 1980s, identity politics was linked to a new wave of social-movement activism.[73]

Identity politics became an industry in academia and other institutions. Many students who favored identity politics became lawyers and achieved careers in social policy, social services, media, teaching, higher education, and nonprofit advocacy groups. These careers became platforms for influence. The power base has been criticized as being an elite class because of its "progressive" social policy. And its unwillingness to consider broader issues. Questioning a policy in order to combat a racial or gender disparity is often countered by "racism" or "sexism" even though the argument may have legal or constitutional basis.[74]

The entertainment industry and mass media promote identity-based themes and make sure to go to great lengths to show ethnic and gender diversity. This has as much to do with demographic targeting for advertisers as it does with ideology.

Political correctness "is used to describe language, policies, or measures that are intended to avoid offense or disadvantage to members of particular groups in society. Since the late 1980s the term has come to refer to avoiding language or behavior that can be seen as excluding, marginalizing, or insulting groups of people considered disadvantaged or discriminated against, especially groups defined by sex or race. In public discourse and the media, it is generally used as a pejorative, implying that these policies are excessive."[75]

The phrase "politically correct" was associated with the dogma of Stalinist doctrine in the early to midtwentieth century. This referred to the communist party line, which indicated the "correct" positions on many political matters. "Thereafter, the term was often used as self-critical satire. Debra L. Shultz said that 'throughout the 1970s and the 1980s, the New Left, feminists, and progressives . . . used their term 'politically correct' ironically, as a guard against their own orthodoxy in social change efforts."[76]

This far-left term became a commonplace lexicon of the conservative social and political challenges to speak against progressive teaching methods and curriculum changes in the secondary school and universities in America. President George H. W. Bush used the term in a speech in May 1991 at a commencement ceremony at the University of Michigan—"The notion of political correctness has ignited controversy across the land. And although the movement arises from the laudable desire to sweep away the debris of racism and sexism and hatred it replaces old prejudice with new ones. It declares certain topics off-limits, certain expression off-limits, and even certain gestures off-limits."[77]

Race

"And He made from one [common origin, one source, one blood] all nations of men to settle on the face of the earth, having definitely determined [their] allotted periods of time and the fixed boundaries of their habitation [their settlements, lands, and abodes]" (Acts 17:26).

"And we know [understand, recognize, are conscious of, by observation and by experience] and believe [adhere to and put faith in and rely on] the love God cherishes for us. God is love, and he who dwells and continues in love dwells and continues in God, and God in him. We love Him because He first loved us. If anyone says, I love God, and hates [detests, abominates] his brother [in Christ], he is a liar, for he who does not love his brother, whom he has seen, cannot love God, Whom he has not seen. And this command [charge, order, injunction] we have from Him: the he who loves God shall love his brother [believer] also" (1 John 4:16, 19–21).

According to God's Word, there is only one race—the human race. All people are valuable to God with no distinction based on race. Racial issues have divided people and it has been a force used by the evil one to divide us, harbor hate, and in some instances violence against our fellow human being. "For God shows no partiality [undue favor or unfairness; with Him one man is not different from another]" (Rom. 2:11).

"We've always had a race problem in this country, but to deny our progress on this front is to deny reality. That progress, however, is not inevitable, and this political generation—in its mindless rage and commitment to identity politics—threatens to undo the work of generations before. When one side screams that white is wrong, another side will scream that white is right, and the concept of an actual 'racial conversation'—much less the notion of 'racial healing'—will be little more than a sad joke."[78]

Martin Luther King would be rolling over in his grave if he were to come back now and see how politicians have used racism as a tool to manipulate and intimidate people to embrace an ideology that furthers their agenda and political ambitions. It is a divisive force that only seeks to gain power by pretending to take the "higher ground" when in actuality it is a device to rein in supporters to rally their cause.

The progressive movement has been at the forefront of this issue. A classic example is the mantra from the left that President Trump is a racist. It is an all-encompassing term that seeks to demonize him and his supporters because no one wants to be labeled as a racist. It shuts down dialogue to really discuss the issues, and since liberals do not appear to have many answers to certain issues, they use racism as a dart to deflate any progress from conservative views. It is an emotional vehicle that is headed for a crash and a clash as exemplified by the Charlottesville riots.

Religion

The church has played a big role in politics since its founding. The Declaration of Independence is based on Biblical principles, "We hold these truths to be self-evident, that all men are created equal all men are created equal, that they are endowed by their Creator with certain unalienable rights, that among these are Life, Liberty, and the pursuit of Happiness."

Clergymen like Charles Finney and Theodore Weld and daughter of abolitionist Lyman Beecher motivated people to support abolition. John Wesley also said that human bondage was "the sum of all villainies" and spoke about its abuses. Charles Finney said that slavery was a moral sin and supported its abolition. "Had made up my mind on the question of slavery, and was exceedingly anxious to arouse public attention to the subject. In my prayers and preaching, I so often alluded to slavery, and denounced it."[79]

Rev. Martin Luther King Jr. and other pastors taught on the equality of all of God's children and led a movement to end segregation. They took this movement from the pulpits to the streets. Thank God they were not intimidated like some pastors who are afraid to speak from the pulpit about political issues such as prolife, marriage between one man and one woman, etc.

The media and the powers that be have come after the church, trying to squelch its voice because it does not fit into the ideology of the liberal culture.

Senator Lyndon Johnson's 1954 Amendment to the tax code was designed to silence his political enemies who were attacking his political aspirations because of his far-left politics. This was a way to silence their voices.

Enter President Trump who repealed the Johnson Amendment, keeping his promise to the American people that the government would not interfere with their freedom of speech. There are differing views on whether or not its repeal will accomplish its goal of keeping the government from allowing pastors to preach their ideological Biblically based views from the pulpits. Nevertheless, it is a step in the right direction for religious liberty.

The Bible states that God clearly establishes human authorities to govern, and we as believers have an obligation to submit to those authorities. Does that mean that no matter what the government orders us to do we have to submit to? No—not if it goes against the Word of God. "So they brought them and set them before the council [Sanhedrin], And the high priest examined them by questioning, Saying, We definitely commanded and strictly charged you not to teach in or about this Name, yet here you have flooded Jerusalem with your doctrine and you intend to bring this Man's blood upon us. Then Peter and the apostles replied, We must obey God rather than men" (Acts 5:27-29).

The world does not define who we are as Christians, but we are defined by who we are in Christ. This must be inherent in our worldview so that we will not succumb to the dictates of the world around us but stand up for our beliefs and not be labeled by those who want to shut us down so that they can live in a godless society. The progressive and liberal movement tends to paint Christians as homophobic, xenophobic, Islamophobic, etc. This is an effort to shut down Christian viewpoints because they may not coincide with their liberal agenda. Attack the messenger because you do not like the message.

Media

American adolescents spend on average six and a half hours per day engaging in some form of media. This is a great deal of time when you consider it constitutes a large block of a youth's waking hours. Why is this something to be concerned about? Adolescents use this media as a guide for social comparison. They can be easily influenced for the better or in some cases, depending on what they view, the worst.[80]

Social media can influence how someone perceives themselves in contrast to what they are "fed" on the internet. Stereotypical portrayals of how a person should act, look, or be is rampant on social media. It can heavily influence a youth or even adults to be duped into trying to "copy" what they perceive to be the "cool" thing.

TV can have a big effect on the family. TV has become in many cases a "babysitter" for the youth. With a mother and father in many cases working full time it becomes a way of entertaining their children while they "catch up" on work at home in order to maintain a home and family. "By the time a baby boomer is sixteen, they will have watched between twelve thousand and fifteen thousand hours of TV. This means that by the time an average American is eighteen, they will have spent more time watching TV than doing anything else besides sleep."[81]

It is very evident that television has had a huge impact upon our culture and especially our family. It has become the centerpiece of the family's interaction with some families eating in front of the TV instead of at the dinner table. It has been part of forming our identity as well as the reality within our world. In many cases it has been the pulpit where some have attained their values. Notwithstanding the emergence of Christian Broadcasting Networks, secular programing has become the "Bible" to some. 2 Corinthians 5:17 says, "Therefore if any person is [ingrafted] in Christ [the Messiah] he is a new creation [a new creature altogether]; the old [previous moral and spiritual condition] has passed away, Behold, the fresh and new has come!"

"By the time an American child is twelve, they will have seen eight thousand murders in the media. There is an average of three to five violent acts per hour in prime-time television and over twenty in children's TV. Children, especially boys with aggressive tendencies, tend to copy the aggressive acts that they see modeled on TV as they become desensitized to violence."[82]

Television offers a distorted view of the world. This can have a strong negative impact on the person as well as the family. The commercials on TV, while promoting their products, seem to want to put us into a box of what we should look like and desire as far as material goods and products; in some instances, it changes our way of thinking, etc.

"Narrative Therapy tells us that reality is constructed in social relationships and that our identity is based on the stories that they tell us.

These stories are what shape our lives and relationships; it is where Identity is found."[83]

The evening news seeks to shape the world we live in by the narratives they choose to convey to us. Has anyone ever heard of fake news? They seek to be the dispensers of the news through the filter of, for the most part, the liberal agenda. Thank God there are those in the news media who, through conservative news networks, programs, and radio programs, seek to tell the truth of what is really happening.

That is why it is so important that we, as Christians, cling to the Word of God as our moral compass so that when we, be it through various media sources such as TV, Facebook, the internet, etc. recognize that there is a force out there driven by the evil one who wants to strip us of our Christian heritage and remove God from every aspect of our lives. Having said that, God has used all these mediums to spread the Gospel of the Kingdom into many areas where maybe no one has ever set foot. A tool can be used for something good or something bad. It depends on who is using it!

Academia

John Dewey was an early twentieth-century progressive education reformer whose ideas were influential in forming the modern American school system. He wanted to move the United States away from the individualistic, constitutional republic where people are free to do as they like and worship God. He wanted to move us to a kind of Soviet-type system.

Dewey was also one of the first signers of the first Humanist Manifesto in 1933. The Manifesto states in its first plank "regard the universe as self-existing and not created," which is in stark contrast with the Christian belief of God creating the heavens and the earth.[84]

Dewey knew that the United States could not be taken down by military force, so he said, "You know what? We'll hollow out the foundations. We'll dumb down the students very slowly."[85]

In the early days, during the formation of the American colonies, the Bible had always been read and used as a formative tool for teaching morals and values. Dewey wanted to downplay the importance of literacy and focus on turning children into social animals that would work for the common good.

This dumbing down of children in the school system is not only limited to the United States; the United Nations Educational, Scientific and Cultural Organization (UNESCO) has created a world core curriculum downplaying literacy. This global agenda is sinister, and its goal is to dumb down humanity for the purpose of attacking the Word of God. It appears, in effect, that this is a precursor to the one world government system.

John Holt, an educational theorist and supporter of school reform, started the modern homeschool movement in the 1970s. He argued that formal school's focus on rote learning created an oppressive classroom environment. Holt's friend, educational theorist Raymond Moore, argued that early schooling was detrimental to children and that children should be schooled at home until age eight or nine so that they could attain a firm educational, psychological, and moral foundation.

These new leaders had a different goal and vision. They created a radical social and religious vision in which children would be homeschooled with the purpose of infiltrating government, education, and entertainment industries in order to transform the United States into a nation based on Christian beliefs and principles.

Homeschooling has continued to increase as it has become an acceptable educational alternative. Many families have decided to homeschool for neither pedagogical nor religious reasons but for individual pragmatic reasons such as concerns about the quality of local schools or concerns about bullying.[86]

Schools have become propaganda centers in which the left has imposed its ideas and philosophy upon unassuming young minds. They have taken over the role of the parent and have become the parent teaching values and ideology in which political correctness has gone amuck. Children are being taught to embrace alternative lifestyles which may conflict with Christian values and morals taught at home.

Our identity was given to us by God the Father. The left is promoting a new "Bible" in which Christians need to leave their beliefs and values at the door and not interfere with a new identity that is being pushed by the progressive media.

The universities have now become the bastions of political correctness. When you split students into racial and gender camps, learning becomes almost impossible. "To see a person primarily as a 'white male' or a 'black female' is to diminish both their humanity and their individuality. It suggests that their experience is contained within the group category, and is fundamentally [not just partially] distinct from the experience of those in other categories. It also minimizes the differences within the category between individuals."[87]

Universities are becoming equity advocates as a community of feeling, not a community of reason and learning. They ascribe inner feelings based on race-gender categories. Is it any wonder that we are hearing about safe spaces in colleges now?

Many universities who were founded on Christian principles do not ascribe to the tenets of faith. In fact, these same universities are the opposite. They seek to eliminate any references to God and "preach" an atheistic view of the world. This is not conducive to the values that many a college student brings when they enter college. "A recent nationwide survey found that the number of freshmen attending America's colleges who have left their faith over the past three decades has skyrocketed. The number of college students with no religious affiliation has tripled in the last 30 years- from 10 percent in 1986 to 31 percent in 2016—according to data from the CIRP Freshman Survey Downey reported in the Scientific American."[88]

The ideology at college campuses isn't the only culprit for young adults leaving the church but it could also be because they may need a "break from church," or maybe the very fact that they are away from home and family they are not "pressured" in to going to church, or work responsibilities of just being too busy.

How can one counteract the temptation to leave their faith once they go to college or even if they don't go to college. The following are suggestions from Ashley Tripp, the author of *Why Students Lose Their Faith in College*:[89]

1. Get Plugged into a Ministry

    Whatever your theological background, get plugged in with a group of solid believers who love God and love people. I chose to become involved with Bama Cru, Cru's chapter at Alabama. Surrounding myself with a community of believers, I created relationships and relationships and gained a deeper understanding of the Christian faith. It wasn't until college when I realized Christianity was not just a certain religion, but also a relationship with Jesus.

2. Take on a Leadership Role

    Are you passionate about your faith? Seek after a leadership role on campus. I became my sorority's chaplain and spread the love of Jesus Christ among my Gamma Phi Beta sisters. Some of my friends from Bama Cru led a six-week video series from Matt Chandler on dating, relationships and sex based off the book of Song of Songs in the Bible. Open to anyone, the series was held at different sorority houses each week. In addition, my sorority collaborated with another sorority for a Bible study on Marian Jordan's book, *Radiance*.

3. Attend a Summer Project

    The summer before my senior year in college, I went on a Greek Summit, a summer project led by Cru staff in Destin, Florida. There, I met over one hundred college students from across the nation. The purpose of the mission trip was to learn how to live out one's faith and how to become an influence in your sorority or fraternity. It was probably the best two weeks of my college career. I learned a great deal about the Gospel and what it looks like to share one's faith with your sorority sisters.

4. Make It a Priority

    Reading the Bible and attending church is what "Culture Christianity" tells society is the right way to practice Christianity. I've discovered it's a daily walk and a personal relationship. When I wake up, I do my best to make it a priority to spend time with God, not in a routine manner or because it's my duty as a Christian, but because God is my reason for living. It's almost like brushing your teeth. Do you brush your teeth because it's a part of your routine, or do you do it so your teeth won't rot away?

Freedom of Speech / Hate Speech

"And you will know the Truth, and the Truth will set you free" (John 8:32). We can only be free by knowing the truth as the Scripture says. According to Webster's Dictionary the word *freedom* means, "*The state of being free of restraints.*" The definition of *speech* is, 1. "*The faculty or act of speaking; 2. The faculty or act of expressing or describing thoughts, feelings, or perceptions by the articulation of words.*"[90]

When God created Adam and Eve and put them in the Garden of Eden, He gave them a free will. They were free agents. They had the freedom to choose to obey God or to not obey Him. We can choose good or evil. It is up to us because we are free to choose just like Adam and Eve.

The Founding Fathers, in their wisdom, established this nation by setting forth Biblical principles in the Constitution of The United States and the Bill of Rights. The First Amendment to the Constitution gives us freedom of speech. The amendment was adopted in 1791 and reads: "Congress shall make no law respecting an establishment of religion, or prohibiting the free exercise thereof; of abridging the freedom of speech, or the press; or the right of the people peaceably to assemble, and to petition the Government for a redress of grievances."

Roger Anghis, in an article for *News With Views* states, "One of the greatest things about America is the fact that we have had the right to voice our opinion for the last 241 years. Our founders gave us that because under the tyranny of most countries in Europe at that time you could be punished for putting forth an opinion that differed from those in power. How times have changed."[91] Freedom of speech is under assault in the United States. All you have to do is turn on the TV or pick up a newspaper or go on Facebook. Conservative points of view are being shut down on almost all of our colleges and even some of our high school and elementary schools.

We've seen many a time when a conservative is asked to speak at a University that there are "protests" that are really riots. Look at the one recently in Berkley that is supposed to be the hallmark of free speech ideology. Who is funding many of these protests? George Soros. His Open Society Institute has followed through with their promises to fund hate groups. Virtually all rallies are funded by Soros and he seeks to silence President Trump as well as his supporters.

So who came up with the idea of "hate speech?" I think that it was the left encouraged by the "powers that be" within the progressive framework, coupled by the media and other anticonservative groups. How do you define "hate speech?" Someone said that it is simply whatever the leftist among us hate to hear!

Erwin W. Lutzer states in an article, "The Demise of Religious Freedom in America," that "The censurers, the radicals who are all too ready to deny freedom to those who disagree with them, are perceived in our culture as 'tolerant' and we, who want to express our views, are viewed as 'intolerant.'" In other words, the philosophy of the left is preach tolerance, but practice inflexible intolerance to anyone who has the courage to express a different point of view."

Angela McCaskill was suspended from Gallaudet University for signing a petition to put Maryland's same-sex legislation on the November ballot. The college declared that it was justified because of tolerance. I guess tolerance means censoring all speech that does not agree with yours.[92]

We have heard the story of the Christian baker who denied baking a wedding cake for a same-sex couple. One could argue that they are just baking a cake for a wedding but a wedding cake is a celebratory act, and no one should have to do something that is against their Biblical beliefs.

Many evangelical pastors refuse to speak about the controversial issues of the day as it relates to same-sex marriage, abortion, freedom of speech, etc. They want to preach a watered-down Gospel that makes one feel warm and fuzzy all over. The fact is that Jesus came and He was radical in His day but He came to present the Truth and He spoke about sin and the consequences of it and what to avoid but He also taught about love and His Kingdom. A parent who does not discipline a child does not really love that child because he or she is not preparing them for the real world and not protecting them from the world.

Jesus is God incarnate. He is the Second Person of the Holy Trinity. He is perfect in every way and yet the people, during the time that He walked the earth, were shocked by many of His statements and many of the things that He did. He did not fit in with all the beliefs and culture at that time and did things that were "unlawful." I imagine the news of the day could have read something like this: "Jesus of Nazareth has been seen eating with Levi, the tax collector and other scum and was even heard to have said that 'sick people need a doctor not healthy ones.'" It was the Sabbath and Jesus was seen walking over to the synagogue in Capernaum. He saw a man with a withered hand and asked him to come up in front of the congregation and asked, "Is it all right to do kind deeds on Sabbath days? Or is this a day for doing harm? Is it a day to save lives or to destroy them?" No one answered so Jesus said, "Reach out your hand." The man's hand was instantly healed. Jesus broke a very sacred law! He healed a man on the Sabbath! On another occasion Jesus spoke to the Jewish leaders and rebuked them about the many laws that they follow only doing them for show and called them hypocrites. Who does this man think that he is? His speech and his actions are offensive and do not line up with our beliefs and attitudes. Mark 2:13–17; Mark 3:1–5; Matthew 23. Yes, Jesus did come to overturn the establishment of those days!

America's Lost Identity

On February 21, 1861, Abraham Lincoln visited Independence Hall and spoke these words to his audience, "I have never asked anything that does not breathe from those walls. All my political warfare has been in favor of the teachings coming forth from that sacred hall. May my right hand forget its cunning and my tongue cleave to the roof of my mouth, if ever I prove false to those teachings." These statements paraphrase the fifth and sixth verses of Psalm 137. "If I forget you, O Jerusalem, let my right hand forget its skill (with the harp). Let my tongue cleave to the roof of my mouth if I remember you not, if I prefer not Jerusalem above my chief joy!"

It appears that Lincoln spoke these words as if comparing America almost to "a chosen people." The Pilgrims saw themselves as new Israelites introduced this major stream of thought coming from the Biblical idea of covenant. These covenant ideas helped form the foundation of the United States and have continued to influence American life.

On November 11, 1620, the Mayflower Compact occurred and remains the first hallowed document of the American constitutional tradition[93] *(typed in the "old English written form" / Covenant and the American Founding by Daniel J. Elazar/Jerusalem Center for Public Affairs).*

> In the name of God, Amen. We whose names are underwriten, the loyall subjects of our dread soveraigne Lord, King James, by the grace of God, of Great Britaine, Franc, and Ireland king, defender of the faith, etc., having undertaken for the glorie of God, and advancement of the Christian faith, and honour of our king and countrie, a voyage to plant the first colonie in the Northerene parts of Virginia, doe by these presents solemnly and mutualy in the presence of God, and one of another, covenant and combine our selves together into a civill body politick, for our better ordering and preservation and furtherance of the ends aforesaid; and by virtue hearof to enacte, constittions, and offices, from time to time, as shall be thought most meete and convenient for the general good of the colonie unto which we promise all due submissioin and obedience.

> In witness wherof we have hereunder subscribed our names at Cap Codd the 11, of November, in the year of the raigne of our soveraigne lord, King James, of England, France, and Ireland the eighteenth, and of Scotland the fiftie fourth. Ano: Dom. 1620

The Declaration of Independence had many of the characteristics of the Biblical covenant at Sinai. The opening paragraph states that Americans are no longer transplanted Englishmen, but a separate people who are entitled to their political independence. This was a separation from tyranny in which Americans made up of individuals bound in partnership to a common enterprise. This was the identity that we as Americans singled us out among the other nations. We became an entity unto ourselves with shared beliefs essentially coming from our Judeo-Christian heritage. This was similar to the Sinai covenant that formally created the people of Israel.[94]

A Quinnipiac University survey released early April, 2016 showed that 57 percent of Americans strongly or somewhat agree that "America has lost its identity." Seventy-nine percent of Republicans agreed that America had lost its identity and 85 percent of Trump reporters agreed.[95]

This poll also showed that Republicans and Trump supporters felt their "beliefs and values are under attack, the government has gone too far in assisting minority groups and public officials don't care much what people like me think."[96]

In a more recent poll by the Associated Press-NORC Center for Public Affairs Research found that Republicans are more likely to say that our culture was founded on Christian beliefs and traditions of early European immigrants and that this was essential to US identity. There may be disagreement between both parties as to the loss of U.S. identity but regardless of party, they say the country is losing that identity.[97]

One only need to turn on the television or listen to the radio or go on the internet to see the many ways that America is losing its identity. There are struggles between many groups—Black Lives Matter, ANTIFA, white supremacists, etc., and our freedoms slowly being challenged by those who would disagree on the meaning of free speech and hate speech. If your ideology is different you are labeled a racist. No one wants to be labeled in such a manner, but it goes to heart of the matter, which is "attack the messenger if you don't like the message."

Summary

Identity politics and political correctness go hand in hand. Never before has it been more evident than in the last election and continuing even to this day. It has become the avoidance of language that is deemed offensive by some because, in my opinion, it is a war against the very values that we, as a country were founded on Judeo-Christian principles. The catchall phrase, if you disagree with a liberal, is "you are a racist." It is a term that elicits anger and hate on the Left to disparage anyone with conservative views.

Martin Luther King Jr. was a perfect example of bringing a terrible wrong—segregation—into the light. He never advocated violence but did stand for what he believed was an injustice. He saw people as individuals with God given rights and he sought to shine the light on that, but he did it with eloquence and honor. His strategy should be the blueprint for all of us who seek to stand up for our own beliefs, especially those of us who are Christian and/or conservative.

Religion or the Church has played a vital role in forming who we are in Christ and who we are as individuals who live in a country founded on Biblical principles. Since the Johnson Amendment in 1954 the Church's voice has been squelched. Many a pastor or clergyman is afraid to speak out about Christian beliefs because of this amendment.

Where are the voices who will speak out? President Trump did repeal it, but time will tell if there is any effect on the Church as it struggles to still be a light in the darkness.

The media is one of the biggest culprits for shaping our identity or at least they are trying to. Television has become the "parent" or the "teacher" in today's society, telling us how we should look and feel and what products to buy so we can be "perfect" in every way. Media is all around us—at home, on our cell phone, the internet, and wherever we go. Most of the media is far left in its ideology, and as a result we see so much "fake news." One commentator on a network said something to the effect that *they* were the dispensers of what we are supposed to be thinking.

The far left has been using propaganda to infiltrate academia from pre-school to universities. These institutions have become a target for their ideology. This big push came in 1962 when prayer was officially removed from the schools. Some suggest that there is a causal relationship between taking prayer out of schools and other things that have happened in society. However statistics do show correlations: after 1963, teen pregnancies increased 187 percent in the next fifteen years; after 1963, divorce rates increased 300 percent each year for the next fifteen years; there has been a decline in SAT scores for eighteen consecutive years after 1963; since 1963, violent crime has increased 544 percent.[98]

Freedom of speech is currently being attacked, and we as individuals and a nation need to stand for our rights because if we don't, who will? Countless men and women have died to protect our rights. We need to honor them by not giving in to pressure from those who would seek to squelch opinions and ideology that disagrees with theirs. Hate speech is only a term from the left that is used as a defense for shutting down any ideology or beliefs not consistent with theirs.

America's identity is slowly being lost, and we need to go back to the principles and Biblical beliefs of our Founding Fathers who established this nation "under God." We, in many respects, are a covenant nation with God. Just as God made a covenant with Israel, the Pilgrims in 1620 dedicated this land to the Creator. We, as Americans, are the living, breathing soul of a nation founded by God to be a beacon of light to all the nations of the world.

America's identity is being erased by the left to create their own socialistic view of the world. From the removal of the Ten Commandments in public places to defacing or taking down statues, using the language of hate speech to silence voices and rewriting history in textbooks at the school level; it all points to the fact that they are really trying to take God out of our lives by preaching the gods of self, materialism, and divisiveness.

Chapter Eight

Gender Identity

Male and Female: God's Plan

"So God created man in His own image, in the image and likeness of God He created him; male and female He created them" (Gen. 1:27). We need to be what God created us to be. It was His idea to create gender. It is inherent in our very being as human beings. When we do not recognize who we are then we cannot truly be who God intended us to be. It's about our spirit and our soul. We live in a body that was created by God for a purpose, and we use this "tent" to glorify Him. Should we say that God made a "mistake" when he created me a female or a male? God does not make mistakes because He is perfect. I believe that it has been Satan's plan throughout the ages to seek to diminish who God has created and those of us who do not have a strong spiritual foundation succumb to the lie.

God created us to be male and female. Two genders. If God had wanted to create another gender He would have created it. Our society is on the verge of becoming a godless society. We have rejected the Bible even to the extent of abolishing public display of the Ten Commandments. Man is slowly becoming the god of his own making. What did Satan try to do from the beginning? He tricked Eve into believing that she and Adam would not die if they ate of the Tree of Knowledge. God had warned Adam, "And the Lord God commanded the man, saying, You may freely eat of every tree of the garden; But of the tree of the knowledge of good and evil and blessing and calamity you shall not eat, for in the day that you eat of it you shall surely die" (Gen. 2:16–17).

"While the culture now tells us that gender is arbitrary and switching genders will solve all our problems, God tells us that only He can give us lasting joy and peace."[99]

The Catholic Church reaffirms the beauty and sovereignty of God's design in each person, which includes their gender. We need not alter the biological sex that God has given us. Pope Francis has said, "It is one thing to be understanding of human weakness and the complexities of life, and another to accept ideologies that attempt to sunder what are inseparable aspects of reality. Let us not fall into the sin of trying to replace the Creator. We are creatures, and not omnipotent. Creation is prior to us and must be received as a gift."[100]

During the last year, agencies of the federal government issued new regulations that redefine discrimination based on "sex," including "gender identity" and also to include "termination of pregnancy." The Department of Education has told public schools across the country receiving federal funds they must provide "equal access" restrooms.

The US Department of Health and Human Services has required most employers, medical providers, educational institutions, and health insurers—including dioceses, parishes, schools, and Catholic charities to cover transgender services in their health plans. As a result, the Diocese of Fargo and other Catholic Charities in North Dakota and The Catholic Benefits Association along with other Catholic Institutions have filed a lawsuit in federal court to halt the implementation of these new rules.[101]

The gender confusion that we are experiencing today, which has put us in such social turmoil, has been the rejection of the Bible as the Word of God. God is the one who created the universe, and it was His idea to create two separate and distinct entities—male and female. The man-made concept of gender as a choice instead of being born with a body that denotes one's gender is a social issue that goes against God's plan. Those that promote it label people who reject the notion as narrow-minded and chauvinistic misogynists.[102]

God gave each of us a free will and he gave us the power to make our own choices. People are also free to think what they believe in. We as Christians have a worldview that revolves around the Bible and God's Holy Word. The problem that occurs is that the concept of gender is being pushed on others as the way it should be. There is no acceptance of the Biblical point of view and if you disagree you are said to be disseminating "hate speech."

Biblical Marriage vs. Same-Sex Marriage

"And great throngs accompanied Him, and He cured theme there. And the Pharisees came to Him and put Him to the test by asking, Is it lawful and right to dismiss and repudiate and divorce one's wife for any and every cause? He replied, Have you never read that He Who made them from the beginning made them male and female, And said for this reason a man shall leave his father and mother and shall be united firmly (joined inseparably) to his wife, and the two shall become one flesh? So they are no longer two but one flesh, What therefore God has joined together, let not man put asunder" (Matt. 19:2–6).

By definition, according to the Bible, marriage is heterosexual. When asked about divorce, Jesus referred them to creation in Genesis 1:27, "So God created man in His own image, in the image and likeness of God He created him; male and female He created them." "And the Lord God caused a deep sleep to fall upon Adam; and while he slept, He took one of his ribs or a part of his side and closed up the [place with] flesh. And the rib or part of his side which the Lord God had taken from the man He built up and made into a woman, and He brought her to the man. Then Adam said, This [creature] is now bone of my bones and flesh of my flesh; she shall be called Woman, because she was taken out of a man" (Gen. 2:21–23). There are those, even Christians, who have picked apart the Bible, essentially arguing that the Church needs to change its view on same-sex marriage. The argument in some cases is that the great commandment found in Matthew 22:37 and 39 that states, "And He replied to him, You shall love the Lord your God with all your heart and with all your soul and with all your mind."

And the second is like it: "You shall love your neighbor as [you do] yourself"—causes us to just look at love and forget what God has said in His Word about marriage.[103]

Jesus did not openly speak about same-sex marriage because he talked about creation and about creating male and female so by definition, same-sex marriage is excluded. If He had wanted to talk about same-sex marriage He could have done it then, but He did not because it would be a contradiction of His own Word.

Some would argue that same-sex marriage doesn't harm anyone so we should accept it morally and should have the right to choose what to do. Yes, God gave each of us a free will. Just because we choose to do something doesn't necessarily mean that it is a godly thing to do.

Male and female was God's design and he said in His Word what marriage is. We are all morally responsible before God. We are all sinners and fall short of the glory of God. We will all be judged.[104] Not only is the culture of our time trying to extinguish any knowledge of God, but unfortunately, they are suppressing this inherent knowledge from creation about God's design and trying to normalize it. So much so, that on June 25, 2015, same-sex marriage was made into law. The courts have become the law and the Law of God has become the enemy. This is a tactic of the enemy, the evil one who began his deception in the Garden of Eden by questioning God and His sovereignty and propagating a lie that we are our own gods. Where were we, as Christians when this was made into law? Where were we, as Christians when they took God out of the schools? Where were we as Christians when Roe V. Wade went into effect? We need to take a stand and not be afraid. Remember there are Christians all over the world that are being beheaded because they confess that they are Christ's. What are we willing to sacrifice for the sake of the Gospel?

Feminism and Male Identity Crisis

"Within feminism, identity politics has taken two often-related forms which, together I believe to be hegemonic today. One is generally referred to as difference or essential feminism, and the other as victim feminism. Difference feminism emphasizes the unique identity of women as a group, stressing and usually celebrating essential female characteristics which it believes make women different from—indeed even opposite to—me. Victim feminism also assumes that women have a unique identity, but the focus of that identity is women's victimization on the basis of sex, typically at the hands of men."[105]

Feminism also focuses on equality of the sexes. It is the belief that women should be equal to men. It is a movement to promote a change in society to end any disadvantages women may have in economic, social, political, and cultural arenas as it relates to power and rights. There is also a belief that men have an advantage in a system that is sexist.[106]

During the sixties, feminism was called Women's Liberation. This movement called upon women to define themselves and did not want men to define their identity. Women had claimed the right to name and define the world around them. On August 26, 1970, twenty thousand women marched down New York's Fifth Avenue identifying themselves with the Women's Liberation Movement.

The Women's Liberation Movement campaigned for women's rights, including the same pay as men, equal rights in law, and the freedom to plan their families. It also has included (universal suffrage)—the right to vote; to hold public office; to work and fair wages for equal pay; to own property; to education; to serve in the military; to enter into legal contracts; and to have marital, parental, and religious rights.

Many of these rights that have emerged as a result of this movement have been positive. For example, the right to vote, equal pay, etc. The problem is that it has resulted in gender confusion and the rejection of the Bible as the authentic Word of God, which in turn has compromised the clear teaching of scripture on the role of women.

God created man in His own image. He created *both* male and female in His own image and likeness. Woman has the same spiritual essence as man and has the same potential of good and evil as well as equal dignity with man.

Women are treated with respect in God's system. God is even considered in His Word to have womanly traits, "[And the Lord answered] Can a woman forget her nursing child, that she should not have compassion on the son of her womb? Yes, they may forget, yet I will not forget you" (Isa. 49:15). God is talking about his relationship with Israel and how His love is never ending. In Isaiah 66:13 the Lord says, "As one whom his mother comforts, so I will comfort you; you shall be comforted in Jerusalem."

Jesus treated women with respect. Mary was elevated as the mother of Jesus. She was well equipped to take on the task of raising Jesus. She was not only His mother but also a homemaker, counselor, domestic engineer, nurse, clerk, teacher, home economist, cook, etc. She was faithful even unto the cross. Not only was she faithful but Mary Magdalene and Mary the mother of James and Salome were faithful as well. They did not run and hide like most of the disciples. Jesus chose to appear first to a woman, Mary Magdalene, after His resurrection. Mary Magdalene, and Joanna and Mary the mother of James and other women with them reported His resurrection to the apostles.[107] "But these reports seemed to the men an idle tale (madness, feigned things, nonsense), and they did not believe the women" (Luke 24:11).

There are many women throughout the Bible that God used in a mighty way. He used Esther and Rahab to save the Jewish people from annihilation and He used the vessel of the womb of Mary to bring forth the Messiah for the salvation of the whole world.

What does the Bible have to say about the role of women? In Proverbs 31, it details the ideal woman. "A capable, intelligent, and virtuous woman—who is he who can find her? She is far more precious than jewels and her value is far above rubies or pearls. The heart of her husband trusts her confidently and relies on and believes in her securely, so that he has no lack of [honest] gain or need of [dishonest] spoil" (Prov. 31:10–11). She is intelligent, confident, stable, and mature woman.

A Christian woman should remember that she has equal access to all spiritual blessings in Christ. She should not fall into the trap of the feminist movement. Both men and women have a God-given privilege to fulfill God's plan for their lives. This divisive movement has resulted in the destruction of the relationship between husbands and wives which in turn has destroyed the family.

Not only has the role of the woman taken on new meaning over the last several decades, but the role of men has been assaulted in our society and as a result, it has resulted in an "identity crisis" for men.

God's Word gives us a framework for the value, responsibility and place of men in society. "For the husband is head of the wife as Christ is the Head of the church, Himself the Savior of [His] body" (1 Corinthians 3:23). The term "head" means the husband's leadership role in the home. He is responsible to lead his wife and his family as Christ is the head of the church and loves the church. "Husbands, love your wives, as Christ loved the church and gave Himself up for her. Even so husbands should love their wives as (being in a sense) their own bodies. He who loves his own wife loves himself" (Eph. 5:25 and 28).

"But as for you, O man of God, flee from all these things; aim at and pursue righteousness [right standing with God and true goodness] godliness [which is the loving fear of God and being Christlike], faith, love, steadfastness [patience], and gentleness of heart" (1 Tim. 6:11).

God ordained a man to be a leader, a teacher, a protector, a provider and the head of the household. Does that mean that a woman cannot be any of these?—of course not, but God in His divine wisdom always looks at order. The single mother has to be able to be the sole provider of all of these responsibilities. Does this order diminish a woman—no because women have many strong and necessary attributes that compliment a man and God uses these differences of the sexes to accentuate the positive in each.

Male identity is under assault and this crisis is growing due to economic insecurity, marital instability, absentee fathers, negative media images, and lack of role models. "Nature abhors a vacuum, so without clearly defined rules and guidelines for manhood, society fills the void. Gangs for example replace what young men need from a father—structure, identity and belonging," explains Paul Louis Cole, President of Christian Men's Network (CMN), host of "lions roar" ("Where Are All the Men? Solutions for the Worldwide Male Identity Crisis" / October 7, 2015).

Male bashing from negative media and feminists such as Camille Paglia's "men are obsolete" and the Economist article which calls men "the weaker sex" has helped to fuel a culture war on men. Add to this the increasing number of fatherless homes and this leaves a void for role models for young men, which is critical in helping them find identity, respect, and courage.

Research shows that men and boys are in a crisis with men committing 70 percent of all suicides and boys are under-achieving in schools with male college enrollment down to 43 percent. There has also been a loss of fatherhood in society that has caused confusion and frustration in younger generation males because of a lack of a specific role model and are less able to find their role in society.[108]

Around the world, young men are treated and in some instances forced to go to lectures, workshops to teach them their masculinity. Incoming freshmen at Gettysburg College were ordered to watch a film on toxic masculinity and at Duke University and the University of North Carolina, there are seminars for men to "deprogram" themselves of their so-called toxic masculinity. This is teaching men that the core of their identity is negative and not productive which has caused some men to become angry or confused.[109]

Guy Garcia who is the author of *The Decline of Men: How the American Male Is Tuning Out, Giving Up and Flipping Off His Future*, says, "Women really have become the dominant gender; what concerns me is that guys are rapidly falling behind. Women are becoming better educated than men, earning more than men, and, generally speaking, not needing men at all. Meanwhile, as a group, men are losing their way."[110]

Homosexuality/Transgender—a Biblical Perspective

In the Old Testament, homosexuality lifestyle is discussed in the Old and the New Testaments. Leviticus 18:22 says, "You shall not lie with a man as with a woman; it is an abomination." This prohibits homosexual acts. In Genesis 19 is the story of the attempted gang rape of Lot's visitors, who were male angels, by the men of Sodom.

In the New Testament it also forbids homosexual behavior. In 1 Corinthians 6:9-10 Paul writes, "Do you not know that the unrighteous and the wrongdoers will not inherit or have any share in the kingdom of God? Do not be deceived [misled]; neither the impure and immoral, nor idolaters, nor adulterers, not those who participate in homosexuality." He goes on to list many other sins such as "drunkards, robbers, greedy graspers" will inherit the kingdom of God.

The homosexual lifestyle is one of many sins that will exclude a person from entering into eternal life with Jesus. It is a focal point, not because it is the greatest of sins but because gender is a focus of this chapter. God is merciful and He hates sin but loves the sinner, and in His Word we can know the truth and the truth will set us free to be who we were created to be in Christ.

God is very clear in His Word that He created man and woman in His own image. The union of man and woman as husband and wife is clearly stated in God's own words and since He is the creator, His design, plan, and purpose is best for us. There are those who do not accept the teachings in God's Holy Word. Since the Garden of Eden, Satan, the deceiver, has tried to steal our identity in any way that he can

In Romans chapter 1, it specifically points our homosexuality as an example of persistent rebellion against God. "For this reason God gave them over and abandoned them to vile affections and degrading passions. For their women exchanged their natural function for an unnatural and abnormal one, And the men also turned from natural relations with women and were set ablaze [burning out consumed] with lust for one another—men committing shameful acts with men and suffering in their own bodies and personalities the inevitable consequences, and penalty of their wrongdoing and going astray, which was [their] fitting retribution. And so, since they did not see fit to acknowledge God or approve of Him or consider Him worth the knowing, God gave them over to a base and condemned mind to do things not proper or decent but loathsome" (Rom. 1:26-28).

Is homosexuality genetic or "natural"? There are differing articles on this issue. As of 2013, there has been no genetic or DNA links for homosexuality. However, whether or not it be genetic in some way should not be a deciding factor whether it is moral or not. Theoretically one could have a genetic predisposition for drug or alcohol abuse. This does not change the morality of these issues and whether or not something "natural" is necessarily moral.[111]

Sexual activities make an impact on who we are, but God's grace can forgive our sins and cleanse us from all of our unrighteousness. No matter what the sin may be, God is forgiving as we reach out to Him for help. "Let us then fearlessly and confidently and boldly draw near to the throne of grace [the throne of God's unmerited favor to us sinners], that we may receive mercy [for our failures] and find grace to help in good time for every need [appropriate help and well-timed help, coming just when we need it]" (Heb. 4:16).[112]

Dr. Paul R. McHugh, the Distinguished Service Professor of Psychiatry at Johns Hopkins University and former psychiatrist-in-chief for Johns Hopkins Hospital, has studied transgender people for forty years. He says, "Transgendered men do not become women, nor do transgendered women become men." He explained in his article for the Witherspoon Institute, that these people, "become feminized men or masculinized women, counterfeits or impersonators of the sex with which they 'identify'" ("John Hopkins Psychiatrist: 'Transgendered Men Don't Become Women,' they Become 'Feminized Men,' 'Impersonators'" / CNS News).

According to Dr. McHugh, "there is plenty of evidence showing that "transgendering" is a "psychological rather than a biological matter." "In fact, gender dysphoria—the official psychiatric term for feeling oneself to be of the opposite sex—belongs in the family of similarly disordered assumptions about the body, such as anorexia nervosa and body dysmorphic disorder." Dr. McHugh also stated that since the 1970s, John Hopkins has stopped offering sex-change surgery because it brought "no important benefits."[113]

Our manhood and our womanhood was given to us by God when He created us. Does an apple seed decide it would rather be a pear than an apple? No, I don't think so. Everything that God created, He created for a purpose. Speaking of apples, Satan has sought to usurp the created order of God. He targets man and woman, God's greatest creation to tear us down. God brings life and Satan seeks to destroy it. Western culture is not helping but going along with the agenda of hate and destruction in order to create their own god of "self."[114]

"We should celebrate the beauty of God's creative design. The Christian church and the godly family should be a festival of happiness. We should rejoice that God in His sovereign wisdom has opened our eyes to see that He has made us according to His perfect design. Manhood and womanhood aren't Plan B. God Himself has made us as we are. We are the pinnacle of His creation."[115]

Identity Theft

No, I am not talking about someone stealing your social security number or your bank account number or even your personal identification. There has been an identity theft going on since the Garden of Eden. The theft I am talking about is how Satan has tried to corrupt our true God given identity throughout all time.

The Hebrew word for "sons of God" is *B'nai Ha Elohim*, which means "heavenly beings," referencing fallen angels. "When men began to multiply on the face of the land and daughters were born to them, The sons of God saw that the daughters of men were fair, and they took wives of all they desired and chose. There were giants on the earth in those days—and also afterward—when the sons of God lived with the daughters of men, and they bore children to them. These were the mighty men who were of old, men of renown" (Gen. 6:1, 2, 4).

The Nephilim ("fallen ones, giants") were the offspring of sexual relationships between the sons of God and daughters of men in Genesis 6:1-4. There is much debate as to the identity of the "sons of God." It is our opinion that the "sons of God" were fallen angels [demons] who mated with human females or possessed human males who then mated with human females. These unions resulted in off-spring, the Nephilim, who then mated with human females. These unions resulted in offspring, the Nephilim, who were "heroes of old, men of renown."[116]

What the demons did was abhorrent to God so He punished them with the flood and imprisonment. "For God did not [even] spare angels that sinned, but cast them into hell, delivering them to be kept there in pits of gloom till the judgment and their doom. And He spared not the ancient world, but preserved Noah, a preacher of righteousness, with seven other persons, when He brought a flood upon the world of ungodly [people]. And He condemned to ruin and extinction the cities of Sodom and Gomorrah, reducing them to ashes [and thus] set them forth as an example to those who would be ungodly" (2 Peter 2:4-6).

As stated earlier, it is a subject of debate as far as the true identity of the Nephilim. I believe that they are part fallen angels and man because there is a speculation that the demons wanted to pollute the human bloodline in order to prevent the coming of the Messiah. In the Garden of Eden, God promised to crush the head of the serpent, Satan. "And I will put enmity between you and the woman, and between your offspring and her Offspring, He will bruise and tread your head underfoot, and you will lie in wait and bruise His heel" (Gen. 3:15). There has been a war between the evil one and God throughout the millennia.

One of the primary reasons for the flood, besides the wickedness of man, in Noah's time, were the Nephilim. "The Lord saw that the wickedness of man was great in the earth, and that every imagination and intention of all human thinking was only evil continually. And the Lord regretted that He had made man on the earth, and He was grieved at h earth" (Gen. 6:5-6). The Lord then decided that He would wipe always man and animals and creeping things and all the birds of the air. "But Noah found grace [favor] in the eyes of the Lord." He told Noah to build an ark to save him and his family.

The Nephilim were on the earth before the flood and seemingly afterward as the ten spies, whom Moses sent out, went to spy out the land of Canaan. They reported that they had seen giants in the land. Were they Nephilim? "There we saw the Nephilim [or giants], the sons of Anak, who come from the giants; and we were in our own sight as grasshoppers, and so we were in their sight" (Num. 13:33). The Bible does not specifically say that they saw Nephilim, but the spies thought that they did. Could it be that demons again mated with human females or some think that traits of the Nephilim were passed on through the heredity of one of Noah's daughters-in-law?

Satan has been conspiring to try to thwart God's plan of creation and redemption for humanity.

Noah was "perfect in his generations." His lineage was 100 percent human so he would be able to carry on the lineage that would lead to the Messiah (Genesis 6:9). The flood was a necessary act to prevent the extinction of humanity, so that Jesus Christ's lineage was preserved through Noah.

Summary

God has a plan, and it started at creation when He created Adam and Eve. He made us in His own image and made us male and female. He has a plan and purpose for our lives giving us a free will to love Him and serve Him.

Marriage, as stated in the Bible, is between one man and one woman. That is God's plan and we, as His creation, should not doubt our Creator and question His plan. We are the creation and He is the Creator. He is a loving God who only wants what is best for us. Satan has always tried to steal our identity and it started in the Garden of Eden. All he had to do was to put a small doubt into Eve's mind by asking her, "Can it really be that God has said, You shall not eat from every tree of the garden?" (Gen. 3).

Satan not only tricked Eve into doubting what God had told her not to do (eat from the Tree of Knowledge) but he continues to this day, if not by corrupting humanity in the flesh like the Nephilim, but assaulting our identities as a woman or a man. A man's identity has been bashed by the progressive left and feminist movement. They want to destroy God's plan by using gender confusion or a new definition of gender based solely on who I think I am rather than who I was created to be. If the evil one can tear down who we are, then he can try to tear down who God is and make Him obsolete.

The conspiracy to "corrupt the seed of woman" is also evident in the conspiracy to change gender. If we can change our gender, then there really is no purpose for marriage. If a man's sperm can be used to impregnate an egg for procreation there is no need for a man and a woman to be joined together for a child to be born.

The Nephilim were a part of this conspiracy changing the DNA of man to serve his purpose in destroying the bloodline of the Savior, Jesus Christ. God destroyed the Nephilim in the flood, but it appears that they reappeared upon the earth. David killed Goliath, whom some believe was a descendant of the Nephilim.

After Adam and Eve had disobeyed God, He told the devil, "And I will put enmity between you and the woman, and between YOUR OFFSPRING and her Offspring; He will bruise and tread your head underfoot, and you will lie in wait and bruise His heel" (Gen. 3:15) This scripture is referring to the seed of the devil (the Nephilim) and Jesus who would come from the seed of the woman to crush the head of Satan. David beheaded Goliath and buried his head at Golgotha, the place of the skull, where Jesus was crucified. Jesus literally crushed the head of the devil on Golgotha! Victory was won!

"We should celebrate the beauty of God's creative design. The Christian church and the godly family should be a festival of happiness. We should rejoice that God in His sovereign wisdom, has opened our eyes to see that

He has made us according to His perfect design. Manhood and womanhood aren't Plan B. God Himself has made us as we are. We are the pinnacle of His creation."[118]

Will the Nephilim reemerge? Will they take on a different form? "Many speculate the alien phenomenon could be a 'disguise' for this. But the main point for the Christian is to not be deceived by any of this. Instead, let us rejoice in knowing that no matter what the adversary attempts, the ultimate victory lies with Jesus Christ our Risen Savior."[117]

Chapter Nine

Progressive Agenda

Progressive Movement

"Progressivism was the reform movement that ran from the late nine-teenth century through the first decades of the twentieth century, during which leading intellectuals and social reformers in the United States sought to address the economic, political, and cultural questions that had arisen in the context of the rapid changes brought with the Industrial Revolution and the growth of modern capitalism in America. The progressives believed that these changes marked the end of the old order and required the creation of a new order appropriate for the new industrial age" (William A. Schambra and Thomas West / the Progressive Movement and the Transformation of American Politics).

Our Founding Fathers believed that all men are created equal and have unalienable rights given to us by God, our Creator. We should respect the rights of others as we in turn respect our own rights—the Golden Rule? The main rights were life and liberty which comprised the right to organize your own church, to associate with whomever you please and use your own talents to acquire and keep your own property. They believed in these rules to guide and maintain our lives.

The progressives rejected these claims and believed that we are not born free. John Dewey wrote that freedom is not "something that individuals have as a ready-made possession." He also believed that freedom is not a gift of God or nature but a product of human making and a gift of the state. Since we, as human beings, according to Dewey, are not naturally free, there can be no natural law or rights. He thought that these rights only exist in mythology and social zoology.

"For the Founders, then, the individual's existence and freedom in this crucial respect are not a gift of government. They are a gift of God and nature. Government is therefore always and fundamentally in the service of the individual, not the other way around. The purpose of government, then, is to enforce the natural law for the members of the political community by securing the people's natural rights. It does so by preserving their lives and liberties against the violence of others. In the founding, the liberty to be secured by government is not freedom from necessity or poverty. It is freedom from the despotic and predatory domination of some human beings over others."[119]

Progressives believe that freedom is the fulfillment of human capacities and the primary purpose of the state. The founders believed in individual freedom and that political society is "formed by a voluntary association of individuals: it is a social compact, by which the whole people covenants with each citizen, and each citizen with the whole people, that all shall be governed by certain laws for the common good" (Massachusetts Constitution of 1780).

The social compact was treated by the progressives with scorn. The belief was that the government was responsible for remolding man by bringing out his real aspirations and capacities.

Christians and Jews, during the founding of our country, believed in the God of the Bible that gave us our liberty and moral laws by which we are guided toward our duties and happiness. Some of the progressives redefined that our human freedom did not come from God but through the right political organization. Some even claimed God to be a myth.

The founders and the progressives had two diametrically opposing views of the world. One believed in limited government and one believed in big government. One believed that the divine was the source of our freedom and rights and the other that the government in effect was the divine and dictated what our rights are. Some progressives openly spoke of themselves to be socialists.[120]

Saul D. Alinsky, a hard left progressive community organizer, wrote a playbook of tactics for a generation of change agents such as Bill Ayers, Bernardine Dohrn, Bill and Hillary Clinton, Frank Marshall Davis, and President Barack Obama.

The main goal of the Alinsky philosophy is to cause social instability through subversive and divisive rhetoric. One way is to control the outcome of the education system by lowering the standards to create a dependent class of people. Once they create a problem, "order through chaos," they propose themselves as the answer and use the method of espousing rights as a method to bring about "equality."[121] Many of us do not even realize that we are being manipulated by the left here in this country. That's why we need to educate ourselves so that we won't have "the wool pulled over our eyes" anymore. Nowadays with so much media, one can't help but think that more and more people are being informed. I don't necessarily think that it is a lack of information, but that people choose to believe what they want to believe and what benefits them and ignore the truth in many cases.

Alinsky's Twelve Rules for Radicals

1. "Power is not only what you have, but what the enemy thinks you have." Power is derived from two sources—money and people. "Have-nots" must build power from flesh and blood.
2. "Never go outside the expertise of your people." It results in confusion, fear, and retreat. Feeling secure adds to the backbone of anyone.
3. "Whenever possible, go outside the expertise of the enemy." Look for ways to increase insecurity, anxiety, and uncertainty.
4. "Make the enemy live up to its own book of rules." If the rule is that every letter gets a reply, send thirty thousand letters. You can kill them with this because no one can possibly obey all of their own rules.
5. "Ridicule is man's most potent weapon." There is no defense. It's irrational. It's infuriating. It also works as a key pressure point to force the enemy into concessions.
6. "A good tactic is one your people enjoy." They'll keep doing it without urging and come back to do more. They're doing their thing and will even suggest better ones.
7. "A tactic that drags on too long becomes a drag." Don't become old news.
8. "Keep the pressure on. Never let up." Keep trying new things to keep the opposition off balance. As the opposition masters one approach, hit them from the flank with something new.
9. "The threat is usually more terrifying than the thing itself." Imagination and ego can dream up many more consequences than any activist.

10. "If you push a negative hard enough, it will push through and become a positive." Violence from the other side can win the public to your side because the public sympathizes with the underdog.
11. "The price of a successful attack is a constructive alternative." Never let the enemy score points because you're caught without a solution to the problem.
12. "Pick the target, freeze it, personalize it, and polarize it." Cut off the support network and isolate the target from sympathy. Go after people and not institutions; people hurt faster than institutions.[122]

Do any of these tactics sound familiar? "Don't like the message, attack the messenger." What about "don't let any tragedy go to waste." Unfortunately, at this writing, that is exactly what the Left is doing now to politicize the tragedy at Las Vegas by pushing more gun laws. How about changing language to make it sound better such as "pro-abortion to pro-choice or reproductive rights" or euthanasia, which generally means mercy killing, or the term "right to die." How about the term "fetus" instead of baby? The left is seeking to inoculate the masses with their lies and propaganda to hide their sinister motives. How about the term social justice?

Social Justice

What is social justice? It is a term used to organize with others to accomplish ends that benefit the whole community. In progressive terms it means a uniform distribution of society's advantages and disadvantages. It was originally a Catholic concept that was later taken over by secular progressives.

There are five common usages of social justice.

1. *Distribution*. The original premise of social justice was not distribution. This new term that was added suggests that a special human force does the distribution which is usually a powerful human agency, usually the state.
2. *Equality*. This implies equality of the burdens and the advantages and the opportunities of citizenship. The concept of equality is at the heart of this term. Although equality is good, this expresses an ideology of enforcement. This would entail a "redistribution"

of resources from those who have "unjustly" gained them to those who justly deserve them.

3. *Common good.* The common good sounds benign but the problem is: Who is going to decide what is the common good? This actually becomes an excuse for total state control. If this be the case, one would have to hope and pray that the leader or leaders making the decisions are moral and kind. God help us if the leader or leaders are evil!

4. *Progressive agenda.* For centuries, there has been an attack the unfairness and inequity of the commercial system. The world went from primarily people who worked on their own farms to people no longer growing their own food and working in factories. This became a problem because these workers became dependent on their wages. They lost their independence and the solidity of their old way of life.

5. *Compassion.* The third term in association with social justice is *compassion*. Reproductive rights came about from the notion that poor women do not have the economic security to raise many children and the privileged of this world can control the number of children that they have but not the poor. What the progressives really did was introduce a concept of reproductive rights which meant abortion. Abortion is now promoted as social justice and reproductive rights.[123]

The gospel is a message of salvation, not redistribution. Michael Youssef states: "The Christian gospel is a message of salvation, not a message of income redistribution and raising our neighbor's taxes." Jesus said that the way to serve the poor is by giving generously of our own resources. "But when you give a banquet," He said in Luke 14, "invite the poor, the crippled, the lame, the blind, and you will be blessed. Although they cannot repay you, you will be repaid at the resurrection of the righteous."

Michael Youssef goes on to say, "The Religious Left is very generous—with other people's money. In fact, I believe the founder of the Religious Left was none other than Judas Iscariot. When Mary, the sister of Lazarus, anointed Jesus with costly perfume just days before the crucifixion, Judas lectured her and said, 'Why wasn't this perfume sold and the money given to the poor?'"[124]

It is the Church's responsibility to care for the poor, not the government's. In my opinion, social justice is used as a ploy to make everyone, except the elites, dependent on the government. "Income redistribution is not Christianity. It's Marxism—and mixing the two only pollutes the Gospel and betrays the Great Commission" (Michael Youssef, PhD, "Social Justice Is Not Socialism").

Abortion

> "For You did form my inward parts; You did knit me together in my mother's womb. I will confess and praise You for You are fearful and wonderful
> And for the awful wonder of my birth!
> Wonderful are Your works, and that my inner self knows right well.
> My frame was not hidden from You when I was being formed in secret [and] intricately and curiously wrought [as if embroidered with various colors]
> In the depths of the earth [a region of darkness and mystery].
> Your eyes saw my unformed substance, and in Your book all the days [of my life] were written before ever they took shape, when as yet there was none of them." (Ps. 139:13–16)

During the time of Jesus, the Romans permitted abortion, infanticide and child abandonment. Abortion is never mentioned in the Bible despite the fact that it has been practiced since ancient times by a variety of means.[125]

Abortion was legal in some of the fifty states prior to Roe V. Wade decision in 1973, which ruled that a woman has a right to an abortion during the first trimester of pregnancy. Depending on the source, there have been close to sixty million abortions in the United States since Roe V. Wade.

A 2010 census reveals that Planned Parenthood is targeting minority neighborhoods through abortion, according to *Protecting Black Life*. Seventy-nine percent of surgical abortion facilities are walking distance of Latino and/or African American communities. More African American babies have been killed by abortion since 1973 than the number of deaths in the African American community. The founder of Planned Parenthood,

Margaret Sanger, was a staunch evolutionist and racist. Sanger spearheaded the eugenics movement in the 1930s and 1940s, which resulted in the sterilization of sixty thousand vulnerable people such as people with mental challenges.[126]

The Bible condemns the shedding of innocent blood. "Keep far from a false matter and [be very careful] not to condemn to death the innocent and the righteous, for I will not justify and acquit the wicked" (Exod. 23:7). "You shall not commit murder" (Exod. 20:17). "There are six things the Lord hates, indeed, seven are an abomination to Him: A proud look [the spirit that makes one overestimate himself and underestimate others], a lying tongue, and hands that shed innocent blood" (Prov. 6:16–17).

"And at that time Mary arose and went with haste into the hill country to a town of Judah. And she went to the house of Zachariah and, entering it, saluted Elizabeth. And it occurred that when Elizabeth heard Mary's greeting, the *baby* leaped in her womb, and Elizabeth was filled with and controlled by the Holy Spirit. And she cried out with a loud cry, and then exclaimed, Blessed [favored of God] above all other women are you! And blessed (favored of God) is the Fruit of your womb! And how [have I deserved that this honor should] be granted to me, that the mother of my Lord should come to me? For behold, the instant the sound of your salutation reached my ears, the *baby* in my womb leaped for joy" (Luke 1: 39–44).

The Greek word *brephos* describes the unborn, newborns and youth. "For behold, the instant, the sound of your salutation reached my ears, the *baby* in my womb leaped for joy." This describes the unborn found in Luke 1:44. A newborn baby is described in Luke 2:12, "And this will be a sign for you (by which you will recognize him): you will find [after searching] a *Baby* wrapped in swaddling clothes and lying in a manger." A young child is referred to in Luke 18:15, "Now they were also bringing [even] *babies* to Him that He might touch them, and when the disciples noticed it, they reproved them."[127]

The personhood of a baby has been the root of the problem. It has been seeking to dehumanize a baby within the mother's womb, thus justifying that a fetus is not really a human but just a blob of cells. How could God say that before we were born that He knew us?

That means that not only are we a physical being but also a spiritual being with a soul. Every child within his/her mother's womb was created for a purpose by God even before that child was conceived.

Believe it or not, there are people today who lived through their mother's abortion. Melissa Ohden is the founder of *Abortion Survivors Network* and has been in contact with 202 survivors and/ or immediate family members of survivors. Gianna Jessen, who is one of these survivors says: "I think someone who was burned in her mother's womb for eighteen hours [me] deserves to be heard, as we face the horror of Planned Parenthood."

Both Melissa and Gianna survived saline abortions. This is a procedure where a salt solution was injected into their mother's wombs, and they were burned inside and out by the solution. In this case, usually the mothers will give birth to a dead baby hours or days later. Both Gianna and Melissa were born alive. When this happens, usually babies are killed immediately or left in a bucket to die. By the grace of God, in their case, a compassionate worker had mercy on them and took them for medical care. They were both later adopted and speak out about their abortion stories.

Other survivors escaped death because, in some cases, an abortion was attempted and failed because the mother remained pregnant or the mother was pregnant with twins neither the mother nor the abortionist realized there was another baby in the womb after the abortion. All these survivors carry emotional scars and can identify with the aborted babies in a way only they can.

Carrie Fischer, an abortion survivor says: "When I see the baby body parts, my heart breaks, because I realize that I could have been one of those babies, I feel the pain and horror each baby must have felt, because I experienced that same pain when my mother tried to abort me. I survived, but so many millions of others have lost their lives to the monstrous atrocities of abortion."

"Where was *my* choice?" This is a question that abortion survivors ask. It is appalling to them for people to say that they were not actually human or that they did not deserve to live.

Most abortion survivors speak of forgiving their birth mothers. They realize that on some level their mothers were lied to or exploited to some extent. Those that spoke to Health Impact News did not show any hatred toward their mothers but forgave them and were compassionate toward them and other women who have had abortions.

Melody Olson, an abortion survivor and a postabortive woman talks about the power of forgiveness: "These women need to know that they are truly forgiven. That's why they don't feel worthy of love. We have to love out of our overflow."[128]

Some of the potential emotional effects from an abortion include regret, anger and guilt, shame, sense of loneliness or isolation, loss of self-confidence, insomnia or nightmares, relationship issues, suicidal thoughts and feelings, eating disorders, depression and anxiety.

Women who have a higher probability of having a negative emotional or psychological side effect are: individuals with previous emotional or psychological concerns; have been coerced, forced, or persuaded to get an abortion; religious beliefs that conflict with abortion; moral or ethical views that conflict with abortion; obtained an abortion in later stages of pregnancy and without support from significant others or their partner and women who have obtained an abortion for genetic or fetal abnormalities.[129]

Rachel's Vineyard provides weekends for healing after an abortion in locations throughout the United States and Canada and additional sites throughout the world. It is a ministry of Priests for Life. Mothers, married couples, fathers, grandparents, and siblings of aborted children as well as persons who have been involved in the abortion industry have participated in Rachel's Vineyard retreats seeking peace and inner healing.[130]

There have been many healings from these retreats and the following are some comments by a couple of women attending the retreats: "For the first time in twenty years, I was able to share my grief, my guilt, my anger. I was able to mourn the loss of my baby. But most important, I was able to believe that she now lives with Jesus. For a short time I could almost touch her and hold her and see her. For this, I will always be grateful. I felt Jesus calling, pulling me back. A feeling I can't forget or deny." "Daily for ten years I'd regretted and mourned alone my abortion decision. I couldn't change what I'd done and I couldn't go on with the pain and guilt. In spite of my fear of bringing up the past I went to a Rachel's Vineyard retreat where I found safety, comfort and understanding. And more pro-foundly, I experienced the forgiveness of God, a hope for tomorrow and for the day I meet my baby."[131]

Euthanasia

What is generally meant by euthanasia is mercy killing which is the deliberate ending of a person's life to reduce their suffering. The "right to die" is more commonly used today. These words sound compassionate, but they still mean that a doctor can kill someone. Remember how progressives change terms to sound less innocuous? It is actually a form of homicide, and now people are calling it an acceptable medical practice.[132]

The Hippocratic Oath that doctors are supposed to abide by is one of the oldest binding documents in history. It was written by Hippocrates and is still held sacred by physicians. There are many versions of the oath now with one of the new ones written by Louis Lasagna in 1964 who was the acting dean of the School of Medicine at Tufts University.

One of the paragraphs of the original Hippocratic Oath states: "I will never give a deadly drug to anybody who asked for it, nor will I make a suggestion to this effect. Similarly I will not give to a woman an abortive remedy. In purity and holiness I will guard my life and my art." Interestingly so, this new version does not contain anything similar to this statement. Is anyone surprised? Roe V. Wade happened in 1973 and now we have euthanasia.[133]

We were created by God for a purpose and our lives have an intrinsic value. This is the source of the "sanctity of life" at all stages of life. Secular humanism views life differently. It maintains that every life has a "quality" attached to it. This means that circumstances, abilities, suffering make a life better or worse. If the standard is happiness or contentment, then if one is suffering, it is reasonable to believe that death would be the preferred choice.

The humanist's worldview sees people as autonomous (self-ruling) biological entities whose life's purpose is pleasure and sees life as only valuable for what it offers and sees little value in suffering. According to this, life should only be lived if it is a "wanted life." They see suffering as a negative and therefore there are some lives not worth living.

Suffering is a part of life and a part of God's providence. "You must submit to and endure [correction] for discipline; God is dealing with you as with sons. For what son is there whom his father does not [thus] train and correct and discipline?" (Heb. 12:7). The purpose of suffering for the Christian is sanctification. "For our light, momentary affliction [this slight distress of the passing hour] is ever more and more abundantly preparing and producing and achieving for us an everlasting weight of glory [beyond all measure, excessively surpassing all comparisons and all calculations, a vast and transcendent glory and blessedness never to cease!]" (2 Cor. 4:17).

The term "quality of life" is a term introduced in the 1960s to refer to the overall welfare of a population. The prodeath movement has adopted it since the 1970s. This term has evolved from "quality of life" to "quality of living" to the "value of life." This has promoted the belief that life with low quality is not worth living. Unfortunately, this way of thinking has been used to justify the killing of unborn babies with Down Syndrome and other genetic defects. It has also included starving to death severely handicapped infants and brain-damaged adults.[134]

This was the case with Terri Schiavo in 1998 when the court ordered that her feeding tube be removed. This was based on a testimony by her husband, Michael Schiavo, and his brother and wife that years earlier Terri had casual statements indicating that she did not want to be kept alive by artificial means. Terri's parents said that the Schaivo's testimony was fabricated and testified that they believed in the sanctity of life. Their testimony failed to persuade Judge George Greer and their seven-year battle in the courts came to an end on March 18. Terri died from dehydration thirteen days later. According to an estimate by a medical examiner who performed the autopsy, removing the feeding tube hastened her death by a decade.

Also, her treating physician had testified that she was neither terminally ill nor suffering and that she was relatively healthy.[135]

The same mind-set for abortion is the same mind-set for euthanasia. Quality of life or value of life or quality of living—no matter what you call it, it is the same evil spirit—the spirit of death. This concept is a slippery slope because it recognizes that there are competent people who are better off dead and therefore it logically follows, from their perspective, that incompetent people are better off dead. This provides a basis for euthanasia for the competent terminally ill or chronically suffering to involuntary euthanasia for the demented, severely handicapped or comatose.

In the Netherlands, courts are now permitting euthanasia not only for terminally ill but also infants with serious handicaps but comatose patients, and even people suffering from severe depression. In the Netherlands a third of lethal injections are given without the patient's consent and despite the requirement for persistent request, 59 percent of cases occur on the same day they are asked for and 10 percent within the same hour. There is evidence that shows that physicians frequently falsify death certificates and disregard requirements for consulting a second physician.[136]

Most terminally ill patients do not want euthanasia. If euthanasia is an option, then these vulnerable people may feel like they are a burden and feel forced to justify their decision to remain alive. Euthanasia could also result in a loss of autonomy because the final choice rests with the physician not the patient.

As Christians, we need to speak out with one voice against the culture of death that is permeating not only the world, but our country in particular. Our country was founded on life, liberty, and the pursuit of happiness! We are in a spiritual battle not only for our very souls but our very lives that were given to us by our Creator.

Artificial Intelligence

"The existential risk from artificial general intelligence is the threat that substantial progress in artificial intelligence (AI) could someday result in human extinction (or some other unrecoverable global catastrophe)."[137]

Artificial intelligence becoming "superintelligent" by surpassing humanity in intelligence poses a threat of becoming powerful and difficult to control. Experts who attended a conference hosted by the Association for the Advancement of Artificial Intelligence met in 2009 to discuss "whether computers and robots might be able to acquire any sort of autonomy, and how much these abilities might pose a threat or hazard." They also noted, "That some robots have acquired various forms of semi-autonomy, including being able to find power sources on their own and being able to independently choose targets to attack with weapons." They also noted that some computer viruses can evade elimination and have achieved "cock-roach intelligence." They concluded that self-awareness as depicted in science fiction is probably unlikely, but that there were other potential hazards and pitfalls.[138]

This brings up the moral question—if artificial intelligence is on its way to autonomy and morality is part of the definition for intelligence, then one could conceive by definition that a superintelligent machine would behave morally. While there are many definitions of intelligence, none reference morality. Most artificial intelligence research focuses on algorithms that "optimize" the achievement of an arbitrary goal.

Stephen Hawking told the BBC in 2014, "Once humans develop artificial intelligence, it would take off on its own, and redesign itself at an ever-increasing rate. Humans, who are limited by slow biological evolution, couldn't compete and would be superseded."[139] The difference between we, as humans, is the fact that we have a soul comprised of our mind, will and emotions. We were created in God's image and we are a reflection of Who God is. We are intended to glorify God. Could an AI do such a thing?

James McGrath, a professor of religion at Butler University toyed with the question of asking a computer to pray for them and observe what happened. The students found out that the computer was more comfortable with commands like "What is prayer?" rather than "Pray for me." The computer, when asked "Pray for me," responded with "I'm not programmed to do that." If this computer was programmed to do that would it be a valuable action?—and if so, how would God receive it?

In the Nicene Creed, it speaks of Jesus as "the only Son of God, begotten, not made." Christians believe that God created humans, but humans make machines and by this logic, it would conclude that AI could not be considered God's children or possess a soul.[140]

Abraham van de Beek, a professor emeritus at Vrije Universiteit Amsterdam, says, "Who we are is not found in looking inward at ourselves but outward toward our Creator. This is because when we look inward, we only see an illusion of ourselves—an identity we created to cover over our true identity, which can only be discovered in relation to our Creator. Only when we deny ourselves can we know who we are."[140]

Anthony Levandowski, a former Google and Uber executive has filed papers with the IRS to "set up a nonprofit religious organization that can be seen as a church of artificial intelligence, where technology would be worshiped and a godhead would be created."[142] The name of the new church is "Way of the Future." The following are some highlights:

- The "Way of the Future" church will have its own gospel called "The Manual," public worship ceremonies, and probably a physical place of worship.
- The idea behind his religion is that one day—"not next week or next year"—sufficiently advanced artificial intelligence will be smarter than humans, and will effectively become a god.
- "Part of it being smarter than us means it will decide how it evolves, but at least we can decide how we act around it," Levandowski told Wired. "I would love for the machine to see us as its beloved elders that it respects and takes care of. We would want this intelligence to say, 'Humans should still have rights, even though I'm in charge.'"
- Levandowski is not the only tech luminary to worry about a superintelligent AI, which others refer to as "strong AI" or the singularity, although he prefers the term *transition*.[143]

Globalization / One World Order

What is the New World Order? According to *Got Questions Ministries*, "The New World Order is a conspiracy theory which posits a new period of history bringing about a major change in the world with the balance of world power. This New World Order is theorized by some to involve a group or groups of elitist people bent on ruling the world through a single worldwide system of government. The appeal of this New World Order lies in its proposal to free the world of wars and political strife, and its promises to eradicate poverty, disease, and hunger. Its purpose is to meet the needs and hopes of all mankind through worldwide peace."[144]

One way to unify the planet would be to do away with any borders. Does this sound familiar? This concept would emphasize tolerance through the promotion of other cultures and values and ideologies. Its ultimate goal being a sense of unity with all people speaking the same language. Does this also seem familiar?—the Tower of Babel maybe? Other objectives would be a single world-wide currency and oneness in religion, politics and moral values.[145] This sounds like a setup for the entrance of the Antichrist rule that is coming according to the scriptures. Revelation 13:8: "And all the inhabitants of the earth will fall down in adoration and pay him homage, everyone whose name has not been recorded in the Book of Life of the Lamb that was slain [in sacrifice] from the foundation of the world."

We can already see the emergence of a New World Order taking shape within our midst. Who is ultimately behind it? "For we are not wrestling with flesh and blood [contending only with physical opponents], but against the despotisms, against the powers, against [the master spirits who are] the world rulers of this present darkness, against the spirit forces of wickedness in the heavenly [supernatural] sphere" (Eph. 6:12). From the Garden of Eden to present age, it has been the devil who has been in constant warfare with God's creation. He has been in a battle against God "How have you fallen from heaven, O light-bringer and daystar, son of the morning! How you have been cut down to the ground, you who have been weakened and laid low [the nations]. O blasphemous, satanic king of Babylon! And you said in your heart, I will ascend to heaven; I will exalt my throne above the stars of God; I will sit upon the mount of assembly in the uttermost north. I will ascend above the heights of the clouds; I will make myself like the Most High" (Isa. 14:12–14).

We as Christians need to be discerning of the times that we are living in. It's one thing to be Christian in name and another to be a born-again believer who searches the scriptures and knows seasons and times that we are living in. In Matthew 24 the disciples asked Jesus "What will be the sign of Your coming and of the end [the completion, the consummation] of the age?" Jesus told them about many signs but the first sign He said was, Jesus answered them, "Be careful that no one misleads you [deceiving you and leading you into error]. For many will come in [on the strength of] My name [appropriating the name which belongs to Me], saying, I am the Christ [the Messiah], and they will lead many astray" (Matt. 24:4–5). Jesus continued on with other signs. It seems to me that deception is one of the big signs of His Second Coming.

Christians need to focus on the Bible and Jesus is saying that we need not be deceived by what the world is doing or saying. We need to be the light shining in the darkness and when things around us are falling apart and we wonder what is going on, we need to look to the truth that sets us free and know that God has prepared us and is preparing us for what is coming upon the earth.

Summary

I believe that the progressive agenda is a setup for globalization just like it began in the Tower of Babel. Man was trying to reach the heavens. God was not pleased with their arrogance.

According to Marjorie Rubright, an associate professor in the department of English, "The Tower of Babel story was, for Judeo-Christians, the first globalization narrative, and one that powerfully shaped ideas of self and other in the Renaissance."[146]

Progressives have sought to redefine terms to conform to their way of thinking. The world according to the humanistic view is seen through the eyes of man and not God. Man has become his own god. As man reaches closer and closer to remake who he is, he is preaching to others what and who they should be. If we fall into this trap, we are all going to walk blindly into the depths of deception that will follow and unless we are anchored in our faith, we will be deceived.

Man is trying to find peace and unity through his own means. The government is becoming a god to many people, and there will never be any true peace until the Messiah, Jesus Christ, comes back and his feet touch the Mount of Olives and His Kingdom reigns forever and ever!

Chapter Ten

Who Is Jesus?

He was born in an obscure village, the child of a peasant woman. He grew up in another village. He worked in a carpenter shop until He was thirty and then for three years was an itinerant preacher. He never wrote a book. He never held an office. He never owned a home. He never traveled two hundred miles from the place where He was born. He never did one of the things that usually accompany greatness. He had no credentials but Himself.

Although He walked the land over, curing the sick, giving sight to the blind, healing the lame, and raising people from the dead, the top established religious leaders turned against Him. His friends ran away. He was turned over to enemies. He went through the mockery of a trial. He was spat upon, flogged, and ridiculed. He was nailed to a cross between two thieves. While He was dying, the executioners gambled for the only piece of property He had on earth, and that was His robe. When He was dead, He was laid in a borrowed grave through the pity of a friend.

Nineteen wide centuries have come and gone, and today He is the central Figure of the human race and the Leader of the column of progress.

All the armies that ever marched, and all the navies that were ever built and all the parliaments that ever sat, and all the kings that ever reigned put together, have not affected the life of man upon this earth as has that One Solitary Life. (Source unknown)

Genealogy

"The Book of the ancestry [genealogy] of Jesus Christ [the Messiah, the Anointed], the son [descendant] of David, the son [descendant] of Abraham. Abraham was the father of Isaac, Isaac the father of Jacob, Jacob the father of Judah and his brothers, Judah the father of Perez and Zerah, whose mother was Tamar, Perez the father of Hezron, Hezron the father of Aram, Aram the father of Aminadab, Aminadab the father of Nahshon, Nahshon the father of Salmon, Salmon the father of Boaz, whose mother was Rahab, Boaz the father of Obed, whose mother was Ruth, Obed the father of Jesse, Jesse the father of King David, King David the father of Solomon, whose mother had been the wife of Uriah, Solomon the father of Rehoboam, Rehoboam the father of Abijah, Abijah the father of Asa, Asa the father of Jehoshaphat, Jehoshaphat the father of Joram [Jehoram], Joram the father of Uzziah, Uzziah, the father of Jotham, Jotham the father of Ahaz, Ahaz, the father of Hezekiah, Hezekiah the father of Manasseh, Manasseh the father of Amon, Amon the father of Josiah, and Josiah became the father of Jeconiah [also called Coniah and Jehoiachin] and his brothers about the time of the removal [deportation] to Babylon. After the exile to Babylon Jeconiah became the father of Shealtiel [Salathiel], Shealtiel the father of Zerubbbabel the father of Abiud, Abiud the father of Eliakim, eliakim the father of Azor, Azor the father of Sadoc, Sadoc the father of Achim, Achim the father of Eliud, Eliud the father of Eleazar, Eleazar the father of Matthan, Matthan the father of Jacob, Jacob the father of Joseph, the husband of Mary, of whom was born Jesus, Who is called the Christ [the Messiah, the Anointed] so all the generations from Abraham to David are fourteen, from David to the Babylonian exile [deportation] fourteen generations, from the Babylonian exile to the Christ fourteen generations" (Matt. 1:1–17).

Elizabeth, Mary's cousin, had miraculously conceived a child in her old age and was in her sixth month of her pregnancy with John the Baptist when Gabriel, God's messenger, appeared to Mary with great news. "Now in the sixth month [after that], the angel Gabriel was sent from God to a town of Galilee named Nazareth, to a girl never having been married and a virgin engaged to be married to a man whose name was Joseph, a descendant of the house of David and the virgin's name was Mary. And he came to her and said, Hail O favored one [endued with grace]! The Lord is with you! Blessed [favored of God] are you before all other women! But when she saw him, she was greatly troubled and disturbed and confused at what he said and kept revolving in her mind what such a greeting might mean. And the angel said to her, Do not be afraid, Mary, for you have found grace [free, spontaneous, absolute favor and loving-kindness] with God. And listen! You will become pregnant and will give birth to a Son, and you shall call His name Jesus. He will be great [eminent] and will be called the Son of the Most High; and the Lord God will give to Him the throne of His forefather David, and He will reign over the house of Jacob throughout the ages; and of His reign there will be no end. And Mary said to the angel, How can this be since I have no [intimacy with any man as a] husband? Then the angel said to her, the Holy Spirit will come upon you, and the power of the Most High will over shadow you [like a shining cloud]; and so the holy [pure, sinless] Thing (Offspring) which shall be born of you will be called the Son of God. And listen! Your relative Elizabeth in her old age has also conceived a son, and this is now the sixth month with her who was called barren. For with God nothing is ever impossible and no word from God shall be without power or impossible of fulfillment. Then Mary said, Behold, I am the handmaiden of the Lord, let it be done to me according to what you have said. And the angel left her" (Luke 1:26–38).

Clearly this states that not only was Jesus a man, who would be born like each and every one of us, but He clearly was the Son of God by the power of the Holy Spirit coming upon Mary in order for her to conceive Jesus.

Identity of Jesus

There are five things that Gabriel said about Mary's child:

1. He said that His name would be Jesus—in Hebrew: Joshua, which means *savior* or *deliverer*. He, in effect, is telling Mary that her child will be her Savior—Jesus.
2. He said that Jesus would be great. "He is the sole expression of the glory of God [the Light-being, the out-raying or radiance of the divine], and He is the perfect imprint and very image of [God's] nature, upholding and maintaining and guiding and propelling the universe by His mighty word of power. When He had by offering Himself accomplished our cleansing of sins and riddance

of guilt, He sat down at the right hand of the divine Majesty on high" (Heb. 1:3).

3. He said that He would be called Son of the Most High. Gabriel says that Jesus is great, He is king and He is eternal. Jesus's sonship is not like ours. Even the demons recognized this. A demon cried out to Jesus, "What have you to do with me, Jesus, Son of the Most High? I beseech You, do not torment me." Jesus is the Son of God and because of this He has the authority to torment the forces of Satan.

4. Jesus will sit on David's throne. It is inevitable and fitting for Jesus to be king. He will fulfill all the prophecies that a son of David will rule over Israel. "And it shall be in that day the root of Jesse shall stand as a signal for the peoples; of Him shall the nations inquire and seek knowledge, and His dwelling shall be glory (His rest glorious)!" (Isa. 11:10).

5. He said that His Kingdom shall never end. Jesus's Kingdom shall reign forever and forever. He is the King of Kings and the Lord of Lords! Christ Conceived by the Holy Spirit / John Piper.[148]

Even before the birth of Christ, God, through His prophets, foretold His coming. "Therefore the Lord Himself shall give you a sign: Behold the young woman who is unmarried and a virgin shall conceive and bear a son, and shall call his name Immanuel" (Isa. 7:14). "For to us a Child is born, to us a Son is given; and the government shall be upon His shoulder and His name shall be called Wonderful Counselor, Mighty God, Everlasting Father [of Eternity], Prince of Peace. Of the increase of His government and of peace there shall be no end, upon the throne of David and over his kingdom, to establish it and to uphold it with justice and with righteousness from the [latter] time forth, even forevermore. The zeal of the Lord of hosts will perform this."

Isaiah 9:6-7: "Surely He has borne our griefs [sicknesses, weaknesses, and distresses] and carried our sorrows and pains [of punishment], yet we [ignorantly] considered Him stricken, smitten by God [as if with leprosy]. But He was wounded for our transgressions, He was bruised for our guilt and iniquities; the chastisement [needful to obtain] peace and well-being for us was upon Him, and with the stripes [that wounded] Him we are healed and made whole" (Isa. 53:4-5).

Jesus Himself proclaimed Who He was and what His purpose was. "Jesus replied, I am the Bread of Life. He who comes to Me will never be hungry and he who believes in and cleaves to and trusts in and relies on Me will never thirst anymore [at any time]. But [as] I told you, although you have seen Me, still you do not believe and trust and have faith. All whom My Father, gives [entrusts] to Me will come to Me; and the one who comes to Me I will most certainly not cast out [I will never, no never, reject one of them who comes to Me]. For I have come down from heaven not to do My own will and purpose but to do the will and purpose of Him Who sent Me. And this is the will of Him Who sent Me, that I should not lose any of all that He has given Me, but that I should give new life and raise [them all] up at the last day. For this is My Father's will and His purpose, that everyone who sees the Son and believes in and cleaves to and trusts in and relies on Him should have eternal life, and I will raise him up (from the dead) at the last day" (John 6:35–40).

Satan tried to steal Jesus's identity when he tempted Him in the desert. "And He stayed in the wilderness –[desert] forty days, being tempted [all the while] by Satan; and He was with the wild beasts, and the angels ministered to Him [continually]" (Mark 1:13). After Jesus had been in the desert for forty days and forty nights without food and was very hungry. "And the tempter came and said to Him. **If You are God's Son**, command these stones to be made [loaves of] bread. But He replied, It has been written, Man shall not live and be upheld and sustained by bread alone, but by every word that comes forth from the mouth of God" (Matt. 4:3–4).

The devil himself tried to put doubt into Jesus's mind about His divinity. He waited for a time when Jesus's flesh was weak to tempt Him. Jesus rebuked him and used the Word of God to refute what he had said. Satan tempted Him again and used the same words, "**If You are the Son of God**, throw Yourself down; for it is written, He will give His angels charge over you, and they will bear you up on their hands, lest you strike your foot against a stone." "Jesus said to him, On the other hand, it is written also, Yu shall not tempt, test thoroughly, or try exceedingly the Lord your God" (Matt. 4:6–7).

In His own words, Jesus said:

> Jesus replied, I am the Bread of Life. He who comes to Me will never be hungry, and he who believes in and cleaves to and trusts in and relies on Me will never thirst any

more [at any time]. But [as] I told you, although you have seen Me, still you do not believe and trust and have faith. All whom My Father gives [entrusts] to Me will come to Me; and the one who comes to Me I will most certainly not cast out [I will never, no never, reject one of them who comes to Me].

For I have come down from heaven not to do My own will and purpose but to do the will and purpose of Him Who sent me. And this is the will of Him Who sent Me, that I should not lose any of all that he has given me, but that I should give new life and raise [them all] up at the last day. For this is My Father's will and His purpose, that everyone who sees the Son and believes in and cleaves to and trusts in and relies on Him should have eternal life and I will raise him up [from the dead] at the last day. (John 6:35-40)

"Once more Jesus addressed the crowd. He said I am the Light of the world. He who follows Me will not be walking in the dark, but will have the Light which is life" (John 8:12). "I have come as a Light into the world, so that whoever believes in Me [whoever cleaves to and trusts in and relies on Me] may not continue to live in darkness" (John 12:46).

"I am the Good Shepherd. The Good Shepherd risks and lays down His [own] life for the sheep. But the hired servant [He who merely serves for wages] who is neither the shepherd nor the owner of the sheep, when he sees the wolf coming, deserts the flock and runs away. And the wolf chases and snatches them and scatters [the flock]. I am the Good Shepherd; and I know and recognize My own, and My own know and recognize Me—Even as [truly as] the Father knows Me and I also know the Father—and I am giving My [very own] life and laying it down on behalf of the sheep" (John 10:11-15).

"Jesus said to her, I am [Myself] the Resurrection and the Life. Whoever believes in [adheres to, trusts in, and relies on] Me, although he may die, yet he shall live; and whoever continues to live and believes in [has faith in, cleaves to, and relies on] Me shall never [actually] die at all. Do you believe this?" (John 11:25-26).

"Jesus said to him, I am the Way and the Truth and the Life; no one comes to the Father except by [through] Me. If you had known Me [had learned to recognize Me], you would also have known My Father. From now on, you know Him and have seen Him" (John 14:6-7).

The Disciples

Even though He proclaimed Who He was and what His purpose was, there were those, even His own disciples were not sure Who He was. "Now when Jesus went into the region of Caesarea Philippi, He asked His disciples, Who do people say that the Son of Man is? And they answered, some say John the Baptist; others say Elijah; and others Jeremiah or one of the prophets. He said to them, But who do you [yourselves] say that I am? Simon Peter replied, You are the Christ, the Son of the living God. Then Jesus answered him, Blessed [happy, fortunate, and to be envied] are you, Simon Bar-Jonah, for flesh and blood [men] have not revealed this to you, but My Father Who is in heaven" (Matt. 16:13-17).

The disciples were not really sure who Jesus was but Peter said that Jesus was the Christ and the Son of the living God. Jesus said that it was a spiritual conviction given to him by His Father in heaven.

In John 6:32-35, Jesus is talking about the bread of life. The disciples had already experienced the miracle of the multiplication of the loaves of bread. Jesus is trying to explain to them that He is the Bread of Life. He also told them that even though they have seen Him they still did not have faith and trust in Him. They were looking for a physical sign and Jesus was trying to tell them that He is the sign! When Jesus spoke about the Bread of Life pertaining to feeding on His flesh and blood, many of His disciples left but the twelve remained.

When Jesus calmed the storm the disciples were amazed, "What kind of man is this that even the winds and the sea obey Him!" (Matt. 8:27). There was another storm and the disciples were in the boat and fearful but then they saw Jesus walking on the water and Peter got out of the boat and walked on the water until he started to sink because he took his eyes off of Jesus. When Jesus got into the boat the disciples said, "And those in the boat knelt and worshipped Him, saying, Truly You are the Son of God!" (Matt.14:33).

When Peter saw Jesus in glory at the Transfiguration, he became very frightened. During the Transfiguration of the Lord God even spoke from a cloud saying, "This is My Son, the [most dearworthy] Beloved One. Be constantly listening to and obeying Him!" How could they then not believe who Jesus really was? Jesus told the disciples to keep it a secret about the Transfiguration until He had risen from the dead and the disciples began to question among themselves what "rising from the dead" meant. Instead of asking Jesus about it they discussed it among themselves.[149]

I think sometimes we forget and fail to realize that the disciples were mere mortals like you and

> I. How would we have responded to Jesus and His teachings if we had lived during His time upon the earth? Maybe we would have questioned what He did or doubted as Thomas did when he said that he would only believe if he could actually see the scars in Jesus's hands and feet and the scar in his side. Sometimes I think we need to just believe without truly understanding because faith would not be necessary if we understood everything about God and His purpose and plan.

Did Mary and Joseph understand who Jesus really was? I am not sure they truly understood. When Jesus was twelve and disappeared from their sight, they searched for three days and found Him sitting in the court of the temple listening to the teachers and asking them questions. They asked Him why He had treated them like this because they had anxiously been looking for Him for three days. When they found Him, Jesus said, "And He said to them, How is it that you had to look for Me? Did you not see and know that it is necessary [as a duty] for Me to be in My Father's house and (occupied) about My Father's business?" (Luke 2:49).

The Pharisees

"And He came into the world, and through the world was made through Him, the world did not recognize Him [did not know Him]. He came to that which belonged to Him [to His own—His domain, creation, things, world], and they who were His own did not receive Him and did not welcome Him" (John 1:10–11). Jesus was born among a chosen people, the Israelites but they rejected the Messiah while He was living with them.

In 1 Peter 2:8, Peter states that the reason the Jews did not believe in Jesus was because they were not first obedient to God, "because they disobey and disbelieve [God's] Word, as those [who reject Him] were destined –[appointed] to do." When someone is disobedient, they live their lives according to their own will and not the will of God. Jesus taught the truth to the Jews but most of them, including the Pharisees turned away from the truth.

They were also very stubborn and refused to believe who Jesus was. They lived in a delusion that they had figured God out. They were self-righteous in and rejected anyone teaching them differently.[150] "Brethren, [with all] my heart's desire and goodwill for [Israel], I long and pray to God that they may be saved. I bear them witness that they have a [certain] zeal and enthusiasm for God, but it is not enlightened and according to [correct and vital] knowledge. For being ignorant of the righteousness that God ascribes [which makes one acceptable to Him in word thought and deed] and seeking to establish and righteousness [a means of salvation] of their own, they did not obey or submit themselves to God's righteousness" (Rom. 10:1–4).

They were looking for signs but closed their eyes to what they saw and questioned Jesus about the law every time they could just to see if they could trip Him up. They did not believe Jesus because He was not meeting their expectations and they did not understand His purpose. Jesus did not act like they expected Him to act, and so they rejected Him.[151] "And all the people who heard Him, even the tax collectors, acknowledged the justice of God [in calling them to repentance and in pronouncing future wrath on the impenitent], being baptized with the baptism of John. But the Pharisees and the lawyers [of the Mosaic Law] annulled and rejected and brought to nothing God's purpose concerning themselves, by [refusing and] not being baptized by him [John]" (Luke 7:29–30).

Some of the Jews rejected Jesus because they feared for themselves. "And yet [in spite of all this] many even of the leading men [the authorities and the nobles] believed and trusted in Him. But because of the Pharisees they did not confess it, for fear that [if they should acknowledge Him] they would be expelled from the synagogue; For they loved the approval and the praise and the glory that come from men [instead of and] more than the glory that comes from God. They valued their credit with men more than their credit with God" (John 12:42–23).

The Character of Jesus

What is one of the first things we think of when we think of Jesus? I think of His great love for us because He willingly came down from heaven to offer His life as a ransom for ours. He was the perfect expiator of our sins. A sinless, perfect Lamb of God whose sacrifice for our sins has allowed us access to the Father. "No one has greater love [no one has shown stronger affection] than to lay down [give up] his own life for his friends" (John 15:13).

The character traits of Jesus are innumerable. He is Holy, He is love, joy, peace, patience, kindness, goodness, faithfulness, gentleness, forgiving, humble, wise, compassionate, obedient, meek, long suffering, and the list goes on. More importantly, do we as Christians reflect the character of Jesus in our everyday lives?

A *Dallas Morning News* reported that an elderly couple, the Davenports, were sitting in their home and after finishing their meal, a burglar broke into their home and pointed a gun at them demanding money. While Mrs. Davenport was looking through her purse for money, the burglar asked the husband what program he was watching and he said *The 700 Club*. The burglar asked, "Are ya'll Christians?" And the man replied, "Yes" and the burglar said, "Me too."[152] Was the criminal really a Christian? Did he exhibit the character of Jesus? I don't think that he really was and his character did not reflect that he was.

In Matthew 7:16, it says, speaking about Christians, "You will fully recognize them by their fruits. Do people pick grapes from thorns, or figs from thistles? Our character should reflect the character of the one whom we serve, Jesus. In 1 John 2:6 it says, "Whoever says he abides in Him ought [as a personal debt] to walk and conduct himself in the same way in which He walked and conducted Himself [Jesus]."

In Mark 10:14–16, Jesus is asked to bless the children, and His disciples rebuked the people, and Jesus said, "Allow the children to come to Me—do not forbid or prevent or hinder them—for to such belongs the kingdom of God. Truly I tell you, whoever does not receive and accept and welcome the kingdom of God like a little child [does] positively shall not enter it at all. And He took them [the children up one by one] in His arms and [fervently invoked a] blessing, placing His hands upon them."

As disciples of Christ we should reflect the character of Jesus in everything we do or say. Even more so in what we do because people watch what we do more than sometimes what we say because they are seeing faith in action.

Dan Clark, who is an actor, songwriter, and recording artist, and video producer wrote an article that exemplifies faith in action.

Once when I was a teenager, my father and I were standing in line to buy tickets for the circus. Finally, there was only one family between us and the ticket counter. This family made a big impression on me. There were eight children, all probably under the age of 12. You could tell they didn't have a lot of money. Their clothes were not expensive, but they were clean. The children were well-behaved, all of them standing in line, two-by-two behind their parents, holding hands. They were excitedly jabbering about the clowns, elephants and other acts they would see that night. One could sense they had never been to the circus before. It promised to be a highlight of their young lives.

The father and mother were at the head of the pack standing proud as could be. The mother was holding her husband's hand, looking up at him as if to say, "You're my knight in shining armor." He was smiling and basking in pride.

The ticket lady asked the father how many tickets he wanted. He proudly responded, "Please let me buy eight children's tickets and two adult tickets so I can take my family to the circus." The ticket lady quoted the price. The man's wife let go of his hand, her head dropped, the man's lip began to quiver. The father leaned a little closer and asked, "How much did you say?" The ticket lady again quoted the price. The man didn't have enough money.

How was he supposed to turn and tell his eight kids that he didn't have enough money to take to tame them to the circus?

Seeing what was going on, my dad put his hand into his pocket, pulled out a twenty-dollar bill and dropped it on the ground. (We were not wealthy in any sense of the word.) My father reached down, picked up the bill, tapped the man on the shoulder, and said, "Excuse me, sir, this fell out of your pocket."

The man knew what was going on. He wasn't begging for a handout but certainly appreciated the help in a desperate, heart-breaking, embarrassing situation. He looked straight into my dad's eyes, took my dad's hand in both of his, squeezed tightly onto the $20 bill, and with his lip quivering and a tear streaming down his cheek, he replied, "Thank you, thank you, sir. This really means a lot to me and my family."

My father and I went back to our car and drove home. We didn't go to the circus that night, but we didn't go without.[153]

St. Paul, in his epistle to the Philippians says, "Do all things without complaining and disputing, that you may become blameless and harmless, children of God without fault in the midst of a crooked and perverse generation, among whom you shine as lights in the world" (Phil. 2:15). This is one thing that we need to be and that is a light in the darkness. As the world gets darker and darker, our lights must shine because when a light shines in the darkness, it makes the darkness disappear. It also brings out that which is hidden. So many things that have been hidden in the world seem to be coming to light. "Let your light so shine before men that they may see your moral excellence and your praiseworthy, noble, and good deeds and recognize and honor and praise and glorify your Father Who is in heaven" (Matt. 5:15).

The Cross—the Resurrection

During the Napoleonic Wars, there was a lottery in which men were drafted into the French Army to go off to war. In very rare cases you may be able to get someone to take your place.

One day, some authorities from the government told a certain man that his name had come up in the lottery. He refused to go with them saying, "I was killed two years ago." He claimed that the records showed he had been killed in action. They were puzzled and asked how it could be and he explained that when his name came up in the lottery, his friend said, "You have a large family but I am not married and nobody is dependent on me. I'll take your name and address and go in your place." This case was referred to Napoleon himself and the country decided that *he was free because another man had died in his place.*[154]

Jesus bore your sins on the cross. "He personally bore our sins in His [own] body on the tree [as an altar and offered Himself on it], that we might die [cease to exist] to sin and live to righteousness. By His wounds we are healed" (1 Pet. 2:24).

Many years ago, a vehicle rear-ended me. Some compassionate people, who witnessed the accident, checked on my well-being and one said he would follow the vehicle that had rear-ended me. We found the person at a house nearby and the family of the youth said that they would repair the car at no cost. A police officer present asked if I was going to bring any charges against the youth and I said, "No." The officer said, "Okay, *it will be as if nothing happened.*"

When Jesus died on the cross, He took upon Himself the punishment for our sins. It was the punishment we deserve. It was Jesus who paid the price. When we ask for His forgiveness, He takes our sins and remembers them no more as if they were never committed.

Jesus did die on the cross, but He rose again on the third day! "At early dawn, [the women] went to the tomb, taking the spices which they had made ready. And they found the stone rolled back from the tomb, but when they went inside, they did not find the body of the Lord Jesus. And while they were perplexed and wondering what to do about this, behold two men in dazzling raiment suddenly stood beside them. Luke 24:1-4 They told them, He is not here, but has risen. Remember how He told you while He was still in Galilee" (Luke 24:6).

The resurrection of Jesus is important because he is alive and living in us. All leaders of other religions, such as Mohammed, Buddha, etc. do not have empty tombs. We serve a Risen Savior Who is alive and continues to do His work in and through us. We have taken on His identity because of the shedding of His blood on Calvary that redeemed us and gave us new life. We can use His blood and His Name as a powerful weapon against the evil one.

In 1432, a terrible plague broke out in Lisbon, Portugal. Thousands of men, women and children died. A Monsignor Andre Dias lived in a monastery of St. Dominic. He urged the people to call on the Holy Name of Jesus. He told them to say "Jesus, Jesus" and write His Name on cards and place them under their pillows, on doors and in a very short time all Portugal was freed from the terrible plague.[155]

Summary

Jesus fulfilled over 350 prophecies. According to a Hebrew requirement that a prophecy must have a 100 percent rate of accuracy, the one who is the true Messiah must fulfill them all or else he is not the Messiah. Did Jesus fulfill these Old Testament prophecies? Peter Stoner, professor of mathematics gave six hundred students a math probability problem that determines the odds for one person fulfilling eight specific prophecies. These students calculated the odds of one person fulfilling all these prophecies and concluded that these eight prophecies are "astronomical"— one in ten to the twenty-first power. Stoner gave the following example to illustrate this: "First, blanket the entire Earth land mass with silver dollars 120 feet high. Second, specially mark one of those dollars and randomly bury it. Third, ask a person to travel the Earth and select the marked dollar, while blindfolded, from the trillions of other dollars."

For all those skeptics out there, the *American Scientific Association* stated, "The mathematical analysis . . . is based upon principles of probability which are thoroughly sound, and Professor Stoner has applied these principles in a proper and convincing way."[156]

The following is a list of the eight prophecies that were fulfilled:

1. Christ to be born in Bethlehem; Micah 5:2, "But you, Bethlehem Ephratah, you are little to be among the clans of Judah; (yet) out of you shall One come forth for Me Who is to be Ruler in Israel, Whose goings forth have been from of old, from ancient days [eternity]." Fulfilled in Matthew 2:4–6: He was born in Bethlehem.
2. Born of a virgin. Isaiah 7:14, "Therefore the Lord Himself shall give you a sign; Behold, the young woman who is unmarried and a virgin shall conceive and bear a son, and shall call his name Immanuel [god with us]." Fulfilled in Matthew 2:22–23—He was born of a virgin.
3. The Messiah would be born from the lineage of David. Jeremiah 23:5, "Behold, the days are coming, says the Lord, when I will raise up to David a righteous Branch [Sprout], and He will reign as King and do wisely and will execute justice and righteousness in the land." Fulfilled 3:23, 31—Jesus, the Son of David.
4. The Messiah would be betrayed for thirty pieces of silver. "And the Lord said to me, Cast it to the potter [as if He said, To the dogs!]— the munificently [miserable] sum at which I [and My shepherd] am priced by them! And I [Zechariah] took the thirty pieces of silver and cast them to the potter in the house of the Lord" (Zechariah 11:13). Fulfilled in Matthew 26:15—"They gave him thirty pieces of silver."
5. The Messiah would have his hands and feet pierced. "For [like a pack of] dogs they have encompassed me; a company of evil-doers has encircled me, they pierced my hands and my feet" (Psalm 22:16). Fulfilled in Luke 23:33—They came to a place called the Skull. All three were crucified there. Jesus on the center cross, and the two criminals on either side.
6. People would cast lots for the Messiah's clothing. "They part my clothing among them and cast lots for my raiment [a long, shirtlike

garment, a seamless undertunic]" (Psalm 22:18). Fulfilled in John 19:23–24—Then the soldiers took His garments . . . and also His tunic . . . they cast lots for it.
7. The Messiah would appear riding on a donkey. "Rejoice greatly, O Daughter of Zion! Shout aloud, O daughter of Jerusalem! Behold, your King comes to you; He is [uncompromisingly] just and having salvation [triumphant and victorious], patient, meek, lowly, and riding on a donkey, upon a colt, the foal of a donkey" (Zechariah 9:9). Fulfilled in Matthew 21:7, "They brought the donkey and the colt and laid their coats upon them [the clothing]."
8. A messenger would be sent to herald the Messiah. Malachi 3:1, "Behold, I send My messenger, and he shall prepare the way before Me. And the Lord [the Messiah], Whom you seek, will suddenly come to His temple; the Messenger or Angel of the covenant, Whom you desire, behold, He shall come, says the Lord of hosts." Fulfilled in John 1:26—"John answered them, I [only] baptize in [with] water. Among you there stands One Whom you do not recognize."[157]

Jesus is who He says He is. The prophets of old foretold His identity before He was born in Bethlehem. Of course before Jesus was born with a physical body, He always existed "In the beginning [before all time] was the Word [Christ], and the Word was with God, and the Word was God Himself. He was present originally with God.

All things were made and came into existence through Him; and without Him was not even one thing made that has come into being" (John 1:1–3).

The Pharisees and even at times his own disciples, did not truly understand who He was. The religious at that time were close minded and probably felt threatened by someone claiming to be the Messiah. Had they taken the prophecies seriously they would have known that He was who He said He was. "So the chief priests and Pharisees called a meeting of the council [the Sanhedrin] and said. What are we to do? For this Man performs many signs [evidences, miracles]. If we let Him alone to go on like this, everyone will believe in Him and adhere to Him, and the Romans will come and suppress and destroy and take away our [holy] place and our nation [our temple and city and our civil organization]" (John 11:47–48).

It appeared that their hearts were hardened so that God's purpose would be fulfilled.

Jesus is who He says He is. God, through His prophets, lit the way to the appearing of His Son, Jesus. Jesus Christ is the embodiment of all that is good and powerful and loving. We are the righteousness of God through faith in Jesus Christ. Without Jesus in the flesh, I don't think that we would ever have known the love God has for us and His plan for our lives through His Son.

Chapter Eleven

Identity in Christ

Who We Are in Christ

In Jonathan Cahn's *Book of Mysteries*, he speaks about our identity shaped by God. "We see ourselves as we are. But God sees us not as we are, but as He called us to be. He gives you an identity not based on your past but based on your future, what you are to become. The secret is to receive that identity and believe it before you see it. Live as if it is. So your name is no longer *Rejected*, but *Beloved*; no longer *Weak*, but *Mighty*; no longer *Defeated*, but *Victorious*. He has given you a name of that which is not. Receive it and it will be. Live by your prophecy name. It is as simple as, 'Let there be light.'"[158]

Remember Gideon and Joseph and Abraham? God spoke into their lives what their destiny would be. God changed Abram's name to Abraham (father of multitudes). Joseph's name, Yosef in Hebrew, means *increase*, and Gideon or Giddone in Hebrew means *to strike down*. Every time their name was spoken, their prophecy was decreed. In the Beatitudes, Jesus is talking about humility, charity, and brotherly love. He teaches about the transformation of the inner person and love becoming the primary motivation as a Christian. The Beatitudes also initiate one of the main themes of Matthew's Gospel, which is that the Kingdom is not of this world but the Kingdom of Heaven.

"Blessed are the poor in spirit, for theirs is the kingdom of heaven." "Poor in spirit" means to be humble. Humility brings and openness and an inner peace that opens us up to seeking the Word of God and doing God's will.

"Blessed are they who mourn, for they shall be comforted." When we acknowledge that we are made in the image and likeness of God and realize that which was lost in the Garden of Eden through disobedience, we mourn that which was and seek the Comforter, the Holy Spirit to enable us to live as Christ showed us how to live in a world where many reject Him.

"Blessed are the meek, for they shall inherit the earth." A meek person becomes gentle and kind even in the face of adversity. We should be obedient and submissive to the will of God. A meek person is one who has self-control. These virtues can not only bring inner peace but help to bring peace in a world full of strife and the lust for power.

"Blessed are they who hunger and thirst for righteousness, for they shall be satisfied." Righteousness is more than observing the law but an expression of love. A strong desire for justice and moral perfection is a necessary ingredient for seeking holiness. Yes, we are not perfect, but if we seek perfection because of our love for the Lord, He, through the Holy Spirit, will help to fulfill the desires of our heart. "Delight yourself also in the Lord, and He will give you the desires and secret petitions of your heart" (Ps. 37:4).

"Blessed are the merciful, for they shall obtain mercy." We need to be merciful just as our Heavenly Father is merciful toward us. Showing mercy by forgiving someone is so important that God the Father echoed it through Jesus in the *Lord's Prayer*: *Forgive us our trespasses as we forgive those who trespass against us.* Also in Matthew 25:35: Jesus talks about being merciful; "For I was hungry and you gave Me food, I was thirsty and you gave Me something to drink, I was a stranger and you brought me together with yourselves and welcomed and entertained and lodged Me."

"Blessed are the pure of heat, for they shall see God." When we are pure of heart, we are free of all selfish intentions and self-seeking desires. No man can see God but if you are pure of heart you will see Him. I think this means that we will see God's true essence.

"Blessed are the peacemakers, for they shall be called children of God." In John 14:27, Jesus says, "Peace I leave with you. My [own] peace I now give and bequeath to you. Do not let your hearts be troubled, neither let them be afraid. [Stop allowing yourselves to be agitated and disturbed; and do not permit yourselves to be fearful and intimidated and cowardly and unsettled.]" Peace is one of the fruits of the Holy Spirit. We need to have peace within our hearts if we want to pass it on to those who are in need of it. The world can be changed one person at a time; just look at what Jesus did!

"Blessed are they who are persecuted for the sake of righteousness, for theirs is the Kingdom of Heaven." When we come under persecution, we need only remember that Jesus went through it and He will not ask us to endure anything He did not first endure. Here in the United States many Christians who are brave enough to stand for their faith are being persecuted. We need to pray that we all will stand when the time comes. Christians in the Roman era suffered martyrdom. Millions of Christians around the world are suffering persecution even to the point of giving up their own lives for the Gospel.[159]

The Fruit of the Spirit

"But the fruit of the [Holy] Spirit [the work which His presence within accomplishes] is love, joy [gladness], peace, patience [an even temper, forbearance] kindness, goodness [benevolence], faithfulness, gentleness [meekness, humility], self-control [self-restraint, continence]. Against such things there is no law [that can bring a charge]. And those who belong to Christ Jesus [the Messiah] have crucified the flesh [the godless human nature] with its passions and appetites and desires. If we live by the [Holy] Spirit, let us also walk by the Spirit. [If by the Holy Spirit we have our life in God, let us go forward walking in line, our conduct controlled by the Spirit]" (Gal. 5:22–25).

Jesus Christ embodied all the nine fruits of the Holy Spirit. In John 15:4 Jesus says, "Dwell in Me, and I will dwell in you. [Live in Me, and I will live in you.] Just as no branch can bear fruit of itself without abiding in [being vitally united to] the vine, neither can you bear fruit unless you abide in Me. I am the Vine; you are the branches. Whoever lives in Me and I in him bears much [abundant] fruit. However, apart from Me [cut off from vital union with Me] you can do nothing. When you bear [produce] much fruit, My Father is honored and glorified, and you show and prove yourselves to be true followers of Mine" (John 15:4–5; 8).

The fruit of the Spirit is the outgrowth of Christ living in us. Our character is formed each day as we yield more and more to Jesus seeking to know Him. Our flesh and our spirit are in a constant battle. Without Christ, we can do nothing.

The Fruit of Love

"Beloved, let us love one another, for love is [springs] from God; and he who loves [his fellowmen] is begotten [born] of God and is coming [progressively] to know and understand God [to perceive and recognize and get a better and clearer knowledge of Him]" (1 John 4:7).

It is not so much that we love God but that God loves us. He sent His only begotten Son to die on a cross to save us from our sins. "And He replied to him, You shall love the Lord your God with all your heart and with all your soul and all your mind [intellect]. This is the great [most important principal] and first commandment, and a second is like it: You shall love your neighbor as [you do] yourself" (Matt. 22:37-39). "This is My commandment, that you love one another just as I have loved you" (John 15:12).

This scripture sums up the definition of love as written by Paul in 1 Corinthians 13:4-8: "Love endures long and is patient and kind; love never is envious nor boils over with jealousy, is not boastful or vainglorious, does not display itself haughtily. It is not conceited [arrogant and inflated with pride]; it is not rude [unmannerly] and does not act unbecomingly. Love [God's love in us] does not insist on its own rights or its own way, for it is not self-seeking; it is not touchy or fretful or resentful; it takes no account of the evil done to it [it pays no attention to a suffered wrong]. It does not rejoice at injustice and unrighteousness but rejoices when right and truth prevail. Love bears up under anything and everything that comes, is ever ready to believe the best of every person, its hopes are fadeless under all circumstances, and it endures everything [without weakening]. Love never fails [never fades out or becomes obsolete or comes to an end]. As for prophecy [the gift of interpreting the divine will and purpose], it will be fulfilled and pass away; as for tongues, they will be destroyed and cease; as for knowledge, it will pass away [it will lose its value and be superseded by truth]." "And so faith, hope, and love abide [faith—conviction and belief respecting man's relation to God and divine things; hope—joyful and confident expectation of eternal salvation; love-true affection for God's love for and in us], these three; but the greatest of these is LOVE."

The Fruit of Joy

Joy is not happiness because happiness is an emotion that is dependent on positive circumstances or situations. Happiness only appears in the Bible 26 times and joy in one form or the other 330 times.

Joy is a gift from God. Joy comes from God. Jesus said in John 15:11, "I have told you these things, that My joy and delight may be in you, and that your joy and gladness may be of full measure and complete and overflowing." Joy in the midst of trials is possible. When Paul and Silas were in prison they were praying and singing hymns and suddenly there was an earthquake and they were freed. They had joy in the midst of a storm. Jesus endured the cross because He knew what the end result would be—the salvation of the world. "He, for the joy [of obtaining the prize] that was set before Him, endured the cross, despising and ignoring the shame, and is now seated at the right hand of the throne of God" (Heb. 12:2).

"Consider it wholly joyful, my brethren, whenever you are enveloped in or encounter trials of any sort or fall into various temptations. Be assured and understand that the trial and proving of your faith bring out endurance and steadfastness and patience" (James 1:3). Sometimes trials can be blessings because they draw us closer to God. When we feel helpless then we can feel hopeful in God that God is allowing a trial in our life to draw us closer to Himself. We can look at trials with joy knowing that God is working everything for our good. Romans 28:8 says, "We are assured and know that [God being a partner in their labor] all things work together and are [fitting into a plan] for good to and for those who love God and are called according to [His] design and purpose" (Rom. 8:28).

The Fruit of Peace

"Great peace have they who love Your law; nothing shall offend them or make them stumble" (Ps. 119:165). Peace is defined as "a sense of calm and complete absence of hostility and fear in the heart, enabling one to devote his/her total energies with poise and purpose to the task at hand."

Jesus said in John 14:27, "Peace I leave with you; My [own] peace I now give and bequeath to you. Not as the world gives do I give to you. Do not let your hearts be troubled, neither let them be afraid. [Stop allowing yourselves to be agitated and disturbed; and do not permit yourselves to be fearful and intimidated and cowardly and unsettled.]" If we truly trust God, then we will have peace.

In this world where there is so much strife, hatred, and violence, we need a supernatural peace that can only come from God. There are many things to be fearful of today with the threat of wars and devastating hurricanes and earthquakes, so we need to be the calm in the storm so that others will see the peace that we reflect and we can give glory to God.

The Fruit of Patience

"The Lord does not delay and is not tardy or slow about what He promises, according to some people's conception of slowness, but He is long-suffering [extraordinarily patient] toward you, not desiring that any should perish, but that all should turn to repentance" (2 Peter 3:9).

Have you heard the old expression, "Lord, give me patience and I want it right now." Sometimes you have to be careful what you pray for because usually God will bring circumstances into your life that require you to be patient. It is kind of "on-the-job training."

Patience or a description of it, is mentioned fifty times in the Bible so it must be pretty important. The two basic principles for patience is "bearing up under suffering or despair" and "self-restraint in the face of unsatisfied desires." Ephesians 4:2 says, "Living as becomes you with complete lowliness of mind [humility] and meekness [unselfishness, gentleness, mildness], with patience, bearing with one another and making allowances because you love one another."

Jesus must have had so much patience to have to wait until He was about the age of thirty to start His ministry. With all of His wisdom and knowledge and gifting, it must have been hard for Him to wait, but God the Father, had a set time for His ministry to begin and also to be ultimately fulfilled on the earth. His disciples thought that Jesus's Kingdom would be coming very shortly but it did not. The Church has been waiting for His Second Coming, and He has not come yet, but God the Father knows the day and the hour and we, as the Body of Christ, need to be patient looking forward to the "blessed hope."

The Fruit of Kindness

True kindness is being compassionate. Being compassionate means being empathetic, not sympathetic. If you are sympathetic you are "feeling sorry for" and if you are being empathetic toward someone, you are "feeling sorry with." You are actually putting yourself in the other person's place. Who else, but Jesus was compassionate and He is our example of compassion and empathy.

Having a forgiving heart is essential in being kind to another. We are all sinners and have many shortcomings. When we sin, we ask God to forgive us so should we not forgive others that have hurt us if they ask for forgiveness and even if they don't ask for forgiveness. "And become useful and helpful and kind to one another, tender hearted [compassionate, understanding, loving-hearted], forgiving one another as Christ has loved us and gave Himself up for us, a slain offering and sacrifice to God [for you, so that it became] a sweet fragrance" (Eph. 4:32) Jesus also said in Matthew 6:15, "But if you do not forgive others their trespasses [their reckless and willful sins, leaving them, letting them go, and giving up resentment], neither will Your Father forgive you your trespasses."

The Fruit of Goodness

By definition, what is good or goodness? If God is a good God and God is love, then goodness comes from God. Some people think that "good people" will make it into heaven. If that were the case, then why did Jesus die on the cross to forgive us of our sins? "Since all have sinned and are falling short of the honor and glory which God bestows and receives" (Rom. 3:23).

"Let your light shine before men that they may see your moral excellence and your praiseworthy, noble good deeds and recognize and honor and praise and glorify your Father in heaven" (Matt. 5:16). John Wesley the great preacher said: "Do all the good you can, by all the means you can, in all the ways you can, in all the places you can, at all the times you can, as long as you can, do good!"[160]

Even Jesus gave glory to the Father when he said, "And Jesus said to him. Why do you call me [essentially and perfectly morally] good? There is no one [essentially and perfectly morally] good—except God alone" (Mark 10:18).

"And Moses said, I beseech You, show me Your glory. And God said, I will make all My goodness pass before you, and I will proclaim My name, THE LORD, before you; for I will be gracious to whom I will be gracious, and will show mercy and loving-kindness on whom I will show mercy and loving-kindness."

The Fruit of Faithfulness

The word *faithful* is used in the Old Testament as meaning "stability" as well as "truth." It is found in the Bible 109 times and is also used in a moral sense as to be true or certain. *Faithfulness* in the New Testament is being used for "trustworthy" or "sure and true."

In Revelation 19:11, it says, "After that I saw heaven opened, and behold, a white horse [appeared]! The One Who was riding it is called Faithful [Trustworthy, Loyal, Incorruptible, Steady] and true, and He passes judgment and wages war in righteousness [holiness, justice, and uprightness]."

Faithfulness in our lives doesn't mean that we have to be perfect. It means that in spite of our mistakes, our sins, even at times doubting God, we continue to forge ahead believing in God to forgive us, direct us, sustain us, and ultimately, save us through His death and Resurrection.

The Fruit of Gentleness

"In the Septuagint [an ancient translation of the Hebrew Old Testament into the Greek New Testament], the word *gentleness* is translated and used as 'one who is humble in disposition and character: one who is submissive under the divine will.' The English translation of *gentleness* refers to *meekness*, suggesting the submission to another without the resistance to the wrongs of others."[161]

Meekness does not mean weakness. It means strength and control just like a soldier who carries weapons for war but only acts when it is proper to do so. God is gentle with us because He is patient and kind toward us as a loving Father would be.

The Fruit of Self-Control

The New Testament translates self-control as "to have an inward strength." Our flesh is so weak especially when it comes to our emotions. Self-control is really a culmination of the fruit of the spirit because if you are loving, joyful, at peace, patient, kind, good and faithful, you will have self-control.

"And in [exercising] knowledge [develop] self-control, and in [exercising] self-control [develop] steadfastness [patience, endurance], and in [exercising] steadfastness [develop] godliness [piety]" (2 Pet. 1:6). Self-control is something that needs to be developed over time. It is like a seed that has been planted and needs to be nourished and begins to grow because it has all the elements it needs to flourish [soil, sun, and water].[162]

As we mature as a Christian, God will pour into our hearts all that we need to glorify Him just as He did with Jesus His Son. God will give us all the tools that we need so that a world that is in darkness will see His light shining through us and give glory to God!

Salt and Light

"You are the salt of the earth, but if salt has lost its taste [its strength, its quality], how can its saltiness be restored? It is not good for anything any longer but to be thrown out and trodden underfoot by men. You are the light of the world. A city set on a hill cannot be hidden. Nor do men light a lamp and put it under a peck measure, but on a lampstand, and it gives light to all in the house. Let your light shine before men that they may see your moral excellence and your praiseworthy, noble, and good deeds and recognize and honor and praise and glorify your Father Who is in heaven" (Matt. 5:13–16).

Jesus is talking about attributes of the Christian life. We need to be the light in the darkness so that others will see and be attracted to us just like a moth is attracted to the light. Light dispels darkness. Salt is a preservative, and it gives flavor to food. We need to be salt in the world adding substance to what it is to live a Christ-centered life. It is a life that is not dull or ordinary but accentuates all the good gifts that God has given us.[163]

What good is it to hide our faith, the light of Christ, and not let it shine? What if Jesus had kept His love of the Father to Himself and never shared it with anyone else? Would people have been saved?

St. Patrick was a fifth-century missionary in Ireland. When he was sixteen years old he was captured by Irish pirates and brought to Ireland where he was sold into slavery. His master was a high priest of Druidism, a pagan sect. During his six years of captivity, Patrick became deeply devoted to Christianity. In a vision, he saw children of pagan Ireland reaching out their hands to him. This vision gave him determination to convert the Irish to Christianity. He eventually escaped to France, studied to become a priest, and after being ordained a bishop he was sent by Pope Celestine I to Ireland to spread the gospel to the nonbelievers and provided support to a small number of Christians already living there.[164]

Many of us may never go to a distant land or have the special privilege of converting thousands to Christianity, but we can be salt and light to our neighbor, our friends, our family, and even strangers that we come across.

Life-Changing Identity in Christ

Author and blogger, stay-at-home mom, Sarah Walton, lists four ways that our identity in Christ changes our lives (adaptation with my own commentary).[165]

1. *We no longer chase after the desires of our flesh but instead seek to bring God glory in all areas of our life.* "Do not love the world or the things in the world. If anyone loves the world, the love of the Father is not in him. For all that is in the world—the desires of the flesh and desires of the eyes and pride in possessions is not from the Father but it is from the world. And the world is passing away along with its desires, but whoever does the will of God abides forever" (1 John 2:15–17).

    We need to seek our identity in Christ alone. If we look to the world to tell us who we are, then we are making a grave mistake because the world's agenda seeks to tear down, not to uplift.

    Looking to Christ we look beyond this life to eternal things. We will see how God sees us and will not be crushed by any failures or weaknesses.

2. *We no longer fear the future.* "For all who are led by the Spirit of God are sons of God. For you did not receive the slavery to fall back into fear, but you have received the Spirit of adoption as sons, by whom we cry, Abba Father" (Rom. 8:14 –15).

    If we truly trust God, then we should have nothing to fear. We need not fear the loss of a job or a loved one or the loss of our home or even our very life because we know that all things are in His hands. Since we are children of God, we have direct access to our Heavenly Father and as a loving Father, He will provide for all of our needs.

3. *We have no need to judge or compare ourselves to others when we seek to please Christ alone, in whom our identity is hidden.* "One person esteems one day as better than another, while another esteems all days alike. Each one should be fully convinced in his own mind. The one who observes the day, observes it in honor of the Lord. The one who eats, eats in honor of the Lord, since he gives

thanks to God, while the one who abstains, abstains in honor of the Lord and gives thanks to God. For none of us lives to himself, and none of us dies to himself. For if we live, we live to the Lord, and if we die, we die to the Lord. So then, whether we live or whether we die, we are the Lord's" (Rom. 14:5-6).

Comparing ourselves to others is a trap that we can so easily fall into. By what standards are we comparing ourselves? We should not be comparing ourselves to the world or the values in the world. We should be comparing ourselves to who we are in Christ. Even as Christians, we tend to compare our gifts to other Christians, but we have to remember that our talents do not define who we are. There's always going to be someone who can sing better than you or play an instrument better than you. If we are doing something for our own glorification, then we are seeking only to please ourselves and the world. What we should be doing is seeking to please God alone.

We should never be judgmental with someone else because they do not share our faith. Do you think someone will be attracted to our character if we come off as a self-righteous, know-it-all? I don't think so. As St. Francis of Assisi said, "Preach the gospel at all times, use words if necessary." This quote has been questioned by some as far as its authenticity. The actual quote is, "Nevertheless, let all the brothers preach by their works." This quote was a sentence from his chapter 17, *Rules of the Friar (1221).*[166] In actuality, people do notice our actions sometimes more than our words.

4. *We should not be surprised when suffering comes, but we can be confident that it will produce things of eternal value.* "The Spirit Himself bears witness with our spirit that we are children of God, and if children, then heirs—heirs of God and fellow heirs with Christ, provided we suffer with Him in order that we may also be glorified with him" (Rom. 8:16-17).

Jesus suffered not only at the cross, but He suffered in so many other ways. He was despised by men; he was betrayed by many of His own disciples at the cross. He was sold for thirty pieces of silver by one of His disciples. He was mocked, ridiculed, and even accused of being a devil.

When He was fasting in the desert, He was tempted by the evil one and even questioned about His own identity, "If you are the Son of God . . ." He never gave up or gave in. Even at the Garden of Gethsemane, He cried out for God to save Him from the cross, but He knew His Father's will, and He willingly gave up His life to save us from our sins.

When we offer our suffering to Christ, He us gives us strength to endure whatever we need to go through. "For I consider that the sufferings of this present time [this present life] are not worth being compared with the glory that is about to be revealed to us and in us and for us and conferred on us!" (Rom. 8:18). Paul, the disciple, went through many trials and sufferings for the sake of Christ. In 2 Corinthians 6:8-9 he says, "Amid honor and dishonor; in defaming and evil report and in praise and good report. [We are branded] as deceivers [imposters], and [yet vindicated as] truthful and honest. [We are treated] as unknown and ignored [by the world], and [yet we are] well-known and recognized [by God and His people]; as dying, and yet here we are alive; as chastened by suffering and [yet] not killed."

We live in a world filled with people who are lost, who are searching for a sense of belonging. People want to fit in. We are living in a time of a spiritual identity crisis even in the Body of Christ. Some of us have been sucked into believing that the Church needs to conform to the world instead of the world conforming to the gospel. This is cultural Christianity like was discussed in a previous chapter. How could this be one would ask? I think that it is because so many of us have been sitting in church pews instead of standing in the public square and standing up for the principles that we believe in. The world wants to change our identity to conform to the world's values and culture. Rosa Parks and Martin Luther King Jr. knew who they were and were not afraid to show by action that who they were was not going to be dictated by the many.

Summary

God has created us to live a life of good works. He has given us His Holy Spirit to empower us, guide us, and comfort us to live in a world that wants to kill, steal and destroy. We need to be the Christ that others have never seen or heard. We need to be a walking and talking gospel so that others will notice and be drawn to us and in so doing we can be a testament to His love and saving grace.

Someone once said, "Jesus came down to earth to become like us so that we could become like Him." Yes, I think that is so. He came to save us from our sins through His death on a cross and Resurrection, but He was the perfect example of who we are supposed to be. He, having gone through temptation, heartache, loss, pain, and extreme suffering, can understand what we go through when we go through various trials and suffering.

God does not see us as we are but what we will be in Him. He always sees the finished product. Not what we are at the moment, but what He has fashioned us to be. Just like the carpenter who sees the finished table or chair in the broken and splintered piece of wood or the sculptor who sees the David in the slab of marble or the potter who sees the beautiful vase in the clay. We are all a work in progress and our identity in Christ is built each day as we surrender our will and our lives to the Father who created us to be salt and light.

Chapter Twelve

Inheritance in Christ

Inheritance

"For [the Spirit which] you have now received [is] not a spirit of slavery to put you once more in bondage to fear, but you have received the Spirit of adoption [the Spirit producing sonship] in [the bliss of] which we cry, Abba [Father]! Father! The Spirit Himself [thus] testifies together with our own spirit, [assuring us] that we are children of God, and if we are [His] Children, then we are [His] heirs also; heirs of God and fellow heirs with Christ [sharing His inheritance with Him]; only we must share His suffering if we are to share His glory" (Rom. 8:15–17).

We have an eternal inheritance through Christ by His promise of eternal life to those who believe in Him and our sins are cleansed by His blood. "Let not your hearts be troubled [distressed, agitated]. You believe in and adhere to and trust in and rely on God believe in and adhere to and trust in and rely also on Me. In My Father's house are many dwelling places [homes]. If it were not so, I would have told you; for I am going away to prepare a place for you. And when [If] I go and make ready a place for you, I will come back again and will take you to Myself, that where I am you may be also" (John 14:1–3).

We also have a spiritual inheritance through Christ living within us. "In Him you also who have heard the Word of Truth, the glad tidings [Gospel] of your salvation, and have believed in and adhered to and relied on Him, were stamped with the seal of the long-promised Holy Spirit. That [Spirit] is the guarantee of our inheritance [the first fruits, the pledge and foretaste, the down payment on our heritage], in anticipation of its full redemption and our acquiring [complete] possession of it—to the praise of His glory" (Eph. 1:13–14).

The Holy Spirit "is the guarantee of our inheritance." In John 16:13–14, Jesus speaks to His disciples, telling them that it is good that He leaves so that the Holy Spirit comes. "But when He, the Spirit of Truth [the Truth-giving Spirit] comes, He will guide you into all the Truth [the whole, full Truth]. For He will not speak His own message [on His own authority]; but He will tell whatever He hears [from the Father: He will give the message that has been given to Him], and He will announce and declare to you the things that are to come [that will happen in the future]. He will honor and glorify Me, because He will take of [receive, draw upon] what is Mine and will reveal [declare, disclose, transmit] it to you. Everything that the Father has is Mine. That is what I meant when I said that He [the Spirit] will take the things that are Mine and will reveal [declare, disclose, transmit] it to you."

Also included in our spiritual inheritance are happiness and joy, peace, victory and freedom from the bondage of sin. We also have the forgiveness of sins and freedom from guilt. We are partakers of the divine nature of Christ. We are colaborers with God and we are seated in heavenly places with Christ. We are given grace and power and anointing in the Holy Spirit. As an heir of Christ, we need to seek after these things by cultivating a Christlike lifestyle by being obedient to the Lord as revealed to us in His Word and also have an active prayer life so we can hear His voice and follow his leading in our own lives.[167]

Prophets, Priests, and Kings

"Christ" comes from the Greek word *Christos*, meaning "anointed one" or "chosen one." This is the Greek equivalent of the Hebrew word *Mashiach*, or "Messiah." "Jesus" is the Lord's human name given to Mary by the angel Gabriel (Luke 1:31). "Christ" is His title, signifying Jesus was sent from God to be a King and Deliverer (see Daniel 9:25; Isaiah 32:1). "Jesus Christ" means "Jesus the Messiah" or "Jesus the Anointed One."[168] "But as for you, the anointing [the sacred appointment, the unction] which you received from Him abides [permanently] in you; [so] then you have no need that anyone should instruct you. But just as His anointing teaches you concerning everything and is true and is no falsehood, so you must abide in [live in, never depart from] Him [being rooted in Him, knit from Him], just as [His anointing] has taught you [to do]" (1 John 2:27).

The Bible refers to believers as prophets, priests, and kings. "Before I formed you in the womb I knew [and] approved of you [as My chosen instrument], and before you were born I separated and set you apart, consecrating you; [and] I appointed you as a prophet to the nations" (Jer. 1:5). Every believer should be able to minister to others, through the Holy Spirit, in these three areas. Jesus revealed by His words and His life that He was the ultimate prophet because He revealed God's character and saving purposes and will for our lives. His priestly ministry was exemplified by His advocacy for the people ministering with mercy and grace.

Jesus stood in our place and, in so doing, bore our burdens and sin. Jesus is the ultimate king. He is the King of Kings and the Lord of Lords. He reigns over the Heavenly Kingdom.

A prophet speaks God's will and plan. We, as believers, can be that voice. John the Baptist was a prophet of God that paved the way for Jesus's appearing. In the book of Joel 2:28-29 it says, "And afterward I will pour out My Spirit upon all flesh; and your sons and your daughters shall prophesy, your old men shall dream dreams, your young men shall see visions. Even upon the menservants and upon the maidservants in those days will I pour out My Spirit."

In Colossians Chapter 3:16 it says that the Word of God dwells in your heart. Every believer needs to read and ponder the Word of God to interpret it correctly so that they can clearly teach one another about the words spoken by Christ.

"Inasmuch then as we have a great High Priest Who has [already] ascended and passed through the heavens, Jesus the Son of God, let us hold fast our confession [of faith in Him]. For we do not have a High Priest Who is unable to understand and sympathize and have a shared feeling with our weaknesses and infirmities and liability to the assaults of temptation, but One Who has been tempted in every respect as we are, yet without sinning" (Heb. 4:15-16).

Revelation 1:6 says, "And formed us into a kingdom [a royal race], priests to His God and Father." We offer up ourselves as priests as living sacrifices. In 1 Peter 2:5 it says that Christians are a "royal priesthood."[169]

As kings of Christ, we allow Christ to reign in our lives. We are given Christ's kingly authority when we are commissioned and authorized to spread the Kingdom of Heaven. Matthew 28:19-20: "Go then and make disciples of all nations, baptizing them into the name of the Father and of the Son and of the Holy Spirit. Teaching them to observe everything that I have commanded you, and behold, I am with you all the days [perpetually, uniformly, and on every occasion], to the [very] close and consummation of the age. Amen [so let it be]."

We are anointed by Christ to be prophets, priests, and kings. Christ is living in us, and by this virtue, His authority and anointing lives in us. We need this anointing as prophets to teach and reveal the word of the Lord to men; as priests to offer sympathy and loving service to anyone seeking compassion, and as kings who reign with Christ in His Heavenly Kingdom.

Citizens of Heaven

Philippians 3:17–4:1 talks about being a citizen of heaven. "But we are citizens of the state [commonwealth, homeland, which is in heaven], and from it also we earnestly and patiently await [the coming of] the Lord Jesus Christ [the Messiah] [as] Savior" (Phil. 3:20). We have a citizenship that is far more important than our earthly citizenship. St. Paul was a Roman citizen, and after they had thrown him and Silas in jail, he complained to the city officials that he was a Roman citizen and should not have been poorly treated. Citizenship does have its privileges.

We are not naturally born into heavenly citizenship. Jesus said, "What is born of [from] the flesh is flesh [of the physical is physical]; and what is born of the Spirit is spirit" (John 3:6). We are natural born sinners and have a sinful nature. Only by a spiritual birth can we enter the kingdom of heaven.

At baptism, we are born of the water and the Spirit. The Holy Spirit came into your life and gave you a new birth. You became a "supernatural born citizen." The blood of Jesus washed away your sins, and you were given a gift of faith.

Our true home and destination is heaven. We are sojourners and pilgrims on this earth until we reach the heavenly kingdom. In Romans 12:2 Jesus said, "Do not be conformed to this world [this age], [fashioned after and adapted to its external, superficial customs], but be transformed [changed] by the [entire] renewal of your mind [by its new ideals and its new attitude], so that you may prove [for yourselves] what is the good and acceptable and perfect will of God even the thing which is good and acceptable and perfect [in His sight for you]."

How can we live on earth and be heavenly minded? We must understand that our role as citizens of heaven is to spread the gospel to the ends of the earth. As a citizen we have rights. What are the heavenly rights that we have? We are who God says we are and we can do what God says we can do. We were created to glorify God in everything we do. Jesus came down and gave us a blueprint of how to live a life that exemplifies our God given authority. It was not God's plan to live separate from man. He walked and talked with Adam and Eve. I guess you could say that heaven is a "holding place" until God recreates the earth at the end of time. As we journey on earth we need to reclaim that which was at the beginning. Jesus came to reclaim our rights, and He showed us how to walk in them.

Just as a government has laws for its citizens, so God gave us the Ten Commandments—not the Ten Suggestions! Why is a law given? It is supposed to be given for the protection and benefit of all.

If you love God with all your heart, soul, and mind and your neighbor as yourself, you really cannot break any of the Commandments. Having said that, there is no one, except Jesus Himself, who is perfect but in seeking perfection we can only achieve a measure of it if we surrender our will to God's will because He alone knows what is best for us because He loves us with and everlasting love.

Peter and his brother Andrew were fishing one day Jesus called them "And He said to them, Come after Me [as disciples—letting Me be your Guide], follow Me, and I will make you fishers of men!" (Matt. 4:19). Peter and Andrew must have thought that they would be fishermen, but God had a different plan. He had a heavenly plan for their lives. They were fishermen, but God saw them as fishers of men. Jesus also told them to follow Him. He would be their guide. He showed them how to walk in His same authority so that they could raise the dead, heal the sick, teach others what He had commanded them to do and make disciples of all nations.

"Our Father Who art in heaven. Hallowed be Thy Name. Thy kingdom come. *Thy will be done on earth as it is in heaven.*" If we are doing God's will here on earth, then we are bringing heaven down to earth. Is there sickness in heaven?—no. Is there violence in heaven?—no. Is there suffering in heaven?—no. We live in a world that is broken and far from the will of God, but if we walk in God's authority perhaps we can be an instrument of change. We can, through the Holy Spirit living in us, heal the sick and raise the dead and preach the great commission.

We can be a change agent in the world. Will we be able to change everyone or everything? I don't think so. Jesus Himself did not change everyone, but He did change the world by showing us Who He is and showing us the love of the Father. All we need to do is accept His will and follow His leading as we walk in "heaven on earth."

God's ways and plans are much greater than we can even imagine or think. "For I know the thoughts and plans that I have for you, says the Lord, thoughts and plans for welfare and peace and not for evil, to give you hope in your final outcome" (Jer. 29:11). In Ephesians 3:20 it says, "Now to Him Who, by [in consequence of] the [action of His] power that is at work within us, is able to [carry out His purpose and] do super abundantly, far over and above all that we [dare] ask or think [infinitely beyond our highest prayers, desires, thoughts, hopes, or dreams]."

A true story about a King of Saudi Arabia who invited a famous golfer to a tournament was written by Joel Osteen in one of his books. The golfer accepted the invitation and before he left to go back to the United States, the Saudi King thanked him for taking the time to come to the tournament. As a gesture of thanks, the king asked the golfer, "I want to give you gifts for coming all this way and making this time so special. *Anything* you want. What could I get you?" The golfer responded, "Oh, please, don't get me anything. You've been a gracious host. I've had a wonderful time. I couldn't ask for anything more."

The king insisted on giving him something that would always remind him of his journey to his country.

Realizing that the king would not take no for an answer, the golfer responded, "Okay, fine. I collect golf clubs. Why don't you give me a golf club?"

On his way home, he kept wondering what type of golf club the king would send him. He imagined it would be solid gold and maybe a sand wedge studded with diamonds and jewels. When he got home, he kept watching the mail for a package and when he received a certified letter in the mail he wondered what had happened to his golf club. When he opened the letter, to his surprise was a deed to a *five-hundred-acre golf course* in America![170]

We need to stop "living as a pauper" and start living as a child of the King. We are sons and daughters of the King, so we should not limit God in what He can do through us and to us to expand the Kingdom of heaven here on earth and change our minds from an earthly perspective to a heavenly perspective!

Authority

What is authority? It is delegated power. "The right and power to command, enforce laws, exact obedience, determine, or judge."[171] Jesus said in Luke 10:19, "Behold, I have given you authority and power to trample upon serpents and scorpions, and [physical and mental strength and ability] over all the power that the enemy [possesses]; and nothing shall in any way harm you." Jesus also said, "But you shall receive power [ability, efficiency, and might] when the Holy Spirit has come upon you, and you shall be My witnesses in Jerusalem and all Judea and Samaria and to the ends [the very bounds] of the earth" (Acts 1:8).

Jesus imparted divine authority to his disciples and to those who would follow Him. The promise of the Holy Spirit was to give the disciples the strength and the wisdom and the spiritual gifts that the Holy Spirit would then impart. We are emissaries for Christ because we represent Him on earth and as a representative, we are given authority to *RE-PRESENT* Him to the world.

We are also ambassadors for Christ. An ambassador is also a ranking government representative in a foreign land. The ambassador is also given authority to protect the citizens of his home country in the foreign country. They are also diplomats of the highest rank formally representing the head of state with full authority to represent the government.

Where we live is not our true home because we are citizens of heaven, and because we are citizens of heaven we can in effect represent the Kingdom of Heaven having been given authority from the King of Kings and the Lord of Lords—Jesus Christ.[172]

The following are biblical examples of Christ's authority working in the lives of believers.

1. Conversion and witness—The Samaritan woman came to the well because she was thirsty, and little did she know that what she was really thirsting for was a touch from God. "She knew that the Messiah was coming, the Anointed One, who would tell them everything that they needed to know" (John 4:25). "Jesus said to her, I Who now speak with you am He" (John 4:26). "As a result of this conversation, she went back to her town and testified to the people that they must come see a man who must be the Christ" (John 4:29).

2. Leading a person into the baptism of the Holy Spirit—The Lord told Ananias, a disciple, in a vision to go to a certain location and lay his hands on Paul who had been blinded on the road to Damascus. Ananias did not want to go because of Paul's reputation but the Lord told him that Paul was a chosen instrument. "So Ananias left and went into the house. And he laid his hands on Saul and said, Brother Saul, the Lord Jesus, Who appeared to you along the way by which you came here, has sent me that you may recover your sight and be *filled with the Holy Spirit*"(Acts 9:17).
3. Deliverance (casting out demons)—"And these attesting signs will accompany those who believe; in My Name they will drive out demons . . ." (Mark 16:17). During Jesus's ministry, He cast out many demons. We have been given this authority too.
4. Heal the sick—Healing the sick is part of the great commission. Whatever Jesus did, the disciples were able to do. It wasn't until they received power from on high at Pentecost that they were unafraid and bold and went out to the other parts of their world and continued the ministry of Jesus.
5. Prayers answered—"Is anyone among you afflicted [ill-treated; suffering evil]? He should pray. Confess to one another therefore your faults [your slips, your false steps, your offenses, your sins] and pray [also] for one another, that you may be healed and restored [to a spiritual tone of mind and heart]. The earnest [heartfelt, continued] prayer of a righteous man makes tremendous power available [dynamic in its working]" (James 5:13, 16). You need to have faith for prayers to be answered. "And Jesus, replying said to them, Have faith in God [constantly]. Truly I tell you, whoever says to this mountain, Be lifted up and thrown into the sea! And does not doubt at all in his heart but believes that what he says will take place, it will be done for him" (Mark 11:23).
6. Walking in the gifts of the Holy Spirit—The nine gifts of the Holy Spirit include—prophecy, the word of wisdom, the word of knowledge, miracles, healing, speaking in tongues, interpreting tongues, faith, and discerning of spirits. "On the morrow, we left there and came to Caesarea; and we went into the house of Philip the evangelist, who was one of the Seven [first deacons]. And stayed with him. And he had four maiden daughters who had the gift of prophecy" (Acts 21:8-9). Every day Christians can manifest all

these gifts. We may not even be aware that we are exhibiting some of these gifts such as a word of knowledge which may come to us as a picture or a thought pertaining to someone who may need that spoken to them as a confirmation for an answer to a prayer that they have been seeking from the Lord. When we lay hands on someone and they recover, we are operating in the gift of healing, the gift of faith, and maybe the word of knowledge knowing how to pray for a specific malady and, if the healing is spontaneous, the gift of miracles.

Authority is given, but if it is not accepted or used, it is useless. We, as Christians, need to accept the mantle of authority so we can walk in it and use it for the glory of God. It is He, working through us, that can manifest the compassion and love that Almighty God is seeking so passionately to bestow on a world that is lost in the darkness of despair and hopelessness.

The Great Commission

The Apostles preached at every opportunity. They sacrificed themselves to fulfill the great commission by going into all the world preaching and teaching the gospel. The Holy Spirit led them and guided them throughout their journey. St. Peter, St. Andrew, St. Matthew, and St. Bartholomew preached in Pontus, Galatia, Cappadocia, Asia Bithynia, Scythia (Russia), Besporan Kingdom Barbarian Lands east of the Black Sea, Turkey and Sebastpolis, Colchis, Apsaros, Trebizond, Amasia, Nicea, Nikomidea, Greece. India, Yemen, Armenia, Persia, and Ethiopia.

St. Thomas, St. Thaddeus, and St. Simon the Patriot preached in Odessa, India, Babylonia, and Syria and St John and St. Philip preached in Asia Minor and St. Paul preached in Damascus, Syria, Tarsus, Antioch, Cyprus, Asia Minor, Derba, Galatia, Ephesus, Greece in Philippi, Thessalonica, Corinth, and Persia, Italy and Spain and finally attained his crown of martyrdom in Rome.[173]

The early Christians typically met in homes. The first church building at Dura Europos on the Euphrates was built in 231. The faith spread mainly through ordinary believers after the Apostle Paul. It was primarily an urban faith. The faith spread as neighbors saw believers living out their faith on a daily basis.

Justin Martyr, an early Christian theologian, described the early believers: "We formerly rejoiced in uncleanness of life, but now love only chastity; before we used the magic arts, but now dedicate ourselves to the true and unbegotten God; before we loved money and possessions more than anything, but now we share what we have and to everyone who is in need; before they hated one another and killed one another and would not eat with those of another race, but now since the manifestation of Christ, we have come to a common life and pray for our enemies and try to win over those who hate us without just cause."[174]

After the death of Jesus Christianity spread throughout the Roman world including the eastern Mediterranean. Christianity was forced underground by the Roman state and because of this Christian communities flourished in different areas. Christians were thought of as traitors by the government and felt threatened by them because they would not give their gods their sacrifices. By the third century persecution became harsher for the Christians.[175]

The Gospel of Jesus Christ continues to spread across the world and Christians continue to be persecuted. Many saints have gone before us and continue to go out into the world and bring Christ to the nations of the world. The Apostle Paul was one of the greatest missionaries of all times. He founded many churches and died a martyr. Saint Patrick (fifth century) was the founder of the Irish Celtic Church. Ramon Llull (1232–1315) was a missionary to the Muslims. He evangelized in North Africa and died a martyr. Bartholomew de las Casas (1484–1566) was a social reformer and Dominican friar. He is best known for protecting the American Indians from mistreatment from Spanish conquistadores. Matthew Ricci (1552–1610) was an Italian priest in China who led one thousand of the aristocracy to Christ. David Brainerd (1718–1747) was an American missionary who worked with the Native Americans. His worked encouraged other Christian missionaries such as Jim Elliot and William Carey. Charlotte "Lottie" Moon (1840–1912) was a Southern Baptist missionary who spent forty years working in China, and she laid a foundation for solid support for missions among Baptists in America. Amy Carmichael (1867–1951) was a missionary in India for fifty-five years and opened an orphanage and founded a mission in Dohnavur. The list goes on, and I am sure there are countless others who are still preaching and teaching the gospel throughout the world not only from our country but many countries around the world.[176]

Campus Crusade for Christ was founded by Bill Bright. It began with college students in 1951 and has since grown into one of the largest international Christian ministries in the world. In 1956 he wrote a four-point booklet known as the *Four Spiritual Laws*. The four points outline how to establish a relationship with Jesus and has been printed in two hundred languages. It has been considered to be the most widely distributed religious booklet in history, and there are 2.5 billion booklets distributed to date. These booklets have since become the standard model for conversion that maintains that Jesus Christ "stands at the door and knocks," but we must open the door of our heart and invite Him into our life. He also used other communication vehicles over the years including books, television, radio, internet, phone banks, billboards, movies, videos, and international teaching conferences. [177]

Bill Bright's Four Spiritual Laws

1. God loves you and offers a wonderful plan for your life (John 3:16, 10:10).
2. Man is sinful and separated from God. Therefore he cannot know and experience God's love and plan for his life (Romans 3:23, 6:23).
3. Jesus Christ is God's only provision for man's sin. Through Him you can know and experience God's love and plan for your life (Romans 5:8; 1 Corinthians 15:3-6; John 14:6).
4. We must individually receive Jesus Christ as Savior and Lord; then we can know and experience God's love and plan for our lives (John 1:12, 3:1-8; Ephesians 2:8-9; Revelation 3:20).[178]

"And this good news of the kingdom [the Gospel] will be preached throughout the whole world as a testimony to all the nations, and then will come the end" (Mark 24:14). It seems that there is an escalation of the preaching of the Gospel throughout the world because of technology and easier distribution of the written Word of God. You can see satellite dishes on top of shacks in third world countries where people are watching Christian programs and being evangelized in their own homes. So it would seem that including all the other signs that we read about in Matthew 24 that the coming of the Lord is near at hand.

Summary

The Holy Spirit is a guarantee of our inheritance because God gave us the Spirit to help us know the Word of God and the book of our life's story. "Your eyes saw my unformed substance, and in Your book all the days (of my life) were written before ever they took shape, when as yet there was none of them" (Psalm 139:16). Kevin L. Zadai writes in his book when He had an encounter in heaven that, "Every person on earth has a book written about them in heaven. God created every person with a plan and purpose in mind. He wrote about each day of your life long ago in a book with your name on it located on a bookshelf in heaven." He also writes that "Because heaven resides outside of time, your future is now, God does not intend for you to be devastated or fail [see Jeremiah 29:11].[179] Jesus, the captain of your salvation, has already won a mighty victory for you and your destiny. He came to give you an exceedingly abundant life [see John 10:10]. You don't have to allow the thief to destroy your destiny. God has assigned a wonderful person called the Holy Spirit to teach you how to walk successfully through this life and to tell you of things to come. We need to learn to live the life we were destined for. Because He is the Spirit of truth, He will lead us along our true path."

We are citizens of heaven, and as citizens we are prophets, priests, and kings who have authority on this earth caring out the King's purpose and plans upon the earth to bring all men to the saving knowledge of Christ who died for our salvation and we are coheirs with Christ in heaven.

Because we are coheirs with Christ, we have been given authority through the great commission to heal the sick, raise the dead, preach the Gospel to the ends of the earth and *RE-PRESENT* Christ upon the earth to anyone who will listen. We are colaborers with Christ through the gifts of the Holy Spirit, which are a manifestation of God's love and compassion and as a sign of His goodness and love to all who will seek Him and make Him Lord of their lives.

Would you like to surrender your life to the Lord right now? Maybe you have, but you have been away from the Lord. Don't hesitate. Now is the acceptable time! Jesus is standing with arms out-stretched to love you, to comfort you and to receive you into His Kingdom. If you are ready pray this prayer:

Salvation Prayer

> *Dear God in heaven, I come to you in the name of Jesus. I acknowledge to You that I am a sinner, and I am sorry for my sins and the life that I have lived; I need Your forgiveness.*
>
> *I believe that Your only begotten Son Jesus Christ shed His precious blood on the cross at Calvary and died for my sins, and I am now willing to turn from my sin.*
>
> *You said in Your Holy Word, Romans 10:9 that if we confess the Lord our God and believe in our hearts that God raised Jesus from the dead, we shall be saved.*
>
> *Right now I confess Jesus as the Lord of my soul. With my heart, I believe that God raised Jesus from the dead. This very moment I accept Jesus Christ as my own personal Savior and according to His Word, right now I am saved.*
>
> *Thank you Jesus for Your unlimited grace which has saved me from my sins. I thank you Jesus that Your grace never leads to license, but rather it always leads to repentance. Therefore Lord Jesus transform my life so that I may bring glory and honor to you alone and not to myself.*
>
> *Thank You Jesus for dying for me and giving me eternal life. AMEN.*[180]

"If we admit that we have sinned and confess our sins, He is faithful and just [true to His own nature and promises] and will forgive our sins [dismiss our lawlessness] and [continuously] cleanse us from all unrighteousness [everything not in conformity to His will in purpose, thought, and action]" (1 John 1:9).

"Confess to one another therefore your faults [your slips, your false steps, your offenses, your sins] and pray [also] for one another, that you may be healed and restored [to a spiritual tone of mind and heart]. The earnest [heartfelt, continued] prayer of a righteous man makes tremendous power available [dynamic in its working]" (James 5:16).

I would encourage you to seek a Bible-believing Church and fellowship with Christians who can help you in your walk of faith. If you are a Catholic, I would recommend the Sacrament of Reconciliation where healing can begin as you confess your sins.

Seek also to be baptized in water because Jesus said in Mark 16:15–16, "Go out into all the world and preach and publish openly the good news [the Gospel] to every creature [of the whole human race]. He who believes [who adheres to and trusts in and relies on the Gospel and Him Whom it sets forth] and is baptized will be saved [from the penalty of eternal death]; but he who does not believe [who does not adhere to and trust in and rely on the Gospel and Him Whom it sets forth] will be condemned."

Chapter Thirteen

God's Healing Touch

Faith

What is faith? Let's see what the Bible has to say about faith:

"Now faith is the substance [the confirmation, the title deed] of the things [we] hope for; being the proof of things [we] do not see and the conviction of their reality [faith perceiving as real fact what is not revealed to the senses]" (Heb. 11:1).

"For we walk by faith [we regulate our lives and conduct ourselves by our conviction or belief respecting man's relationship to God and divine things, with trust and holy fervor; thus we walk] not by sight or appearance" (2 Cor. 5:7).

"So faith comes by hearing [what is told], and what is heard comes by the preaching [of the message that came from the lips] of Christ [the Messiah Himself]" (Rom. 10:17).

"But without faith it is impossible to please and be satisfactory to Him. For whoever would come near to God must [necessarily] believe that God exists and that He is the rewarder of those who earnestly and diligently seek Him [out]" (Heb. 11:6).

These are a few of the scriptures that speak to us about faith. Jesus was truly the consummate manifestation of faith. He never doubted God's plan for His life. He was filled with God's Spirit, and it was through the power of the Holy Spirit that Christ accomplished all that the Father willed for Him to do. In the agony in the Garden of Gethsemane He anguished over his suffering and even asked the Father to save Him from this, but He said, "Father, if You are willing, remove this cup from Me; yet not My will, but [always] Yours be done" (Luke 22:42).

It was through Christ's faith in the Father that He was able to carry out the mission that God had preordained for Him to accomplish. Jesus took God at His word and carried out the will of the Father.

What is great faith? In Luke 7: 2-9, Jesus marveled at the faith of the centurion who had a bond servant who was ill and at the point of death and sent Jewish elders to tell Jesus to come and make his servant well. As Jesus was walking to the centurion's house, the centurion sent friends to tell Jesus, "Lord, do not trouble [Yourself], for I am not sufficiently worthy to have You come under my roof; Neither did I consider myself worthy to come to You, But [just] speak a word, and my servant boy will be healed. For I also am a man [daily] subject to authority, with soldiers under me. And I say to one, Go, and he goes; and to another, Come, and he comes; and to my bond servant, Do this and he does it. Now when Jesus heard this, He marveled at him, and He turned and said to the crowd that followed Him, I tell you, not even in [all] Israel have I found such great faith [as this]." The centurion had great faith because he took Jesus at His word.[181]

It was by faith that Noah believed God and built an ark to save his family from a flood that God had warned him about. Noah believed God and built the ark. The flood came, and he and his family were saved.

God told Abraham to go out to another place to receive his inheritance, and by faith he left along with his family. God also told Abraham that he would be the father of many nations. God promised Sarah, his wife, that she would conceive a child even though she was passed child bearing and "She considered Him faithful Who had promised." Sarah took God at His word.

It was by faith that Moses led the Israelites through the Red Sea and into the wilderness. Moses trusted in God to set his people free and was not afraid of the Pharaoh.

It was by faith that the walls of Jericho fell down after the people of God marched around it for seven days and attained victory.[182] It was by faith that Mary, the mother of Jesus, accepted the will of God to conceive and become the mother of the Savior even though she did not really know exactly how that could be and what the future would be like, but she accepted the will of God for her life and because of her "yes," Jesus was born who would deliver us from our sins and open the doors of heaven by His great sacrifice of redemption. "Christ" comes from the Greek word Christos, meaning "anointed one" or "chosen one." This is the Greek equivalent of the Hebrew word Mashiach, or "Messiah." "Jesus" is the Lord's human name given to Mary by the angel Gabriel (Luke 1:31). "Christ" is His title, signifying Jesus was sent from God to be a King and Deliverer (see Daniel 9:25; Isaiah 32:1). "Jesus Christ" means "Jesus the Messiah" or "Jesus the Anointed One."

Faith is a gift from God. In Ephesians 2:8, it says, "For it is by free grace [God's unmerited favor] that you are saved [delivered from judgment and made partakers of Christ's salvation] through [your] faith. And this [salvation] is not of yourselves [of your own doing, it came not through your own striving] but it is the gift of God."

Faith is not what we feel but what we know is true. The Word of God is true. Standing on His Word is the fuel that we need to keep the fire of our faith burning no matter what situation we encounter in our lives. In Romans 8:28, it says, "We are assured and know that [God being a partner in their labor] all things work together and are [fitting into a plan] for good to and for those who love God and are called according to [His] design and purpose."

We have faith because we trust God. We believe God. When our children come up to us and ask us for something, and we tell them that we will give it to them they accept our word and believe us, and I am sure some of us can appreciate the fact that once you promise a child something, they will *never* forget and they will hold you to your promise! We need to be like little children in our faith and trust in God. "This was so that, by two unchangeable things [His promise and His oath] in which it is impossible for God ever to prove false or deceive us, who have fled [to Him] for refuge might have mighty indwelling strength and strong encouragement to grasp and hold fast the hope appointed for us and set before [us]" (Heb. 6:18).

Grace

There is a story that is told about a train drawbridge operator whose job was to raise and lower a bridge. The bridge would normally remain up due to heavy traffic on the seaway. On this particular day, the drawbridge operator's son came to work with him. The father warned the son to stay close and not go near the tracks and the bridge. When it came time for the drawbridge to be lowered, because there was a train coming, the father looked around for the son and could not find him. He saw his son stuck in the mud on the train track. He knew that if he left the room to help his son, it would cost the lives of all the people coming on the train. He also knew that if he lowered the bridge, his son would be killed. As the train approached, he lowered the bridge, turning his head away as the bridge was lowered. The passengers got off the train and crossed safely, not knowing that the drawbridge operator's son's life was just given for theirs.

This is a very sad story but it represents an act of grace. "For it is by free grace [God's unmerited favor] that you are saved [delivered from judgment and made partakers of Christ's salvation] through [your] faith. And this [salvation] is not of yourselves [of your own doing, It came not through your own striving], but it is the gift of God. Not because of works [not the fulfillment of the Law's demands]. Lest any man should boast. [It is not the result of what anyone can possible do, so no one can pride himself in it or take glory to himself]" (Eph. 2:9–10).

There is another story about the Russian Czar Alexander who used to love to disguise himself among his people to find out what they had to say. One day while visiting an army camp, he saw a young soldier sitting at a table with his head on his arm and sound asleep. Curious about the paper next to the soldier, he tiptoed to the back of the chair, and looking over the soldier's shoulder, he noticed a sheet of paper with a long list of gambling debts. At the end of the list were the words "who can pay so much?" It appeared that the young soldier had gambled away all of his money and was going to take his own life for fear of not being able to meet his debts. Alexander, the Czar, picked up a pen and below the young soldier's question wrote, "I, Alexander, Czar of Russia." The next morning when the soldier woke up he immediately took hold of the revolver, when suddenly he saw writing on his letter that he had not written. At that very moment, a messenger came to his tent with a bag of money from the Czar. His debt had been paid in full and his life had been spared.[183]

A very well-known story in the Old Testament is the story of Joseph. Joseph's father, Israel, loved him more than any of his other sons. He made a beautiful coat of many colors for him. Joseph had dreams, and in those dreams he shared that his family would bow down to him and this fueled the anger of his brothers who threw him in a pit and plotted to kill him but instead sold him to the Ishmaelites (mixed Arabians).

Joseph was put in prison because of a false accusation by Potiphar's wife, and while in prison it is revealed that he can interpret dreams and he interprets the Pharaoh's dream and is promoted to authority next to Pharaoh. The dream interpreted by Joseph was that there would be seven years of abundance followed by seven years of drought. The famine affected the surrounding communities including the land where his father and his brothers lived. His brothers were sent to Egypt to get grain so that they could survive.

His brothers did not recognize Joseph and bowed down to him. Joseph recognized his brothers. Once Joseph told his brothers who he was, they were frightened that he would take revenge on them. In Genesis 45:3-4, Joseph said to his brothers, "I am Joseph! Is my father still alive? And his brothers could not reply for they were distressingly disturbed and dismayed at [the startling realization that they were in] his presence. And Joseph said to his brothers, Come near to me, I pray you. And they did so. And he said, I am Joseph your brother, whom you sold into Egypt! But now, do not be distressed and disheartened or vexed and angry with yourselves because you sold me here, for God sent me ahead of you to preserve life."

Joseph is a type of Jesus. He was hated by his own brothers who even wanted to kill him. Even though Joseph was not guilty, he was put in prison, but he found favor with the Pharaoh and was elevated to authority. He forgave his brothers and restored them and brought them into the Kingdom where he ruled alongside the Pharaoh.[184]

Jesus Christ is the personification of grace. Jesus is the King of kings and the Lord of lords. He willingly gave His life as a ransom for us by dying on a cross even while we were still sinners. He became a sin offering to cleanse us from our sins. He who had no sin, became sin so that we, who are sinful, can be made into the righteousness of God in Christ.

Tozar said, "Grace is the good pleasure of God that inclines Him to bestow benefits on the undeserving." Grace is unmerited. It is undeserving. Why would God send His only Son to die for us? He sent His Son because He loves us! "For God so greatly loved and dearly prized the world that He [even] gave up His only begotten [unique] Son, so that whoever believes in [trusts in, clings to, relies on] Him shall not perish [come to destruction, be lost] but have eternal [everlasting] life" (John 3:16).

Essentially we do not have to do anything to merit grace. It is given freely. A. T. Pierson, who was a well-known preacher, said, "However poor a preacher, I can preach the gospel better than Gabriel can, because Gabriel cannot say what I can say, 'I am a sinner saved by grace.'"[183]

Presence

Brother Lawrence was a humble cook who discovered the greatest secret in the kingdom of God—the art of "practicing the presence of God in one single act that does not end." He discovered that the time spent with the Lord should be the same whether he was on his knees praying or washing dishes or talking to friends. "I am doing now what I will do for all eternity. I am blessing God, praising Him, adoring Him, and loving Him with all my heart."

The following excerpts are from the book *The Practice of The Presence of God* by Brother Lawrence:

The Means of Acquiring God's Presence

The first means of acquiring the presence of God is a new life, received by salvation through the blood of Christ.

The second is faithfully practicing God's presence.

Next, the soul's eyes must be kept on God, particularly when something is being done in the outside world.

It is proper that the heart—which is the first to live and which dominates all the other parts of the body—should be the first and the last to love God. The heart is the beginning and the end of all our spiritual and bodily actions and, generally speaking, of everything we do in our lives. It is, therefore, the heart whose attention we must carefully focus on God.

Then in the beginning of this practice, it would not be wrong to offer short phrases that are inspired by love, such as "Lord, I am all Yours," "God of love, I love You with all my heart," or "Lord, use me according to Your will." However, remember to keep the mind from wandering or returning to the world. Hold your attention on God alone by exercising your will to remain in His presence."

Finally, although this exercise may be difficult at first to maintain, it has marvelous effects on the soul when it is faithfully practiced. It draws the graces of the Lord down in abundance and shows the soul how to see God's presence everywhere with a pure and loving vision, which is the holiest, firmest, easiest, and the most effective attitude for prayer.[186]

When we receive Jesus as our Lord and Savior and ask Him into our hearts and give Him our lives, He truly makes His abode in us. Why would we not want to have an intimate relationship with someone we love and who is living within us? He is ever present and just as one would talk to a friend and seek to deepen that relationship, so it is with our relationship with Jesus.

Jesus and the Father were one. Jesus communicated with the Father all the time. Jesus said that He only did what He saw the Father doing.

John 17:21: "That they all may be one, [just] as You, Father, are in Me and I in You, that they also may be one in Us, so that the world may believe and be convinced that You have sent Me." Jesus had an intimate relationship with His Father, and He wanted us to have that same relationship.

When we have an intimate relationship with someone we listen to them; share time with them; speak to them, and we develop a greater love for them. God desires our hearts. It is a dialogue between God and man that He desires. When we ask Jesus into our hearts we become children of God and as a loving Father desires to be with his children, so God desires to have a relationship with us and we should be more than willing to foster that relationship each day as we make Him a part of our everyday activities focusing on Him and His will and His desires for us.

The Holy Spirit

"God said, Let us [Father, Son, and Holy Spirit] make man-kind in Our image, after Our likeness, and let them have complete authority over the fish of the sea, the birds of the air, the [tame] beasts and over all the earth and over everything that creeps upon the earth" (Gen. 1:26).

The Holy Spirit is the Third Person of the Godhead. "And when Jesus was baptized, He went up at once out of the water; and behold, the heavens were opened, and he [John] saw the Spirit of God descending like a dove and alighting on Him. And behold a voice from heaven said, 'This is My Son, My Beloved, in Whom I delight'" (John 3:16–17). Clearly this shows the Godhead working together for the same purpose.

How can there be three entities distinct in one? I liken it to our own identities. We are made up of body, soul, and spirit. God is in heaven and Jesus is at His right hand so the Holy Spirit, the Third Person of the Godhead, is here on earth with us, living in us, and guiding us and giving us counsel and comfort. Remember when Jesus said that it was good for Him to go away because if He did not, the Holy Spirit would not come. The Holy Spirit is God's Spirit. Jesus is the bodily manifestation of God's glory.

"However, I am telling you nothing but the truth when I say it is profitable [good, expedient, advantageous] for you that I go away, Because if I do not go away, the Comforter [Counselor, Helper, advocate, Intercessor, Strengthener, Standby] will not come to you [into Close fellowship with you]; but if I go away, I will send Him to you [to be in close fellowship with you]" (John 16:7).

"But when He, the Spirit of Truth [the Truth-giving Spirit] comes, He will guide you into all the Truth [the whole, full Truth]. For He will not speak His own message [on His own authority]; but He will tell whatever He hears [from the Father; He will give the message that has been given to Him], and He will announce and declare to you the things that are to come [that will happen in the future]. He will honor and glorify Me, because He will take of [receive, draw upon] what is Mine and will reveal [declare, disclose, transmit] it to you. Everything that the Father has is Mine. That is what I meant when I said that He [the Spirit] will take the things that are Mine and will reveal [declare, disclose, transmit] it to you" (John 16:13–15).

Before Jesus ascended into heaven, He promised them that they would receive power when the Holy Spirit came upon them. Acts 1:8: Not only did He promise that through the Holy Spirit He would be with them but there would be gifts given by the Spirit to help them to do their work in new and powerful ways.

"But earnestly desire and zealously cultivate the greatest and best gifts and graces" (1 Cor. 12:31). We should seek after these gifts. Paul goes on to say that the greatest of these is love. We can have many gifts, but if we do not show love, then we are just going through the motions.

Benny Hinn describes these gifts and they are presented in a synopsis from an article titled "Nine Gifts of The Holy Spirit."

There are nine gifts of the Holy Spirit and they can be divided into three groups:

1. Revelation gifts include the word of wisdom, the word of knowledge, and discerning of spirits.
2. Vocal gifts are tongues, interpretation of tongues, and prophecy.
3. Power gifts include faith, healings, and the working of miracles.

Revelation Gifts

1. Word of Wisdom: the application of knowledge. We experience the word of wisdom when the Holy Spirit gives us supernatural wisdom or understanding through His Word in certain situations.

   You can use the word of wisdom to defeat the purposes of the Enemy by knowing how to apply the Word, and at times it can mean the difference between life and death. In fact, the word of wisdom is essential in the operation of all the other gifts, so it is important to seek this gift.

2. Word of knowledge: receiving facts supernaturally by the Spirit. A word of knowledge can be personal or may be given for you to share with others.

3. Discerning of spirits: perceiving the source of a manifestation. The last of the three revelation gifts helps us perceive whether a spiritual manifestation is from God, man, or the devil.

Vocal Gifts

1. Tongues: three supernatural means of communication.

   a. Tongues unto God "He that speaketh in an unknown tongue speaketh not unto men, but unto God" (1 Cor. 14:2).
   b. Tongues is a sign to the unbeliever. Some people marveled at hearing their own native tongue (Acts 2).
   c. Tongues that edify the body of believers. "Greater is he that prophesiath than he that speaketh with tongues, except he interpret, that the church may receive edifying" (1 Cor. 14:5).

2. Interpretation of Tongues: translation of divine utterances into recognizable language. Only the third type requires interpretation. With this type of tongues, the interpretation of tongues is crucial. The Word shows that interpretation becomes equal to prophecy.

3. Prophecy: revelation for edification. The gift of prophecy builds up and encourages us. It comforts. It encourages and must always be consistent with scriptures.

Power Gifts

1. Faith: the God-given ability to believe Him for the impossible. The gift of faith is the greatest of the power gifts. It's the exceptional ability to rust God to work, even in unusual ways or in particularly challenging situations.
2. Healings: restoration of health. The spoken word is used most often. We read of the laying on of hands and anointing oil.
3. Working of miracles: The power gift of the working of miracles is a supernatural occurrence against the law of nature.

Jesus operated in all the gifts during His ministry here on earth. He said that whatever He did we would do and even greater works (John 14:12). "And afterward I will pour out My Spirit upon all flesh; and your sons and your daughters shall prophesy, your old men shall dream dreams, your young men shall see visions" (Joel 2:28).[187] Would you like to receive the baptism of the Holy Spirit? There are five steps to receive the baptism with evidence of speaking in tongues.

1. Be born again—John 3:3 and Acts 2:38
2. Believe that this is a promise for you—Acts 2:17–18
3. Have a desire for the gift of the Holy Spirit—John 7:37–39
4. Ask for it—Luke 11:13
5. Do the speaking—Acts 2:4

If you are ready to receive the baptism of the Holy Spirit, pray this prayer:

> *Heavenly Father, at this moment I come to You. I thank You that Jesus saved me. I pray that the Holy Spirit might come upon me. Lord Jesus, baptize me now in the Holy Spirit. I receive the baptism in the Holy Spirit right now by faith in Your Word. May the anointing, the glory, and the power of God come upon me and into my life right now. May I be empowered for service from this day forward. Thank You, Lord Jesus, for baptizing me in Your Holy Spirit. Amen. (From CBN.com)*

After you have received, begin by practicing the power of the Spirit, and praise God in a new language. Just praise God out loud in whatever words come to you and tell Him how much you love Him and thank Him and worship Him. If you diligently seek a new prayer language, God will give it to you. Just keep trying. It may not come right away. It may come during the middle of the night. Have faith in God and desire all of His gifts. He is faithful.[188]

Pray and read His Word each day. I know when I received the baptism of the Holy Spirit the first thing I noticed was a hunger for the Word of God. Grow in your relationship with the Lord. As you seek Him, He will manifest Himself to you in many ways. Remember, it's about relationship even more than the gifts! Walk in His Spirit each and every day and His gifts, given freely, will flow as you surrender all to Him.

Healing

In February 2016, a few weeks before our granddaughter Anastasia was born, a routine ultrasound indicated that a tumor was wrapped around one of her kidneys. They said it was malignant and that after she was born, they would remove the affected kidney. We were all shocked because all ultrasounds had not shown anything abnormal. Many, many people prayed for her, and we stood on God's Word according to Matthew 18:19: "Again I tell you, if two of you on earth agree [harmonize together, make a symphony together] about whatever [anything and everything] they may ask, it will come to pass and be done for them by My Father in heaven."

Several days after Anastasia was born, she had surgery to remove her kidney. The surgery was very dangerous because she could have bled to death, but God prevailed and the surgery was a success. The tumor was biopsied, and it was benign, not cancer! Incidentally, during the time of her initial diagnosis, I looked up the meaning of Anastasia and in Greek it means—*resurrection*, so I knew that was a sign from God that she was going to be fine. She is a very healthy toddler now and well into approaching her "terrible twos."

Faith and healing go hand in hand. We know that without faith it is impossible to please God. In Matthew 9:27—31, it says, "As Jesus passed on from there, two blind men followed Him, shouting loudly, Have pity on us, Son of David! Then He touched their eyes saying, According to your faith and trust and reliance [on the power invested in Me] be it done to you; and their eyes were opened."

Faith has a lot to do with receiving the promises of God including our salvation and the forgiveness of our sins. In Luke 5:12-13, it says, "While He was in one of the towns, there came a man full of [covered with] leprosy; and when he saw Jesus, he fell on his face and implored Him, saying, Lord, if You are willing, You are able to cure me and make me clean. And [Jesus] reached out His hand and touched him, saying I am willing; be cleansed! And immediately the leprosy left him."

The centurion and the woman with the issue of blood both had faith. Jesus even said that He had not seen such great faith as the centurion. What did Jesus marvel at? I think He was amazed that just the words that Jesus spoke would be enough to heal his servant. How many of us have faith in God's Word?

How does this apply to us? Who did Jesus leave on this earth to do His work?—us! This is our identity. We are to be His representatives on the earth and in so doing, whatever Jesus did, we should be able to do also. Remember the great commission in which He ordained each of us to go out and proclaim the Good News and heal the sick? Not only did He commission us and give us authority, but He also said, "I assure you most solemnly I tell you, if anyone steadfastly believes in Me, **he will himself** be able to do the things that I do; and **he will do even greater** things than these, because I go to the Father" (John 14:12). How can we do greater things than He? I think it is because as we each become followers, believers in Christ, indwelt with the power of the Holy Spirit, we can do more than He because we are many. Jesus had to die to multiply His glory here on the earth. We are the seeds of His Glory acting on His behalf to do the things that He did and be the manifestation of His love here upon the earth.

Forgiveness also plays a key role in receiving our healing. Some have said unforgiveness is like drinking poison and expecting the other person to get sick. When we do not forgive, we harbor resentment, and it can actually make us sick.

Another reason to forgive is very plainly said by Jesus in Matthew 6:14-15, "For if you forgive people their trespasses [their reckless and willful sins, leaving them, letting them go, and giving up resentment], your heavenly Father will also forgive you. But if you do not forgive others their trespasses [their reckless and willful sins, leaving them, letting them go, and giving up resentment], neither will your Father forgive you your trespasses." It is a very daunting reality but something we each should take to heart.

There is a story that Corrie ten Boom, whom I highlighted earlier in the book, that tells about an experience she had concerning forgiveness.

"My name is Corrie ten Boom and I am a murderer." There was total silence. "You see, when I was in prison camp I saw the same guard day in and day out. He was the one who mocked and sneered at us when we were stripped naked and taken into the showers. He spat on us in contempt, and I hated him. I hated him with every fiber of my being. And Jesus says when you hate someone you are guilty of murder" (1 John 3:15).

"When we were freed, I left Germany vowing never to return," Corrie ten Boom continued. "But I was invited back there to speak. I didn't want to go but I felt the Lord nudging me to. Very reluctantly I went. My first talk was on forgiveness. Suddenly, as I was speaking, I saw to my horror that same prison guard sitting in the audience. There was no way that he would have recognized me. But I could never forget his face, never. It was clear to me from the radiant look on his face while I spoke, that he had been converted since I saw him last. After I finished speaking he came up and said with a beaming smile, 'Ah, dear sister Corrie, isn't it wonderful how God forgives?' And he extended his hand for me to shake.

"All I felt as I looked at him was hate. I said to the Lord silently, 'There is nothing in me that could ever love that man. I hate him for what he did to me and to my family. But you tell us that we are to love our enemies. That's impossible for me, but nothing is impossible for you. So if you expect me to love this man it's going to have to come from you, because all I feel is hate.'"

She went on to say that at that moment she felt nudged to do only one thing: "Put out your hand, Corrie," the Lord seemed to say. Then she said, "It took all of the years that I had quietly obeyed God in obscurity to do the hardest thing I have ever done in my life. I put out my hand." Then, she said, something remarkable happened.

"It was only after my simple act of obedience that I felt something almost like warm oil was being poured over me. And with it came the unmistakable message: 'Well done, Corrie. That's how my children behave.' And the hate in my heart was absorbed and gone. And so one murderer embraced another murderer, but in the love of Christ."[187]

We may feel emotions even after we have forgiven but as we continue to forgive and ask Jesus to heal the memory of the offense, He will bring emotional healing and help us to forgive that person/s from our heart. Healing also comes as we pray for that person whenever the memory surfaces in our lives.

A Prayer for Forgiving

> *Father, thank You for Your mercy and grace toward me, and for forgiving my sins through Your Son's death on the cross. Thank You that You forgive me over and over, for repeated sins and for new sins, big or small. I am so grateful for Your grace.*
>
> *Lord, I need to forgive_____, who has wronged me, hurt me, betrayed me, offended me, and sinned against me. It is hard for me to do this—I am still hurt, angry, confused. So I come asking You for the power to forgive_____. Fill me with Your Spirit and remind me of Your love and mercy to me—and to_____.*
>
> *By Your Spirit, I choose to forgive_____. I choose to extend grace and mercy to him/her, even as You have done for me. I choose, as You enable me, to live at peace with this person. I ask that You bless_____in Your love. Please may we be reconciled and our relationship healed. And if that does not happen, may I continue to love and forgive.*
>
> *Thank You that this is possible in the power of Your Spirit. In Jesus's name.*[190] *(I personally believe that we need to forgive deceased people also because we need to let go of the past.)*

Doctors have said that 80 percent of illnesses are directly associated to stressful situations and can directly cause illnesses.

Who we are consists of our body, soul and spirit and our soul consists of our mind, will and emotions. In 3 John, it says, "Beloved, I wish above all things that you m ay prosper and that you may be in good health, as it goes well with your soul."

There is a strong possibility that illness is connected to a wound in our soul. Getting healed of that wound allows us to prosper and be brought into health even as our soul prospers.

Our souls have been wounded through two main sources: Sin and Trauma:

1. Sin—When we sin against ourselves, for example; adultery, drugs, etc., we are opening a door where these sins can, according to scripture, wound us. Maybe somebody sinned against us, and we were offended and have unforgiveness in our heart toward them and even toward ourselves when we sin against ourselves. These sins and any unforgiveness can wound us.
2. Trauma—Tragic events in our lives leave wounds in our souls such as a tragic accident, death in the family, the loss of a job or relationship, such as a divorce, loss of a child, etc. All these can cause a wound in our soul.[191]

Healing Prayer for a Wounded Heart[192]

Katie Souza (adapted)

> *Jesus, I repent for any sin that may be the root cause of this illness I put the blood of Jesus on it.*
> *I forgive anyone that has sinned against me I put the blood of Jesus on it right now*
> *I plead the blood of Jesus over it now*
> *I also decree that any sin from my ancestors through my blood line Is washed by the blood right now in the Name of Jesus*
> *It is being removed now in Jesus Name I receive the blood of Jesus in my soul*
> *I have been risen to new life*
> *Through the Resurrection and the power of the blood of Jesus Christ My soul is renewed*
> *I am being strengthened and reinforced With mighty power in my spirit*
> *My soul is being filled by the blood of Jesus With Dunamis power*
> *I receive it now I receive it now*
> *My body is being healed by the blood of Jesus Dunamis power is healing my body and my soul I receive it now*
> *I receive it now Amen.*

My husband and I have a ministry called Healing Hearts Ministry. It is a ministry in which we focus on healing through scripture reading and Praise and Worship. We have people pray for each other using five steps that are outlined below. The following testimonies occurred during one of our programs. A woman, named Kathy, said that during prayer she received an emotional healing. "I miscarried a baby . . . I felt a release of guilt and within my mind's eye I saw him [the baby] holding Jesus's hand, and he was very happy." Another woman stated that she had an emotional healing. "I felt contentment and healing of a broken heart that Jesus will give me strength and sustain me." Physical healings also occurred such as less pain in a "rotator cuff and osteoarthritis in knee and neck."

Releasing the Healing, Anointing of Jesus in Prayer (Adapted from "How to Release God's Healing Power Through Prayer"[193] by Mark Virkler, Gary S. Greig, Frank Gaydos)

1. Focus on Jesus / forget about everything else.

    - Focus on Jesus who is always with us.
    - Just receive and don't pray for yourself.
    - With your mind's eye see Jesus. See Him surrounded by light. See Jesus's anointing power radiating onto you and into you. Keep your focus on Him and praise Him in your spirit for His sacrifice on the cross for our sins, and for His love and power.
    - Keep your attention on Jesus. Listen to what Jesus may be saying to you.
    - Possible responses to presence of God and the power of the Holy Spirit: shaking, trembling, laughing, shouting, crying, feeling heat, energy, and/or deep peace.

2. Ask for the Holy Spirit's healing power to be released into the person.

    - "Jesus, please release the healing power and light of Your Holy Spirit on this person. Come, Holy Spirit, release your healing power and light on this person."
    - See the healing power of Jesus as His radiant light enters the person's body.

3. Thank the Lord for His mercy and healing power. Engage prayer as the Spirit leads.

    - Pray as the Lord leads you to, with petition/intercession to God and/or words from God spoken to a condition.
    - The *command prayer* is the most frequent type of healing prayer in the Gospels, so expect the Lord to lead you to use the prayer of command a lot in healing prayer.
    - **First command the pain to leave the person:** "Pain, you leave this person's body [arm, leg, heart, etc.] now! Obey the body and blood of Jesus! It is written, 'By His wounds we are healed' [Isaiah 53:5; 1 Peter 2:24], and we proclaim that by Jesus's wounds this person's body is healed in Jesus's name." Don't be afraid to command pain to leave more than once. Jesus had to pray for the blind man more than once in Mark 8:23. Usually it leaves after two to three times of command prayer.
    - **Then, command the underlying disease (cancer, arthritis, etc.) to leave the person**—treat it like an intruder and tell it to leave and never return in Jesus's name. Notice Jesus "rebuked the fever in Luke 4:39 like He "rebuked" demons elsewhere. He rebuked the evil spirit: "You deaf and mute spirit . . . I command you, come out of him and n ever enter him again!"

4. Remove any inner blocks to healing.

    - Ask questions. "How are you feeling: Better? Worse?
    - Be sensitive to the Holy Spirit. Ask the Holy Spirit to reveal any blocks to your healing (unforgiveness, worry, anxiety, fear, sin).

5. **Keep praying as the Lord leads.** See yourself healed and whole. Thank Jesus to whatever measure of healing you have received.

Summary

It is by faith that we receive Jesus as Lord and Savior in our lives. If we can believe and trust in Jesus to be saved, then we should be able to trust Him in all aspects of our lives. We have all been given a measure of faith. All we need to do is accept it and increase it each day as we read God's Word, which teaches about faith and the great men and women of faith.

Grace is given freely by God. Jesus is the personification of grace. We do not deserve His grace, but we are offered it because God loves us so much. We are a fallen people who need God's grace in order to succeed in the race set before us.

As we walk by faith and receive His grace, we need to constantly seek more of His presence. Brother Lawrence lived a life full of God's presence by living each day totally aware of His presence no matter what he was doing. He saw God's presence everywhere even in the simplest of tasks. Presence is a way of life and an intimate relationship with Jesus.

The Holy Spirit is the giver of gifts that are manifestations of God's glory! We need to seek after the gifts, so we can use them to bring glory and honor to the Lord. The Holy Spirit is our comforter, our counselor, and our guide. We need to seek Him each day and ask for His good counsel.

Forgiveness can be a key to physical and emotional healing. We have all been wounded in one way or another. The blood of Jesus can heal our wounds and make us whole. As Catholics, we believe in the true presence of Jesus in the Eucharist. In the book *The Healing Power of the Eucharist*, Father Hampsch says, "Nonetheless, in spite of the avenues of healing by anointing, laying on of hands, prayers of petition, and intercession, healing through the Eucharist is by far the greatest way healing can occur."[194] Before receiving the Eucharist in the Mass, people recite, "Lord, I am not worthy that you should enter under my roof, but only say the word and *my soul shall be healed.*"

Healing can be instantaneous but many times it is a process and can occur over a period of time. Speaking healing scriptures is a powerful force that can bring about healing. It is important to note that emotional healing is in many instances, a pre-requisite for physical healing.

Chapter Fourteen

The Ultimate Showdown

Satan's Fall

"How have you fallen from heaven, O light-bringer and daystar, son of the morning? How you have been cut down to the ground, you who weakened and laid low the nations [O blasphemous, satanic king of Babylon]! And you said in your heart, I will ascend to heaven; I will exalt my throne above the stars of God' I will sit upon the mount of assembly in the uttermost north. I will ascend above the heights of the clouds; I will make myself like the Most High. Yet you shall be brought down to Sheol [Hades], to the innermost recesses of the pit [the region of the dead]" (Isa. 14:12–15).

Although this passage applies to the King of Babylon, it depicts the earthly king with Satan and his character. Isaiah called the King of Babylon the personification of Satan. His fall was because of his pride. He desired to be God. He was the anointed cherub who was not content in his position. He rebelled against God and was cast out of heaven.[195]

> You were in Eden, the garden of God; every precious stone was our covering, the carnelian, topaz, jasper, chrysolite, beryl, onyx, sapphire, carbuncle, and emerald; and your settings and your sockets and engravings were wrought in gold. On that day that you were created they were prepared. You were the anointed cherub that covers with overshadowing [wings], and I set you so. You were upon the holy mountain of God; you walked up and down in the midst of the stones of fire [like the paved work of gleaming sapphire stone upon which the God of Israel walked on

Mount Sinai]. You were blameless in your ways from the day you were created until iniquity and guilt were found in you. Through the abundance of your commerce you were filled with lawlessness and violence, and you sinned, therefore I cast you out as a profane from the mountain of God and the guardian cherub drove you out from the midst of the stones of fire.

Your heart was proud and lifted up because of your beauty; you corrupted your wisdom for the sake of your splendor. I cast you to the ground; I lay you before kings that they might gaze at you. You have profaned your sanctuaries by the multitude of your iniquities and the enormity of your guilt, by the unrighteousness of your trade. Therefore I have brought forth a fire from your midst; it has consumed you, and I have reduced you to ashes upon the earth in the sight of all who looked at you. All who know you among the people are astonished and appalled at you; you have come to a horrible end and shall never return to being. (Ezek. 28:12-19)

There again it speaks of his arrogance and pride. He wanted to be exalted above all—even to be like God himself. He became impressed with his own power and beauty. This act was the actual beginning of sin in the universe, which preceded the fall of man. He wanted to change his identity so that he could be the ruler of all.

He was banished from living in heaven and his name changed from Lucifer (morning star) to Satan (adversary). He fell from being the highest of God's angels to becoming a power that is completely perverted seeking to steal our God ordained identities by turning all things good into evil.[196]

The Antichrist and the Battle of Armageddon

Before the Second Coming of Christ, the Bible speaks about an Antichrist. He will be an end-time figure who opposes Christ. He opposes and claims to be Christ. "Boys [lads], it is the last time [hour, the end of this age]. And as you have heard that the antichrist [he who will oppose Christ in the guise of Christ] is coming, even now many antichrists have arisen, which confirms our belief that it is the final [the end] time" (1 John 2:18).

There is a spirit of Antichrist right now in the world, which is against Christ. Most eschatology experts believe the Antichrist will be the ultimate embodiment of what it means to be against Christ. He will seek world domination and will try to destroy all followers of Jesus Christ and also the nation of Israel.[197]

During the first century at the time of Jesus, the Jewish believers did not recognize Jesus as the Messiah because they believed He would come to earth as a conquering king to establish the Kingdom of God. This doctrine is an example of a spirit of Antichrist.[198]

In Matthew 24:24, it says that even the elect will be led astray. "For false Christs and false prophets will arise, and they will show great signs and wonders so as to deceive and lead astray, if possible even the elect [God's chosen ones]."

"Let no one deceive or beguile you in any way, for that day will not come except the apostasy comes first unless the predicted great falling away of those who have professed to be Christians has come, and the man of lawlessness [sin] is revealed, who is the son of doom [of perdition]" (2 Thess. 2:3).

The Antichrist will emerge as a world leader who will appear on the scene during a time of great peril and fear. This would cause people to beg for a savior to come and "fix" our problems.

According to the Bible, he would rule the world just before Jesus Christ returns. He would appear as benevolent but would be a figure of evil and a threat to mankind. He would be focused against the Jews.

He would deceive the world by performing great miracles. "The coming [of the lawless one, the Antichrist] is through the activity and working of Satan and will be attended by great power and with all sorts of [pretended] miracles and signs and delusive marvels—[all of them] lying wonders" (2 Thess. 2:9).[199]

The Antichrist is going to appear at a set time, a season. The appearance of the Antichrist signals the return of Christ at the Second Coming. In Matthew chapter 24, Jesus is talking about the signs to look for before the coming of the Lord. There will be wars and rumors of wars.

There will be an increase in earthquakes. With all of the natural disasters that have been happening lately and the turmoil in the nations and the terror of ISIS and the threat by North Korea, it seems that we are living in the last days.

According to Bible prophecy, "Then another angel, a third, followed them, saying with a mighty voice, Whoever pays homage to the beast and his statue and permits the [beast's] stamp [mark, inscription] to be put on his forehead or on his hand" (Rev. 14:9). The followers of the Antichrist will be marked by this seal. We have the technology today to implant chips. The mark of the beast will be the end-times mark, and you will not be able to buy or sell unless you worship the Antichrist. Do not take the mark of the beast! It won't be called the "mark of the beast," but it will be a type of technology that will have control over people.

The Battle of Armageddon refers to the Earth's final battle, which will essentially be between Christ and Satan. The entire world will be involved, and it will be a war between good and evil. It is an all-out effort of Satan to destroy God's people. It is the final battle, of an effort by Satan, to be the God of the universe and take down the people who are God's own. "And you said in your heart, I will ascend to heaven; I will exalt my throne above the stars of God; I will sit upon the mount of assembly in the uttermost north. I will ascend above the heights of the clouds; I *will make myself like the Most High*" (Isa. 14:13–14).[200]

Christ will prevail in the Battle of Armageddon! The armies of heaven will come, and they will be victorious! "After that I saw heaven opened, and behold, a white horse appeared, The One Who was riding it is called Faithful [Trustworthy, Loyal, Incorruptible, Steady] and True, and He passes judgment and wages war in righteousness [holiness, justice, and uprightness]. His eyes [blaze] like a flame of fir, and on His head are many kingly crowns [diadems]; and He has a title [name] inscribed which He along knows or can understand. He is dressed in a robe dyed by dipping in blood, and the title by which He is called is The Word of God. And the troops of heaven, clothed in fine linen, dazzling and clean, followed Him on white horses. From His mouth goes forth a sharp sword with which He can smite [afflict, strike] the nations; and he will shepherd and control them with a staff [scepter, rod] of iron. He will tread the winepress of the fierceness of the wrath and indignation of God the All-Ruler [the Almighty, the Omnipotent]. And on His garment [robe] and on His thigh He has a name –[title] inscribed, KING OF KINGS AND LORD OF LORDS" (Rev. 19:11–16).[201]

Satan will be bound for one thousand years. We who are the beloved of the Lord will reign with Jesus Christ during the Millennium, and there will peace and righteousness shall flourish. After this one-thousand-year reign, Satan will be loosed for a period of time, and he will have the last opportunity to regain power. Then will come the Great White Throne Judgment where believers and unbelievers will be judged. Believers will be judged according to their deeds in order to receive rewards gained or lost. Those whose names are not written in the Book of Life will be lost and will be judged according to their deeds to determine the degree of punishment that they will receive in the lake of fire. Satan will be cast into the lake of fire forever.

Tribulation / Rapture / Second Coming of Christ

The Tribulation is a seven-year period of time when God will be dealing with judgment on nations and His discipline of Israel. It will be unlike any other time since the world began. "And if those days had not been shortened, no human being would endure and survive, but for the sake of the elect [God's chosen ones] those days will be shortened" (Matt. 24:22).

During this period, the Antichrist will allow the Jewish Temple to be rebuilt, which confirms a peace-treaty agreement. This is when many Bible scholars believe that the tribulation period begins.

According to the Bible, the Tribulation period is broken up into three parts:

1. First half of the seven-year agreement (three and a half years) – Revelation 6–10
2. Middle of the seven-year agreement (thirty days) – Revelation 11–13
3. Last half of the seven-year agreement (three and a half years) – Revelation 14–19

The first half starts with a seven-year agreement allowing Temple sacrifice and worship in the Third Temple. This comes about because of the battle of Gog and Magog. Peace is sought because of this worldwide war, and this agreement brings a temporary peace between Israel and the world.

The middle of the Tribulation Satan is cast to earth and loses his position in heaven to accuse believers. He then incarnates the Antichrist who at this time has stopped worship and sacrifice in the Temple and demands that the world and Israel worship him. This is referred to as the "abomination of desolation." Those believers in Jerusalem will flee into the mountains of Judah (Rev. 12:7–12).

The Antichrist will go to war with those who failed to escape. They are the remnant and he pursues those who refuse to worship him. The false prophet helps the Antichrist by performing satanic wonders so that people will worship the beast (Antichrist). The false prophet sets up an economic system in which no one can buy or sell unless they have the mark of the beast—666 on their forehead or hand and those that refuse will be beheaded (Rev. 13:11-15, 16-18).

The last half of the tribulation begin with the "abomination of desolation" takes place and ends with the return of Jesus, the Messiah. This will be Satan's last stand. During this period there will be satanic wonders on earth hoping to deceive humanity. There will be final judgments on the earth. These "Bowl" judgments are seven final plagues that lead to the final battle of Armageddon. Jewish people who have survived and have come to a saving knowledge of Jesus as Messiah will call out to Him to save Israel. During this time, full authority has been given to Satan.

"The coming [of the lawless one, the antichrist] is through the activity and working of Satan and will be attended by great power and with all sorts of [pretended] miracles and signs and delusive marvels—[all of them] lying wonders—and by unlimited seduction to evil and with all wicked deception for those who are perishing [going to perdition] because they did not welcome the Truth but refused to love it that they might be saved. Therefore God sends upon them a misleading influence, a working of error and a strong delusion to make them believe what is false. In order that all may be judged and condemned who did not believe in [who refused to adhere to, trust in, and rely on] the Truth, but [instead] took pleasure in unrighteousness" (2 Thess. 2:9-12). We know that Jesus and the armies of heaven will be victorious in this battle and this will usher in the Second Coming of Jesus, the Messiah.

Jesus came as a baby in His first coming. In His Second Coming, He will return to fulfill the remaining prophecies as written in the Bible. He will return as the conquering King of Kings and Lord of Lords! He will arrive with the armies of heaven at His side to defeat and conquer evil and establish His reign of justice and peace upon the earth defeating the Antichrist and establishing His thousand-year reign.

Rapture comes from the Latin term for "caught up"—*rapturo*. Those of us who have trusted in Christ as Savior will literally be transported into heaven in the "twinkling of an eye." We will meet

Jesus in the air. "Then we, the living ones who remain [on the earth], shall simultaneously be caught up along with [the resurrected dead] in the clouds to meet the Lord in the air; and so always [through the eternity of the eternities] we shall be with the Lord! Therefore comfort and encourage one another with these words" (1 Thess. 4:17–18). The church will be caught up or carried away into the air to be with the Lord. His coming will be with the loud sound of the archangel and a trumpet call of God. The dead "in Christ" will be resurrected first and those of us living will be changed and be caught up to be with Jesus without experiencing death.[202]

There are three views of when this will happen in regard to the seven-year Tribulation period.

1. Pretribulation Rapture—believes that before the tribulation, the church will be raptured and that those left behind will suffer through the seven years of tribulation. During this time, Israel will come to know Jesus as their Messiah, and then the Lord will come to judge the earth at His Second Coming.

    - Arguments for this view are based on several points:
    - Imminence—No man knows the day or the hour (Matt. 24:36, 24:50, 25:13). Other positions would know the day of His return.
    - Distinction between the Church and Israel—the Church will fulfill the "Fullness of the Gentiles" (Rom. 11:25).

    God would not pour out His wrath on His own Church because it was not a method of the past, example—Noah and his family saved from the flood; Lott and family saved from Sodom.

2. Midtribulation Rapture—believes that the Church will go through the first three and half years before the great tribulation when God will pour out His wrath. The Church will be raptured during the middle of the tribulation period and then will return with Christ at the Second Coming.

    - Since the Church was promised tribulation, we will experience a portion of it (Matt. 24:1–9).

- Paul taught that there would be a time of apostasy and perilous times (2 Thess. 2:3; 2 Timothy 3:10).
- God is withdrawing His restraints so that man can reap what he is sowing, and these trumpet and seal judgments are not manifestations of wrath.
- In Revelation 11, the two witnesses are "caught up" into heaven accompanied by the rest of the Church.

3. Post-tribulation Rapture—The Church believes that before the Second Coming they will be raptured and return with Jesus at the Second Coming and the Church will go through the great tribulation.

- Historically this doctrine indicates that this event will precede the Second Coming immediately followed by the judgment seat of Christ in which all men would go before the Throne of Christ.
- Passages in Luke 23:27-31, Matthew 24:9-11, and Mark 13:9-13 are promises of tribulation for the Church and Israel.
- In Matthew 13:24-30, 36-45, it speaks about the wheat and tares and places the "Saints" as wheat and the tares as "Unsaved" growing side by side until the harvest and Jesus saying, "Let both grow together until the harvest." This interpretation views the harvest as the rapture of believers at the end of the tribulation.[203]

We, as believers in Jesus Christ, are the Bride of Christ awaiting with great anticipation the day when we are united with our Bridegroom, Jesus Christ. So we say with great longing and ecstasy—"Come, Lord Jesus!" "He who gives this warning and affirms and testifies to these things says, Yes [it is true]. [Surely] I am coming quickly [swiftly, speedily]. Amen [so let it be]! *Yes, come, Lord Jesus!*" (Rev. 22:20).

Summary

Satan fell because of his pride. He wanted to be like God. He was cast down to the earth, and this has been his domain where he has tried to deceive the nations with his lies and evil working through people who want to destroy God's creation, His laws, and His plan.

The Antichrist will appear at a set season in order to deceive even the elect. His mission is to take over as a world leader who will deceive many in believing that he is God. There will be persecution of believers, and unless you receive the mark of the beast you will not be able to buy or sell. There will be believers that will be beheaded for their faith.

Christians need to make sure they know and understand the Word of God so they can be prepared not to fall into any deceptions and false teachings. There are many such teachings out there right now. The spirit of Antichrist is still out there and we need to be careful.

We do not know when the rapture will occur for certainty. Whatever view you take, pretribulation; midtribulation or post-tribulation, we all need to be ready to meet the Lord whether it be by natural death or "caught up" to meet the Lord in the air. There are those that don't believe in the rapture at all. I believe that there are enough scriptures in the Bible referring to a rapture than any not referring.

The Battle of Armageddon is Satan's last stand. It will be between Jesus and the heavenly armies who will undoubtedly be victorious. This will usher in the Second Coming of Jesus Christ, coming as the King of Kings and the Lord of Lords who will rule with the saints (believers) for a thousand years. Satan will be let lose for a short period of time after the millennium and ultimately, he and any unbelievers judged at the White Throne Judgment whose names are not written in the Book of Life will be cast into the lake of fire forever.

Chapter Fifteen

Reflections

Heaven/Hell

"Then He will say to those at His left hand, Be gone from Me, you cursed, into the eternal fire prepared for the devil and his angels!" (Matt. 25:41). It was never God's plan for a single person to end up in hell. "The Lord does not delay and is not tardy or slow about what He promises, according to some people's conception of slowness, but He is long-suffering [extraordinarily patient] toward you, not desiring that any should perish, but that all should turn to repentance" (2 Peter 3:9).

We were not created for hell. Sin separates us from having a relationship with God. Because we are sinners we are not automatically entitled to enter into God's presence therefore we cannot enter heaven as we are. "So Heaven is not our *default* destination. No one goes there automatically. Unless our sin problem is resolved, the only place we will go is our true default destination . . . Hell."[204]

"Enter through the narrow gate; for wide is the gate and spacious and broad is the way that leads away to destruction, and many are those who are entering through it. But the gate is narrow [contracted by pressure] and the way is straitened and compressed that leads away to life, and few are those who find it" (Matt. 7:13–14). There are many who will not enter Heaven.

Hell is inhabited by all those who have not received God's gift of redemption through Jesus Christ. Jesus speaks more about Hell than anyone else. "Just as the darnel [weeds resembling wheat] is gathered and burned with fire, so it will be at the close of the age. The Son of Man will send forth His angels and they will gather out of His kingdom all causes of offense [persons by whom others are drawn into error or sin] and all who do iniquity and act wickedly, and will cast them into the furnace of fire; there will be weeping and wailing and grinding of teeth" (Matt. 13:40-42).

Can Christians, those who have given their life to the Lord, go to hell? There are differing views on this. There are those that say once you are born again you are saved and your past, present, and future sins are forgiven. I believe that this is true, our sins are forgiven, but it does not mean that we have a "get out of hell" free card. Jesus died to cleanse us from our sins. Jesus forgives us, but we have to ask for forgiveness. We need to be in a state of constant reconciliation with God because we do not know when we will experience death.

It is not enough just to believe. "You believe that God is one; you do well. So do the *demons* believe and shudder." In James 2:19, Jesus said, "*Not everyone* who says to Me, Lord, Lord, will enter the kingdom of heaven, but *he who does the will of My Father* Who is in heaven. Many will say to Me on that day, Lord, Lord, have we not prophesied in Your name and driven out demons in Your name and done many mighty works in Your name? And then I will say to them openly [publicly], I never knew you; depart from Me, you who act wickedly [disregarding my commands]" (Matt. 7:21-23).

There is a Nigerian Pastor named Daniel who gives a testimony of visiting heaven and hell. A video can be seen on YouTube: *Nigerian Pastor who went to Hell* by John Sturm at EternalProductions.com. In the video, the pastor that had this experience relates this experience and how he died and visited heaven and hell.

"An angel accompanied the pastor to heaven and there he saw saints in heaven and beautiful mansions and flowers that actually sang and praised God. Then he was shown hell. There were people in agony and torment there. He saw a pastor that said, 'I'm a pastor, I stole money from the church, I'm ready to repent.' The Angel told Daniel, 'If the Book of your life was to be closed today this would be your portion.' Daniel said, 'No, I'm a pastor, I'm a child of God, I'm born again, I've preached all over this country. No, No!' The Angel said, 'Enough, enough. When you were on your way to the first hospital you were asking God to forgive you, but you would not forgive your wife, and your sins have not been forgiven. It is a matter of reaping what you sow. You cannot sow unforgiveness to your wife and reap forgiveness from God.'" The Angel also said that this would be the last warning for this generation. Daniel was resurrected back to life because believers prayed for him and that is why he is spreading this message.[205]

This is a true story well-documented. It should give all of us as Christians and of course unbelievers pause. God sent His Son into the world so that we would be saved through Jesus's sacrifice on the cross. He forgave all manner of sin, but we still need to confess our sins and it really should be a daily activity. If we truly love the Lord, then we will be sorry for our sins not just to avoid hell but because we have offended the One whom we love.

Does this mean we should live in fear? No, of course not. We know that we have been redeemed by the blood of the Lamb, Jesus Christ, but we need to know that this is an intimate relationship, a covenant. It is like a marriage covenant that can only be broken because of unfaithfulness. Unfaithfulness to His Word and His will by turning away through sin and unrepented sins. Let us all thank the Lord for His mercy and grace living from heaven to earth where there is no sin, and His power is there to redeem our fallen state and just as a loving husband and wife converse and share intimacy with each other, they need to be ever aware of their commitment, their love for each other and as a result always willing to ask for forgiveness when the other has been offended.

Just as there have been people who have experienced the reality of hell, there are those who have witnessed heaven. One very popular movie about this is *Heaven Is for Real*. The young child experiences going to heaven, and he sees things that no one else had told him. For example he meets his sister in heaven. His mother had had a miscarriage, and this child had never been told about it. He also talked about seeing a grandfather that he never knew. There are so many stories and there have been movies made about this subject. There are many scriptures that speak about heaven.

John 14:2—"In My Father's house there are many dwelling places [homes]. If it were not so, I would have told you; for I am going away to prepare a place for you."

1 Corinthians 2:9—"But, on the contrary, as the Scripture says, What eye has not seen and ear has not heard and has not entered into the heart of man, [all that] God has prepared [made and keeps ready] for those who love Him [Who hold Him in affectionate reverence, promptly obeying Him and gratefully recognizing the benefits He has bestowed]."

Matthew 6:19-20—"Do not gather and heap up and store up for yourselves treasures on earth, where moth and rust and worm consume and destroy, and where thieves break through and steal. But gather and heap up and store for yourselves treasures in heaven, where neither moth nor rust nor worm consume and destroy, and where thieves do not break through and steal."

Revelation 21:21-25—"And the twelve gates were twelve pearls, each separate gate being built of one solid pearl. And the main street of one solid pearl. And the main street [the broadway] of the city was of gold as pure and translucent as glass. I saw no temple in the city, for the Lord God Omnipotent [Himself] and the Lamb [Himself] are its temple, and the city has no need of the sun nor of the moon to give light to it, for the splendor and radiance [glory] of God illuminate it, and the Lamb is its lamp."

Randy Alcorn writes in his book *Heaven*: "Perhaps you're afraid of becoming so heavenly minded you're of no earthly good." Relax—you have nothing to worry about! On the contrary, many of us are so earthly minded we are of no heavenly or earthly good. C. S. Lewis observed, "If you read history, you will find that the Christians who did most for the present world were just those who thought most of the next. The Apostles themselves, who set on foot the conversion of the Roman Empire, the great men who built up the Middles Ages, the English Evangelicals who abolished the Slave Trade, all left their mark on Earth, precisely because their minds were occupied with Heaven. It is since Christians have largely ceased to think of the other world that they have become so ineffective in this. Aim at Heaven and you will get earth 'thrown in'; aim at earth and you will get neither."[206]

Why did Jesus come to redeem us? He came because He loved us and wanted to bring us back into a full relationship that we had at the Garden of Eden where He walked and talked to man and woman. We need to get back to being what God intended us to be and what He created us to be. We are made in His image and likeness. Heaven is our destiny and we are on a journey to arrive there but since we are connected through a relationship with God through Jesus we need to be heavenly minded and bring heaven down to earth.

Jonathan Cahn says in his *Book of Mysteries*: "Live from heaven, from the kingdom yet to come, from the life yet to be, even from the *you* you are yet to become. Fight the won battle, run the run race, accomplish the finished work, start from the finish line, begin from the victory, rejoice now from the joy at the end. Live now from what will one day be, and you'll live a life of blessing, and victory, on earth as it is in heaven."[207]

"But he who commits sin [who practices evildoing] is of the devil [takes his character from the evil one], for the devil has sinned [violated the divine law] from the beginning. The reason the Son of God was made manifest [visible] was *to undo [destroy, loosen, and dissolve] the works the devil [has done]*" (1 John 3:8).

Nothing will frustrate or hinder the plan of God. Satan and all of his fallen angels cannot change the will of God but can only fulfill it and for that matter, nothing else will! He will come in His glory and the Second Coming, and He will judge the nations and the people, and He will set up His Millennial Kingdom here on earth and His plans shall be accomplished.[208]

"And [so that you can know and understand] what is the immeasurable and unlimited and surpassing greatness of His power in and for us who believe, as demonstrated in the working of His mighty strength. Which He exerted in Christ when He raised Him form the dead and seated Him at His [own] right hand in the heavenly [places], far above all rule and authority and power and dominion and every name that is named [above every title that can be conferred], not only in this age and in this world, but also in the age and the world which are to come. And He has put all things under His feet and has appointed Him the universal and supreme Head of the church [a headship exercised throughout the church], which is His body, the fullness of Him Who fills all in all [for in that body lives the full measure of Him Who makes everything complete, and Who fills everything everywhere with Himself]" (Eph. 1:19–23).

Why does there appear to be an identity crisis? What does *crisis* mean? *Webster's Dictionary* defines *crisis* as "A crucial or decisive point or situation: *turning point*. An unstable state of political, international, or economic affairs with an impending abrupt or *decisive change*." How does *Webster's* define *identity crisis*? "A state of disorientation and *role confusion* occurring in a social structure, as in an institution."[209]

There is no need to be confused about who we are in Christ. God has outlined who we are in His Word. The following is a list of some identity declarations that we have been given as children of God:

Biblical Identity Declarations

1. *I am blessed with every spiritual blessing in the heavenly places in Christ (Ephesians 1:3).*

2. I am chosen in Christ before the foundation of the world that I may be holy and blameless before the Father (Ephesians 1:4).
3. The Father has accepted me in the beloved (Ephesians 1:6).
4. I have redemption through Jesus Christ's blood and the forgiveness of sins (Ephesians 1:7; Colossians 1:14).
5. God raised me up in heavenly places to sit with Him in Jesus Christ (Ephesians 2:6).
6. I am saved by grace through faith. I am not saved by my own works (Ephesians 2:8–9).
7. I am God's masterpiece. He created me anew in Christ Jesus, so I can do the good things He planned for me long ago (Ephesians 2:10).
8. I am strengthened with might through His Spirit in the inner man according to the riches of His glory (Ephesians 3:16).
9. Christ dwells in my heart by faith. I am rooted and grounded in love (Ephesians 3:17).
10. God gives me the victory through Jesus Christ my Lord (1 Corinthians 15:57).
11. I have the mind of Christ (1 Corinthians 2:16).
12. I am in Christ Jesus and therefore I am a new creation. Old things have passed away and all things have become new (2 Corinthians 5:17).
13. If I sin, I have an advocate with the Father, Jesus Christ the righteous (1 John 2:1).
14. All of God's promises are yes and amen for me because I am in Christ (2 Corinthians 1:20).
15. God my Father has delivered me from the power of darkness and transferred me into the kingdom of His beloved Son (Colossians 1:13).

Igniting Hope Ministries June 10, 2015)
/blog/1-25biblicaldeclarations 210

Stand

We as Christians, need to take a stand. We cannot afford to be on the sidelines and watch as we are being stripped of our very identity in Christ. We are *not* what the world is telling us we are. We do *not* think the way the world thinks. We do *not* live the way the world wants us to live. We *are* who God says that we are. We *do* have the mind of Christ. We *will* live the way Christ wants us to live.

Where was the Church during Roe V. Wade? The Church was silent. Where were we when they took God out of the schools? Where were we when there was a ruling on same-sex marriage? The Church is slowly becoming the Church of Political Correctness, not the Church of Jesus Christ.

We need to take a stand and speak up and not let our voices be silenced anymore. Our true identity is being eroded by the Antichrist spirit living and moving in our politicians, media, and sadly to say in some churches.

In Exodus 32:26, Moses came down from the mountain and saw that some of the people had rebelled against God in his absence, "Then Moses stood in the gate of the camp and said, Whoever is on the Lord's side, let him come to me. And all the Levites [the priestly tribe] gathered together to him."

Yes, I believe that God is saying now that whoever is on His side needs to take a stand by our actions and our words. How can we say we are Christ's when we sit back and let even our Christian faith be mocked? Would there have been an end to racial segregation if Martin Luther King Jr. and others had not taken a stand? We need to take a stand and be who God created us to be and do what He has called us to do and that is to be a light in the darkness because we may be the only witness that others will see and be a testimony to who God is in us through Christ.

The Lord's intervention, being manifested in the election of President Donald Trump, does not mean that we now sit down on our laurels and wait for him to be our savior but it is said by many that we have been given "a reprieve" in which we need to use this time to go forth and be bold with our faith and resist all that the enemy is throwing at us because he knows that his time is short. I believe that we are the remnant that will be ushering in the return of Jesus Christ and as such, we need to stand firm and not give in to what the enemy has been devising since the Garden of Eden and that is stealing our identity in Christ!

Prepare

How are we to prepare? We need to prepare for the Second Coming of Jesus and the "end of the age" by spreading the Gospel message of Salvation. We are to be coworkers with Christ to bring in the final harvest before His return.

We need to make sure that we are ready to meet the Lord whether it be because of the death of our bodies or whether it be in the rapture of the saints. We need to be sure we are not living in sin and quick to ask for God's forgiveness and always keep hatred and unforgiveness far from our hearts.

Today is the acceptable time to come to the Lord if you have not, and if you have been born again you need to be sure you're ready to meet the Lord. Do not put off forgiving your spouse or your neighbor or your child.

In chapter 24 of Matthew, the disciples asked Jesus, "What will be the sign of Your coming and of the end [the completion, the consummation] of the age?" He responded by saying that there would be wars, famine, great earthquakes, and the Good News of the Kingdom [the Gospel] would be preached throughout the whole world. Could it be that we are living in this age that Jesus is talking about? I believe that we are and so do many Christians because one of the great signs is when Israel became a nation in 1948. That appears to be the tipping point for the beginning of the end of the age, and it would make sense because how could the armies come against Israel if Israel was not a nation yet?

If the time before the Second Coming is winding down as many now believe, and one of the signs is famine, we should prepare by storing twenty to thirty year shelf life food and have extra water on hand because we do not know the day or the hour. With all the recent hurricanes and earthquakes and floods, it would seem that it would be a prudent thing to do if only to prepare for disaster.

Summary

It is all about choices. Adam and Eve had a choice in the Garden. Abraham and Moses and Noah and all the great Patriarchs had a choice to believe God and follow Him or not. The Israelites had a choice to be "on the Lord's side" or not. Mary the mother of Jesus had a choice to allow God to use her womb as a sacred dwelling place in which the Savior of the world would be conceived and be born through her. The disciples had a choice to follow Jesus or not follow him. The early followers of Jesus had a choice to live or to die for Him, and there are millions who have been martyred for the sake of Christ since Jesus came. Corrie ten Boom and her family had a choice to help the Jewish people or not. Ruth had a choice to stay with her mother-in-law or leave to another land. Rosa Parks had a choice to sit at the back of the bus or not.

God had a choice to send His only begotten Son, Jesus Christ, to save us from our sin, and He did send Jesus because of His love for us. Jesus chose to give His life freely, as a ransom for us, and to die in our place so that we would be forgiven from our sins.

What is your choice? Will you choose to be a born-again believer and follower of Jesus? Will you choose to live His life in you and truly fulfill the identity that He has given to you so freely? Will you be ready to meet Him and hear His words?—"Well done, good and faithful servant."

Do not let the world and the devil steal your identity! We are who we are in Christ. We are His hands, His feet, and His body that He has chosen to live in so that we can be His ambassadors. Let's not live in an *Identity Crisis* world without showing the world the *Identity Christ Is* living in us!

> *In conclusion, be strong in the Lord [be empowered through your union with Him]: draw your strength from Him [that strength which His boundless might provide]. Put on God's whole armor [the armor of a heavy-armed soldier which God supplies], that you may be able to successfully stand up against [all] the strategies and deceits of the devil. For we are not wrestling with flesh and blood [contending only with physical opponents], but against the despotisms, against the powers, against [the master spirits who are] the world rulers of this present darkness, against the spirit forces of wickedness in the heavenly [supernatural] sphere. Therefore put on God's complete armor, that you may be able to resist and stand your ground on the evil day [of danger], and, having done all [the crisis demands], to stand [firmly in your place]. Stand therefore [hold your ground], having tightened the belt of truth around your loins and having put on the breastplate of integrity and of moral rectitude and right standing with God, and having shod your feet in preparation [to face the enemy with the firm-footed stability, the promptness, and the readiness produced by the good news] of the Gospel of peace. Lift up over all the [covering] shield of saving faith, upon which you can quench all the flaming missiles of the wicked [one]. And take the helmet of salvation and the sword that the Spirit wields, which*

is the Word of God. Pray at all times [on every occasion, in every season] in the Spirit, with all [manner of] prayer and entreaty. To that end keep alert and watch with strong purpose and perseverance, interceding in behalf of all the saints [God's consecrated people]. (Eph. 6:10–18)

Words from the Lord

The following are words I believe that the Lord gave me concerning the times we now live in. It appears that it is later than we think as far as the Lord's Second Coming.

September 15, 2017

"Child of mine, I say to you to be prepared. Watch, pray. Be prepared, for many trials are coming upon the earth. For My voice will be heard be it by thunder, or rain, or flooding. My voice will be heard! Be my voice. Utter My Words. Go before Me like Elijah. Proclaim the Good News. *Revel* in it. For I proclaim to you that heaven and earth will not pass away until My promises, My Word, My Kingdom shall be established upon the earth. It's a *new day*. It's a *new dawn. Walk in it! Walk in it! Walk in it!*"

October 14, 2017

"My child, hear the whistle of the train? See the smoke from the stack from the train as it approaches? When you see these signals, you know that the train is near. The train is nearing, the time for the gathering is near—you can almost hear the sound of the trumpet as the angel prepares to sound the alarm! Be ready! Be ready! Be ready! Call others to the train station. You need a ticket to board!"

1990s

I had a dream in the 1990s about an earthquake in California. In the dream, I was on my way to visit my brother in California, and I stopped at a diner to ask for directions to get to California, and when I asked someone for directions, I saw a map of the state of California on the wall, and half the state was no longer there. When I woke up, I was shaking, and it felt very real to me.

There are prophets who have prophesied this earthquake as well as earthquakes along the western coast of the United States and a great tsunami on the eastern coast of the United States as well as a big earthquake in the middle of the United States if our country divides Israel.

There is no reason to fear. God is merciful and all we need to do is trust in Him and prepare spiritually and physically for any storm or calamity.

The following are the words from Jesus to my husband, Marty, in a dream/vision on July 6, 2018:

Marty was in a meadow, and Jesus appeared along with David, Elijah, John the Baptist, Adam and Eve, the apostles, and a woman whose name He did not mention.

Jesus said, "What you see around you, is, but a small part of creation being celebrated. You celebrate that creation when you are as these, for they chose to live in *My* world and not live *with* the world. They chose to acknowledge and celebrate that they are My image and likeness as a matter of faith, in spite of this world and by doing so, they acknowledged Me and My Father and the Spirit and their unwavering faith and trust in Me and My Father, for when you are as these, you bring the light of My creation to life and express your total faith and trust in Us, by being. For we, Christ, God the Father, and the Spirit, are the guardians and helpmates to your journey home. The challenge is living with the world while living in *My* world." Marty believes that Jesus is saying to live in *His* world.

A Call to Action

In a surprise speech at a Catholic University, Jim Caviezel, the actor who portrayed Jesus in *The Passion of The Christ*, brought a message of faith. The following is an excerpt from the speech:

> Embrace your cross and race towards the goal. I want you to go out into this pagan world and I want you to have the courage to step into this pagan world and shamelessly express your faith in public.
>
> The world needs proud warriors animated by their faith; warriors like St. Paul and St. Luke who risked their

names, their reputations to take this faith; their love for Jesus, into the world.

God is calling each one of us; one of you, to do great things but how often we fail to respond dismissing it as some mental blurp.

It is time for our generation now to accept that call, the call of God urging all of us to give ourselves entirely to Him; to see that gentle hand guiding your path. But you must make the commitment to start praying, to fast, to meditate on the Holy Scriptures; to take the Holy Sacraments seriously for we are in danger of succumbing to our excesses. We must shake off this indifference, this destructive tolerance of evil that only our faith and the wisdom of Christ can save us but it requires warriors ready to risk their reputations, their names, even our very lives to stand for the truth. Set yourselves apart from this corrupt generation. Be saints! **YOU WEREN'T BORN TO FIT IN—YOU WERE BORN TO STAND OUT!**[211]

My husband and I compose and produce Christian music. This song was written by my husband, Marty, and I think that the words convey how we may sometimes reflect on our life and maybe how God looks at us Through His Eyes.

Through His Eyes

Music/lyrics by Marty Ward © 1999.[212]

1. There's a man, staring back, in the windowpane / He's looking at me, through the eyes, of my life / Hoping, that I will see, my life was not in vain
    He's showing me, what He's seen, through the eyes of my life

    Chorus: Through His eyes, the reflection of my journey

    Is seen through the cloudy windowpane, of my eyes / Through His eyes, the measure of my humanity

    Is seen, when my pride and selfishness, dies.

2. Sitting here, and staring out, at the pouring rain / And thinking back on all the years and endless tears / Seeing the world, pass me by, like an endless train / Remembering the failures, sorrows, and all the fears

   Bridge: Lord, what do you see in me?

   Am I a becoming what you would want of me? Lord, what do you see through me?

   Am I a reflection, of You living in me?

3. Watching the sun, breaking through, the parting clouds above / Remembering how, Your light filled my darkest night Even when I failed and sinned, / You forgave me with your love / And blessed all of my days with / Your peace and delight

4. Feeling the warmth, and the hope, of a brand new day / Like the flowers born just after a spring day's rain My Spirit finds new life when I follow your way

   You're the breath of my life seen in that windowpane. Chorus: Through His eyes the reflection of my journey

   Is seen through the cloudy windowpane, of my eyes / Through His eyes, the measure of my humanity

   Is seen when my pride and selfishness, dies

Healing Hearts Ministry is a ministry helping people to encounter the love, mercy, and healing power of God through the message of God's Word and praise and worship renewing the whole person in body, mind, and spirit.

http//:www.mmissary.net/HealingHearts/
http//:www.mmissary.com
https://solaceinGodsworld.blogspot.com

Chapter 16

Heaven's Perspective: The Best Is Yet To Come

Adam and Eve disobeyed God in the Garden of Eden and were removed from the garden. Satan thought he had won, but "the best was yet to come." Abraham obeyed God and went up to a mountain to slay his son, but God stopped him, because "the best was yet to come." Moses led the Israelites out of Egypt but they complained and went around the mountain for 40 years, but "the best was yet to come."

Ruth pleaded before the King for her people even at the risk of death, but "the best was yet to come." Daniel was thrown into the lion's den, but "the best was yet to come." Jesus was nailed to a cross, suffered and died for our salvation and the devil thought he had won, "but the best was yet to come!"

Are you tired of the bad news that is continually being broadcast from most networks? Are you tired of hearing this? Don't let it get you down because "The best is yet to come!" Where have we heard these words of encouragement before? None other than Trump himself. Could it be that God is using Trump's voice to speak to us and give us encouragement? We are at a very low time in our country where the spirit of fear is rampant and the truth is being stifled by many. The false prophets (most of the people in the media) are "preaching" a message of false hope that a change or re-set in our government will solve all of our problems.

I would say, don't be so quick. It isn't over until God says it is over!! The best is yet to come. We, as Christians, can have hope, through Christ, that as long as we keep our minds and hearts fixed on Him, we will get through this time of turmoil and have faith that God will do what *only* He can do.

There are many prophets that have said and are still saying that President Trump will have a second term. "Surely the Lord God will do nothing without revealing His secret to His servants the prophets." (Amos 3:7) Does this mean that we need to look to President Trump being the "savior" of the world? No, I think not, but God is and will be using him as well as other patriots to lead His people out of bondage.

People are waking up. We are in probably the greatest awakening in all of history! This is going to be the biggest and greatest harvest of souls of all time.

No, it's not over until God says it is over!! So don't be disappointed. You need to keep the faith. **The best IS yet to come**. God still has a plan for this country and the world. There is going to be a revival, an awakening, coming that will be ushering in the greatest harvest of souls before the Second Coming of Jesus! God loves us so much that He wants everyone to join Him at the Banquet Table of the Bridegroom (Jesus) and His Church (The Bride of Christ).

I believe the Lord gave me the following words on November 9, 2016:

> *"God is assembling an army, an army of believers to fight the good fight to be victorious and win the battle. He is appointing generals, admirals, and sergeants. He is booting out the chaff. We are all called to this army. Be ready, be ready for battle. Be prepared,* **the best is yet to come**. *There is never a battle without an enemy. The enemy is the left, the evil one. Be strong. Be vigilant. Be calm. For I give you the sword of My Spirit, My Word which will go before you. So march on My people. Be ready for the battle. Know ye this, there can be no victory without the fight. March on. Be calm. Be strong. Watch and wait for My directions."*

I believe the Lord gave me the following words on November 29, 2020:

> *"There will be an avalanche against the enemy. An avalanche of Biblical proportions. One in which My power will know, no bounds. So prepare for this for I will be opening the Red Sea to bring My people across and there will be an avalanche of My power that will overwhelm the enemies*

camp. So rejoice and be exceedingly glad My children. This is the decree of the King of Kings and the Lord of Lords. Prepare; be My re-enforcers of the Kingdom which is to come and which is within you. Be a force for the Kingdom of God. For I AM WHO I AM and no demon in hell will prevent what I am doing now. My voice has spoken and I will do it so prepare army of God. PREPARE, PREPARE, PREPARE!!"

Is the best yet to come? Yes I believe it is and it is in God's Holy Word. Evil has an expiration date and I believe we are living in the greatest time in history but it is up to us to stand for God and our freedoms! Evil has to be constrained so that the Gospel of the Kingdom will be exemplified as well as preached before the Second Coming of Jesus Christ.

"And this good news of the kingdom (the Gospel) will be preached throughout the whole world as a testimony to all the nations, and then will come the end." (Matthew 24:14)

"Then he showed me the river whose waters give life, sparkling like crystal, flowing out from the throne of God and of the Lamb."

Through the middle of the broadway of the city; also, on either side of the river was the tree of life with its twelve varieties of fruit, yielding each month its fresh crop; and the leaves of the tree were for the healing *and* the restoration of the nations.

There shall no longer exist there anything that is accursed (detestable, foul, offensive, impure, hateful, or horrible). But the throne of God and of the Lamb shall be in it, and His servants shall worship Him [pay divine honors to Him and do Him holy service].

They shall see His face, and His name shall be on their foreheads.

And there shall be no more night; they have no need for lamplight or sunlight, for the Lord God will illuminate them *and* be their light, and they shall reign [as kings] forever and ever (through the eternities of the eternities)." (Revelation 22:1-5)

THE BEST *IS* YET TO COME!

NOTES

Chapter 1: AI—Am Who I Am?

1. Herzfeld, Noreen L. 2003, "Creating in Our Own Image: Artificial Intelligence and the Image of God. Zygon": Journal of Religion and Science 37 (2): 303:–316.
2. Williams, Thomas D., PhD, 17 October 2017. "Dan Brown Declares That 'God Cannot Survive Science.'" Accessed on June 6, 2018. http://www.breitbart.com/big-government/2017/10/17/dan-brown-declares-that-god-cannot-survive-science/.
3. Webster's Dictionary II New Riverside University Dictionary (1984). Houghton Mifflin Company.
4. "What does it mean that humanity is made in the image of God (imago dei)?" Accessed on July 17, 2017. https://www.gotquestions.org/image-of-God.html.
5. "The Burning Bush (Exodus 3:1–15) From the Series: Exodus: The Birth of The Nation. Accessed on December 11, 2017. https://bible.org/seriespage/3-burning-bush-exodus-31-15.
6. Armstrong, Herbert W. From the book "The United States and Britain in Prophecy" Accessed on August 9, 2017. https://www.thetrumpet.com/literature/books_and_booklets/44) Https://www.thetrumpet.com/authors/13-herbert-w-armstrong (1967, 1972, 1975, 1980, 2003, 2007, 2009) Philadelphia Church of God.
7. Webster's Dictionary II New Riverside University Dictionary (1984). Houghton Mifflin company.

Chapter 2: God as Father

8. "Characteristics of Father God" Accessed on August 15, 2017. http://receive-healing.com/blog77/characteristics-of-father-god/.
9. "The Our Father: A Reflection" (Mt 6:9–13). Accessed on June 6, 2018. totustuus.com/TheOurFatherAReflection.pdf.
10. "Jesus Speaks of Both His Relation to the Father and His Disciples' Relation to the Father" Accessed August 17, 2017. https://www.biblegateway.com/resources/commentaries/IVP-NT/John/Jesus-Speaks-Both-Relation.

11. IBID
12. IBID
13. IBID

Chapter 3: Men of Faith in the Bible

14. https://www.dictionary.com/browse/abraham.
15. "The Focal Point of Abram's Faith (Genesis 15:1–21) Accessed August 23, 2017. Https://bible.org/seriespage/16-focal-point-abram-s-faith-genesis-151-21.
16. "Double Identity" Based on the teachings of the Lubavitcher Rebbe Courtesy of MeaningfulLife.com. Accessed November 23, 2017.Http://www.chabad.org/parshah/article_cdo/aid/246640/jewish/DoubleIdentity.
17. "Jacob" Accessed September 13, 2017. https://bible.org/article/jacob.
18. "What should we learn from the life of Joseph?" Accessed August 23, 2017. http://www.gotquestions.org/life_Josephhtml.
19. "Study 4: Moses' Cultural And Identity Confusion" Exodus 2. Exodus Bible Studies updated 2013-03-11. https://mem.intervarsity.org/sites/mem/files/Moses%20A%20Tricultural%20Man%20Bible%20S tudy%204%20-%20Ex%202_0.pdf.
20. "Gideon Bible Story Summary With Lesson" posted by David Peach on (October 25, 2012). Accessed July 20, 2017. http://www.whatchristianswanttoknow.com/gideon-bibl-story-summary-with-lesson.
21. IBID
22. IBID
23. "Encyclopedia of the Bible—Elijah" Accessed August 23, 2017. https://www.biblegateway.com/resources/encyclopedia-of-the-bible/Elijah.
24. Moen, Chris., "Jeremiah the Prophet" Accessed July 21, 2017. https://life-hopeandtruth.com/prophecy/prophets/prophets-of-the-bible/jeremiah-the-prophet/.
25. IBID
26. "Daniel's Faith and God's Providence at Work" Daniel 6. Accessed August 23, 2017. http://www.bible.ca/ef/expository-daniel-6.htm.
27. Abrams, Cooper, "Commentary on the Book of Jonah" Accessed July 21, 2017. http://bible-truth.org/Jonah.html.
28. IBID
29. Jackson, Wayne. Accessed August 23, 2017. https://www.christiancourier.com/articles/266-who-was-john-the-baptist/.
30. IBID
31. IBID
32. Hooser, Don. posted on June 14, 2011. Accessed August 28, 2017. https:// www.ucg.org/user/don-hooser/.

Chapter 4: Women of Faith in the Bible

33. "All the Women of the Bible—Rahab" Accessed July 27, 2017. https://www.biblegateway.com/resources/all-women-bibl/Rahab/.
34. IBID
35. Wickramaratne-Rebera, Ranjini E., "Who Are You?" Identity And Difference in the Book Of Ruth" https://www.assembly.uca.org.au/image/stories/_archive/mcm) identity-and-difference-in-the-book-of-ruth/.
36. "A Pair of Queens—The Dual Nature of Queen Esther" Accessed July 21, 2017. http://www.beingjewish.com/yomtov/purim/esther_hamalkah.html.
37. "Esther—Queen—Bible Woman" August 29, 2017. http://www.womeninthebible.net/women-bible-old-new-testaments/esther-queen-bible-woman/.
38. IBID
39. IBID
40. Dunsford, Jenn. "5 Things Women Can Learn from Mary Magdalene" (February 5, 2016). Accessed July 21, 2017. http://www.lifeway.com/films/2016/02/05/5-things-women-can-learn-from-mary-magdalene/.
41. "All the Women of the Bible—Mary Magdalene" Resources Chapter 2. Alphabetical Exposition of Named Bible Women M Mary Magdalene. Accessed July 31, 2017.
https://www.biblegateway.com/resources/all-women-bible/Mary-Magdalene/.

Chapter 5: The Church

42. "The Impact of Christianity" Accessed September 5, 2017. http://faithfacts.org/chirst-and-the-culture/the-impact-of-christianity/.
43. IBID
44. Morley, Patrick/Man in the Mirror "Are You a Cultural Christian or a Biblical Christian? (/opinion/45530-are-you-a-cultural-christian-or-a-biblical-christian) (2017) Charisma Media. Accessed September 4, 2017. http://www.charismamedia.com/.
45. Feeney, Jim., "Our Culture Is a Corrupting Influence on the Church!" Accessed September 4, 2017. http://www.jimfeeney.org/culture-changing-church.html'.
46. Jenkins, Jack "Are evangelicals inventing a new kind of Christianity that's all about sex? Accessed on June 6, 2018. http://thinkprogress.org/ are-evangelicals-inventing-a-new-kind-of-Christianity-that's-all-about-sex?/.
47. Turpin, Simon., The Loss of Free Speech in the UK and How We Should React as Christians" (March 6, 2017). Accessed July 24, 2017. https://answersingenesis.org/blogs/simon-turpin/2017/03/06/loss-free-speech/.
48. IBID
49. "Ake Green" Wikipedia, the free encyclopedia. Accessed November 25, 2017. http://wildernesschristianity.net/info/Ake_Green/wikipedia_Ake_Green/.

50. Mohler, Albert "Criminalizing Christianity: Sweden's Hate Speech Law" Accessed September 4, 2017. http://www.christianheadlines.com/columnists/al-mohler/criminalizing-Christianity-Sweden's-Hate-Speech-Law.
51. Fournier, Deacon Keith "Trump is Right: Repeal the Johnson Amendment That Muzzles Pastors". Accessed on June 6, 2018. https://stream.org/ trump-right-repeal-johnson-amendmen-muzzles-pastors/.
52. Millard, Dr. Catherine "Preachers and Pulpits of the American Revolution". Accessed on June 6, 2018. http://www.christianheritagemins.org/articles/Preachers%20and%20Pulpits%20of%20the%20American%20Revolution.pdf.
53. Terry, Michelle"JohnsonAmendmentandChurches'Freedoms"(July26,2016). Accessed September 7, 2017. https://aclj.org/free-speech/ho-the-johnson-amendment-threatens-churches-freedoms/.
54. "Separation of Church and State, Thomas Jefferson and the First Amendment" Accessed November 27, 2017. http://www.free2pray.info/1separationchurch-state.html.
55. Moyer, Justin Wm. "Christian teen in Colorado drops school prayer lawsuit" (June 10, 2015). Accessed November 27, 2017. https://www.washington-post.com/news/morning-mis/wp/2015/06/10/Christian-teen-in-Colorado-drops-school-prayer-lawsuit/.
56. Levine, Daniel S., "Jack Phillips: 5 Fast Facts You Need to Know" (June 26, 2017). Accessed November 27, 2017. http://heavy.com/news/2017/06/ jack-phillips-supreme-court-colorado-masterpiece-cakeshop-baker-religion/.
57. "What is the Kingdom of God?" Accessed November 27, 2017. https://gotquestions.net/Printer/kingdom-of-God-PF.html.
58. "Christian Persecution" Accessed September 10, 2017. http://www.allaboutfollowingjesus.org/christian-persecion.htm.
59. Wooding, Dan "Modern Persecution" Accessed September 10, 2017. http://www.christianity.com/print/11630665/.
60. Van Hooser, Tamara (October 25, 2014). Accessed September 10, 2017. http://guardianlv.com/2014/10/isis-persecution-forces-iraqi-christians-to-choose/.
61. IBID

Chapter 6: I Have a Dream

62. "Martin Luther King Jr. Minister, Civil Rights Activist (1929–1968)" Accessed September 11, 2017. https://www.biography.com/people/martin-luther-king-jr.-9365086.
63. King Jr., Martin Luther "I Have A Dream . . ." Speech by the Rev. Martin Luther King At the "March on Washington." Accessed on June 15, 2018.
64. IBID

65. "Rosa Parks Activist, Civil Rights Activist (1913–2005). Accessed September 11, 2017. https://www.biography.com/people/rosa-parks-9433715.
66. "Mother Teresa Saint, Nun (1910–1997). Accessed September 11, 2017. https://www.biography.com/people/mother-teresa/9504160
67. "Corrie ten Boom Activist, Activist (1892–1983)" Accessed September 11, 2017. https://www.biographycom/people/corrie-ten-boom-21358155.
68. Christian History "Dietrich Bonhoeffer German theologian and resister" (1906–1945). Accessed September 10, 2017. http://www.christianitytoday.com/history/people/martyrs/dietrich-bonhoeffer.
69. United States Holocaust Memorial Museum "The German Churches and the Nazi State" Accessed September 12, 2017. https://www.ushmm.org/wic/en/article.php?ModuleId=10005206.
70. Worsham, Sabrina Lea "Medias Influence on Social Norms and Identity Development of Youth". Accessed on June 15, 2018. http://www.personal.psu.edu/bfr3/blogs/applied_social_psychology/2011/11/medias-influence-on-social-norms-and-identity-development-of-youth.html.

Chapter 7: Cultural Impact on Identity

71. "Identity Politics" Accessed July 22, 2017. http://rationalwiki.org/wiki/Identiy_politics.
72. Lancaster, Roger "Identity Politics Can Only Get Us So Far" Accessed September 18, 2017. https://www.jacobinmag.com/2017/08/identity-politics-gay-rights-neoliberalism-stonewall-feminism-race.
73. "Identity Politics" Wikipedia. Accessed November 22, 2017 https://en.wikipedia.org/wiki/Identity_politics.
74. IBID
75. "Political Correctness" Wikipedia. Accessed December 15, 2017. https://en.wikipedia.org/wiki/Political_correctness.
76. IBID
77. IBID
78. French, David "Identity Politics Are Ripping Us Apart" (May 18, 2016). Accessed September 20, 2017 http://www.nationalreview.com/node/435567/ print.
79. "Christian Abolitionism" Wikipedia. Accessed November 27, 2017. https://en.wikipedia.or/wiki/Christian_Abolitionism.
80. Worsham, Sabrina Lea "Media's Influence on Social Norms and Identity Development of Youth" Accessed July 21, 2017. http://personal.psu.edu/ bfr3/blogs/applied_social_psychology/2011/11/medias-influence-on-social-norms-and-identity-development-of-youth.html.
81. Bolen, Jackie "TV's Effect on the family" November 21, 2006. Accessed July 31, 2017. http://tvseffect.blogspot.com.

82. IBID
83. IBID
84. "Progressive educator's original goal? Abolish Christianity" Accessed July 26, 2017. http://www.wnd.com/2015/05/progressive-educators-original-goal-abolish-chirstianity.
85. IBID
86. "A Brief History of Homeschooling". Accessed September 22, 2017. https://www.responsiblehomeschooling.org/homeschooling-101/a-brief-history-of-homeschooling.
87. Good, Graham "Identity politics is killing college life" September 23, 2013. Accessed September 22, 2017. http://www.spiked-online.com/newsite/ article/ identiy_politics_is_killing_college_life.
88. Panell, Gary "Why are so many Christians leaving their faith when they go to college?" May 30, 2017. Accessed September 23, 2017. http://bible-christian.org/7628-2/.
89. Tripp, Ashley "Why students lose their faith in college" April 28, 2014. Accessed September 23, 2017. https://www.cru.org/communities/campus/why-students-lose their-faith-in-college/.
90. Webster's Dictionary II New Riverside University Dictionary (1984) Houghton Mifflin.
91. Anghis, Roger News With Views. We're Losing Our Free Speech, Part 3. Accessed on June 6, 2018. https://www.educationviews.org/were-losing-free-part-3/.
92. Lutzer, W. Dr. Erwin Moody Church Media 2014 "The Demise of Religious Freedom in America" Accessed September 23, 2017. https://www.moodymedia.org/articles/demise-religious-freedom-in-america/.
93. Elazar, Daniel J. Jerusalem Center for Public Affairs "Covenant and the American Founding" Accessed September 25, 2017. http://www.jcpa.org/ dje/articles/cov-amer.htm.
94. IBID
95. VOA News "New Survey Reveals Americans Believe Country has 'Lost its Identity'" (April 6, 2016). Accessed September 25, 2017. http://www.voanews.com/a/mht-quinnipiac-survey-reveal-americans-believe-country-has-lost-its-identity.
96. IBID
97. "Poll: 7 in 10 people say America is losing its identity" (March 5, 2017). Accessed September 24, 2017. https://www.cbsnews.com/news/poll-7-in-1 0-people-say-america-is-losing-its-identity/.
98. Brooks, Carol "Prayer in Schools" Accessed September 26, 2017. http://inplainsite.org/what_happened_when_the_praying.html.

Chapter 8: Gender Identity

99. Folda, Most Rev. John T. "Male and female: Our identity in God's plan" (February 2017). Accessed September 26, 2017. http://fargodiocese.org/Male-and-female-Our-identity-in-Gods-plan/.
100. IBID
101. IBID
102. Miller, Dave Ph. D., "Male and Female Roles: Gender in the Bible" Accessed September 26, 2017. http://www.apologeticspress.org/APContent.aspx?category=7&article/
103. Craig, William Lane., "A Christian Perspective on Homosexuality" Accessed September 27, 2017. http://www.reasonablefaith.org/a-christian-perspective-on-homosexuality/
104. Bock, Darrell., "The Bible and Same-Sex Marriage: 6 Common but Mistaken Claims" (July 27, 2015). Accessed September 27, 2017. https://www.thegospelcoalition.org/aritcle/bible-same-sex-marriage-six-mistaken-claims/.
105. Mandle, Joan D., "How Political is the Personal?: Identity Politics, Feminism and Social Change" Accessed November 28, 2017. https://userpages.umbc.edu/-korenman/wmst/identity_pol.html.
106. Lewis, Jone Johnson., "Learn About Feminism: The Ideas, Beliefs, Movements" Updated (June 28, 2017). Accessed September 29, 2017. https://www.thoughtco.com/what-is-feminism-3528958?print.
107. Collins, Martin G., Sermon: "The Role Of Women" January 13, 2001. Accessed September 29, 2017. https://www.bibletools.org/index.cfm/fuseaction/audio.details/ID/625/Role-women.htm.
108. Global Summit Addresses Men's Leadership, Fathers, Mentoring and Character "Where Are All the Men? Solutions for the Worldwide Male Identity Crisis" October 7, 2015 Christian Men's Network. Accessed September 27, 2017. http://www.prnewswire.com/news-releases/where-are-all-the-men-solutions-for-the-worldwide-male-identity-crisis/.
109. Airaksinen, Toni., "Why Colleges Should Stop Teaching "Toxic Masculinity" (November 16, 2016). Accessed September 29, 2017. http://quillette.com/2016/11/16/why-colleges-should-stop-teaching-toxic-masculinity/.
110. "Our male identity crisis: What will happen to men?" (July 19, 2010). Accessed September 27, 2017. https://www.psychologytoday.com/blog/wired-success/201007/our-male-identity-crisis-what-will-happen-to-men/.
111. "Homosexuality: The Biblical-Christian View" Accessed July 26, 2017. https://bible.org/article/homosexuality-biblical-christian-view.
112. IBID
113. "Johns Hopkins Psychiatrist: 'Transgendered Men Don't Become Women,' They Become 'Feminized Men,' 'Impersonators'" Accessed September 27, 2017. http://www.cnsnews.com/print/1034411.

114. Strachan, Owen., "Transgender Identity—Wishing Away God's Design" (July 24, 2016). Accessed September 25, 2017. https://answersingenesis.org/ family/ gender/transgender-identity-wishing-away-God's-design/.
115. IBID
116. "Who/what were the Nephilim?" Accessed October 2, 2017. http://www.gotquestions.org/Nephilim.html.
117. "The Nephilim-Giants In The Bible" by Beginning and End. Accessed June 15, 2018. https://www.beginningandend.com/Nephilim-giants-bible/.
118. Strachan, Owen., "Transgender Identity—Wishing Away God's Design". Accessed June 15, 2018. https://answersingenesis.org/family/gender/transgender-identity-wishing-away-God's-design/.

Chapter 9: Progressive Agenda

119. Schambra, William A. & West, Thomas., "The Progressive Movement and the Transformation of American Politics" (July 18, 2007). Accessed October 4, 2017. http://www.heritage.org/node/15814/print-display.
120. IBID
121. Alinsky, Saul D., "Saul Alinsky's 12 Rules for Radicals" Accessed September 20, 2017. https://www.steelonsteel.com/saul-alinskys-12-rules-for-radicals/.
122. IBID
123. Novak, Michael., "Social Justice: Not What You Think It Is" The Heritage Foundation. (December 29, 2009). Accessed October 4, 2017. http://www.heritage.org/node/9227/print-display.
124. Youssef, Michael "Social Justice Is Not Socialism" Accessed October 5, 2017. https://www.charismanews.com/opinion/41449-social-justice-is-not-socialism/.
125. "What Does the Bible Say About Abortion?" Frequently Asked Questions. Accessed October 6, 2017. http://www.christianbiblereference.org/faq_abortion.htm.
126. Omega, Jan "Abortion Clinic Hidden Agenda: Kill Off Latino and African American Communties" (May 9, 2014). Accessed October 6, 2017. https://www.inquisitr.com/124567/abortion-clinic-hidden-agenda-killing-off-latino-and-african-american-communities/.
127. "Christian View of Abortion" Accessed November 28, 2017. http://www.abortionfacts.com/literature/the-christian-view-of-abortion.
128. LaPoint, Terri., "Babies Who Survived Abortions and are Now Adults: Time for Our Voice to be Heard" (October 6, 2017). Accessed October 6, 2017 https://healthimpactnews.com/2015/babies-who-survived-abortions-and-are-now-adults-time-for-our-voice-to-be-heard.
129. "Abortion Emotional Side Effects—The Emotional Side Effects Many Women Experience After An Abortion" Accessed October 6, 2017. http://

american-pregnancy.org/unplanned-pregnancy/abortion-emotional-side-effects.
130. "What Is Rachel's Vineyard?" Accessed October 6, 2017. http://www.rachels-vineyard.org/aboutus/index.aspx.
131. "Rachel's Vineyard Retreat Ministries of Tucson and Southern Arizona, Inc." Accessed October 6, 2017. http://www.rachelsvineyardtucson.org/testimonies.html.
132. Pankratz, Dr. H. Robert C./Welsh, Richard M., "A Christian Response to Euthanasia"Accessed August 5, 2017. http://www.tkc.com/resources/resources-pages/euthanasia.html.
133. "Hippocratic Oath" Accessed October 7, 2017. https://www.medicinenet.com/script/main/art.asp?articlekey=20909.
134. Pankratz, Dr. H. Robert C./Welsh, Richard M., "A Christian Response to Euthanasia" Accessed August 5, 2017. http://www.tkc.com/resources/resources-pages/euthanasia.html.
135. Lynne, Diana., "Was Terri Schiavo's Death Assisted Suicide?" (October 6, 2005). Accessed October 7, 2017. http://www.wndcom/2005/10/32696.
136. Pankratz, Dr. H. Robert C./Welsh, Richard M., "A Christian Response to Euthanasia"Accessed August 5, 2017. http://www.tkc.com/resources/resources-pages/euthanasia.html.
137. "Existential risk form artificial general intelligence" Wikipedia. (October 7, 2017). Accessed October 7, 2017. https://en.wikipedia.org/wiki/Existential_risk_from_artificial_general_intelligence/.
138. IBID
139. Merritt, Jonathan., "Is AI a Threat to Christianity?—Are you there, God? It's I, Robot" (February 3, 2017). Accessed October 7, 2017. https://www.theatlantic.com/technology/archive/2017/02/artificial-intelligence.
140. IBID
141. Estes, Douglas., "Does 'The Image of God' Extend to Robots, Too?" (February 27, 2017). Accessed October 7, 2017. http://www.christianitytoday.com/ct/channel/utilities/print.html?type.
142. "'Church of Artificial Intelligence' Files For IRS Recognition" (November 16, 2017). Accessed December 19, 2017. http://blackchristiannews.com/2017/11/church-of-artificial-intelligence-files-for-IRS-recognition.
143. Leswing, Kif., "Ex-Google executive Anthony Levandowski is founding a church where people worship an artificial intelligence god" (November 15, 2017). Accessed December 19, 2017. http://www.businessinsider.com/ anthonylevandowski-way-of-the-future-church-where-people-worship-ai-god-2017-11.
144. "What is the New World Order?" Accessed October 7, 2017. https://www.gotquestions.net/NewWorldOrder.
145. IBID

146. "The Tower of Babel and Modern Identity" Fall 2013. Accessed July 24, 2017. http://utsccommons.utsc.utoronto.ca/fall-2013/mosaic/tower-babel-modern-identity.
147. IBID

Chapter 10: Who Is Jesus?

148. Piper, John., "Christ Conceived by the Holy Spirit" Accessed October 10, 2017. https://www.desiringgod.org/messages/christ-conceived-by-the-holy-spirit.
149. "Disciples Who Didn't Understand" Accessed October 11, 2017. https://www.gci.org/gospels/disciples.
150. Baehr, Steve., "Why were the Pharisees so unwilling to believe in Jesus as the Messiah?" (April 25, 2013). Accessed October 11, 2017. https://greenboxanswers.wordpress.com/2013/04/25/why-were-the-Pharisees-so-unwilling-to-believe-in-Jesus-as-the-Messiah?
151. IBID
152. "Reflecting The Character Of Christ" (Part 1). Accessed October 12, 2017. http://www.biblecenter.com/sermons/reflectingthecharacterofchristpart1.
153. IBID
154. Cole, Steven, J., "Lesson 13: The Meaning Of The Cross (I Peter 2:24-25" Accessed June 15, 2018. https://bible.org/seriespage/lesson-13-maning-cross-1-peter-224-25/
155. O'Sullivan, Fr. Paul, O.P. (E.D.M.). The Wonders Of The Holy Name. Tan Book and Publishers, Inc. P.O. Box 424, Rockford, Illinois 61105.
156. "What are the Odds?" Accessed November 29, 2017. http://y-jesus.com/what-are-the-odds/.
157. IBID

Chapter 11: Identity in Christ

158. Cahn, Jonathan. Copyright 2016. The Book of Mysteries. Frontline Pub. Day 172.
159. "The Eight Beatitudes Of Jesus" Accessed October 13, 2017. http://jesus-christsavior.net/Beatitudes.html.
160. Williamson, Daniel "Fruit Of The Spirit Series" (January, 6, 2003). Accessed October 14, 2017. https://sermoncentral.com/Sermons/print? sermonld-33771.
161. IBID
162. IBID
163. Henrickson, Pastor Charles., "Salt of the Earth, Light of the World" (Sermon on Matthew 5:1316) (February 4, 2017). Accessed September 4, 2017. http://steadfastlutherans.org/2017/02/salt-of-the-earth--light-of-the-world.

164. "St. Patrick" Saint (c. 386-461). Accessed October 17, 2017. https://biogra-phy.com/people/st-patrick-9434729.
165. Smith, Pastor Collin "Four Ways Our Identity in Christ Changes Our Lives" (April 9, 2015). Accessed August 17, 2017. http://unlockingthebible.org/four-ways-our-identity-in-christ-changes-our-lives.
166. "What St. Francis Really Said About Preaching" Accessed October 17, 2017. http://garrettkell.com/what-st-francis-really-said-about-preaching-the-gospel.

Chapter 12: Inheritance in Christ

167. Pastor Ken Birks., "Joint Heirs With Christ" http://www.kenbirks.com/outlines/inheritance.pdf.
168. "What Does Christ Mean?". Accessed June 15, 2018. https://www.gotquestions.org/what-does-Christ-mean.html
169. Henrickson, Pastor Charles., "Our Citizenship Is in Heaven" (Sermon on Philippians 3:17-4:1) (February 20, 2016). Accessed September 4, 2017. http://steadfastlutherans.org/2016/02/our-citizenship-is-in-heaven.
170. Bousa, Jess., "Living As A Citizen Of Heaven On Earth" (October 10, 2005). Accessed October 20, 2017. http://www.sermoncentralcom/Sermons/Print?sermonId=83878.
171. Webster's Dictionary II New Riverside University Dictionary (1984) Houghton Mifflin.
172. Feeney, Pastor Jim., Pentecostal Sermons and Bible Studies "The Authority of The Believer" Accessed July 19, 2017. http://www.jimfeeney.org/authority-of-believer.html.
173. "How Did Christianity Spread Throughout the World?" Accessed June 15, 2018. http://www.suscopts.org/.../apostalicagechristianity.pdf.
174. IBID
175. "Christianity and the Roman Empire" Accessed June 15, 2018. http://www.saylor.org/courses/hist101/#6.4.3.
176. Voelkel, Jack., "21 Missionaries You Should Know" (July 16, 2014). Accessed on October 24, 2017. https://www.urbana.org/blog/21-missionaries-you-should-know.
177. "Bill and Vonette Bright Founders of Campus Crusade for Christ, International" Accessed on October 24, 2017. https://www.cru.org/about/our-leadership/our-founders.html.
178. "Bill Bright's Four Spiritual Laws" Accessed on October 24, 2017. http://www.mesacc.edu/-thoqh49081/handouts/bright.html.
179. Zadai, Kevin L. Copyright 2015. Heavenly Visitation A Guide To Participating In The Supernatural. Kevin L. Zadai. www.xulonpress.com.
180. "The Salvation Prayer" Accessed on October 24, 2017. http://salvationprayer.info/home Chapter 13: God's Healing Touch.

Chapter 13: God's Healing Touch

181. "Faith Is Not a Feeling" (excerpt from Ney Bailey's book "Faith Is Not A Feeling" Copyright 2002. Published by WaterBrook Press.) (February 27, 2011). Accessed on October 27, 2017. http://www.startingwithgod.com/knowing-God/what-is-faith/.
182. "What Is Faith?" Hebrews 11 New Century Version (NCV). Accessed on October 27, 2017. https://www.biblegateway.com/passage?search=Hebrews=11&versionNCV.
183. Sparks, Mark., "Grace" (August 20, 2010). Accessed on October 30, 2017. https://sermoncentral.com/Sermons/Print?sermonId=149451.
184. Roberts, Gerald "Grace" (August 12, 2011). Accessed on October 30, 2017. https://sermoncentral.com/Sermons/Print?sermonId=159509.
185. Bester, Jaco "Grace!" (March 30, 2004). Accessed on October 30, 2017. https://sermoncentral.com/Sermons/Print?seronId=67216.
186. Lawrence, Brother. Copyright 1982. The Practice of the Presence of God. Whitaker House.
187. Hinn, Benny., "Nine Gifts of the Holy Spirit" Accessed on October 31, 2017. https://www.bennyhinn.org/nine-gifts-of-the-holy-spirit/.
188. "Baptism in the Holy Spirit" Accessed on November 11, 2017. http://www1.cbn.com/spirituallife/what-is-the-baptism-in-the-holy-spirit.
189. Accessed June 15, 2018. http://www.unionchurch.com/teaching-resources/sermon-archive/forgiveness-letting-go-of-the-hurt/.
190. Douglass, Judy., "A Prayer For Forgiving" June 13, 2012. Accessed on June 15, 2018. https://www.judydouglass.com/2012/06/a-prayer-for-forgiving/.
191. Souza, Katie., "Your Soul is Sabotaging Your Life!" Accessed June 19, 2018. https://www.youtube.com/watch?v=up3vlz_SdYI.
192. Souza, Katie., "Can Sickness and Disorders Be Connected to Our Soul?" Accessed June 19, 2018. https://www.youtube.com/watch?v=z Du-xIYKk
193. Virkler, Mark/Greig, Gary S./Gaydos, Frank., adapted from "How to Release God's Healing Power Through Prayer". Accessed on June 15, 2018. http://cwgministries.org/sites/default/files/files/books/How-to-Release--Healing.pdf.
194. Hampsch, John H. C.M.F. Copyright 1999. The Healing Power of the Eucharist. Servant p.

Chapter 14: The Ultimate Showdown

195. "How, why, and when did Satan fall from heaven?" Accessed November 7, 2017. https://www.gotquestions.net/Printer/Satan=fall=PDF.html.
196. "How Did Lucifer Fall and Become Satan?" Accessed November 7, 2017. http://www.christianity.com/print/11557519/.

197. "What is the Anti-christ?" Accessed November 7, 2017. https://www.gotquestions.net/Printer/what-is-the-antchrist-PF.html.
198. United Church of God "Who is the Antichrist? What does the Bible say about the Antichrist?" October 27, 2010 http://www.ucg.org/bible-study-tools/bible-questions-and-answers/who-is-the-antichrist-what-does-the-bible-say-about.
199. Pack, David C., "The Antichrist All-powerful, Worse Than Any Expect—and Close!" Accessed November 7, 2017. https://rcg.org/books/tawtae.html.
200. "What is Armageddon?" Accessed November 8, 2017. http://www.battleofarmageddon.net/.
201. "What is the Second Coming of Jesus Christ?" Accessed November 7, 2017. https://www.gotquestions.net/Printer/second-coming-PF.html.
202. Stanley, Charles F., "Understanding The End Times: The Rapture" (July 7, 2014). Accessed November 8, 2017. https://www.intouch.org/read/understanding-the-end-times-the-rapture.
203. "The Rapture and the Tribulation" Accessed November 8, 2017. https:// www.truthnet.org/Endtimes/introduction/Rapturetribulation.

Chapter 15: Reflections

204. Alcorn, Randy. 2004. Heaven. Tyndale House Publishers p. 23.
205. "Nigerian Pastor Who Went To Hell" by Johan Sturm on YouTube. https://www.youtube.com/watch?v=UvFlcMH888g.
206. Alcorn, Randy. 2004. Heaven. Tyndale House Publishers p. 21.
207. Cahn, Jonathan. 2016. The Book of Mysteries. FrontLine p. 301.
208. "Satan's part in God's Perfect Plan" Accessed November 7, 2017. https:// bible.org/seriespage/3-satan-s-part-God-s-perfect-plan.
209. Webster's Dictionary II New Riverside University Dictionary Copyright 1984 Houghton Mifflin.
210. Igniting Hope Ministries "25 Biblical Identity Declarations" Accessed August 17, 2017. https://ignitinghope.com/blog/1-25biblicaldeclarations.
211. "Jim Caviezel Surprises Students and Brings A Message of Faith" March 9, 2018. Accessed June 15, 2018. crosswalk.com/culture/features/jm-caviezel-surprises-students-and-brings-a/.
212. Ward, Martin. Song—copyright 1999: Thru His Eyes.

* Bible verses are from *The Everyday Life Bible* containing the Amplified Old Testament and the Amplified New Testament Notes and Commentary by Joyce Meyer, Faith Words Hachette Book Group, New York, New York, First Edition October 2009.

ABOUT THE AUTHOR

Marcella Ward currently lives in Arizona with her husband, Marty. They have two children and eight grandchildren. Marcella was an educator for thirty-two years, and she and her husband of forty-three years have been involved in Christian ministries for many years. They write and produce Christian music. In their Healing Hearts Ministry, they seek to glorify God by helping people to encounter the forgiveness, love, mercy, and healing power of God through the message of God's Word renewing the whole person in body, soul, and spirit.

Marcella believes that this book, which was birthed by divine inspiration, will take you on a journey to discover that you are a reflection of God's image and likeness. He has a perfect plan for your life because of who you are in Him, and He has given many gifts and tools to equip you as a child of God to manifest His glory throughout the earth.

www.ingramcontent.com/pod-product-compliance
Lightning Source LLC
Chambersburg PA
CBHW021441070526
44577CB00002B/243